Lecture Notes
in Business Information Processing 367

More information about this series at http://www.springer.com/series/7911

Ho-Pun Lam · Sajib Mistry (Eds.)

Service Research and Innovation

7th Australian Symposium, ASSRI 2018
Sydney, NSW, Australia, September 6, 2018
and Wollongong, NSW, Australia, December 14, 2018
Revised Selected Papers

 Springer

Editors
Ho-Pun Lam (iD)
CSIRO
Eveleigh, NSW, Australia

Sajib Mistry (iD)
University of Sydney
Sydney, NSW, Australia

ISSN 1865-1348   ISSN 1865-1356 (electronic)
Lecture Notes in Business Information Processing
ISBN 978-3-030-32241-0   ISBN 978-3-030-32242-7 (eBook)
https://doi.org/10.1007/978-3-030-32242-7

Preface

This volume collects the proceedings of the 7th Australasian Symposium on Service Research and Innovation (ASSRI 2018) held in Sydney and Wollongong, NSW, Australia, during September 6 and December 14, 2018, respectively. The symposium aims to bring together a cross-disciplinary group of researchers and practitioners who are engaged in research and development in the area of services-related technologies to exchange research findings and ideas on services-related technologies and practices. It is a premium event for paving ideas, inspiration and information of how software applications should be designed, developed, delivered, and consumed.

For this volume, we selected nine high-quality papers from the ASSRI 2018 submissions for presentation and publication, keeping the acceptance rate at around 40%. Each paper was reviewed by a team of three Program Committee members and selected based on their originality, significance, relevance, and clarity of presentation. These nine papers showcase fresh ideas from exciting and emerging topics on a variety of aspects of research on service-oriented computing, which include crowdsourcing, services technologies, as well as service security, privacy, and trust.

For the first time in the ASSRI symposiums, a service innovation challenge track was offered to consolidate and present a set of real-life triggers for research with impact. The focus this year was on the problems and challenges that appear in the airline industry and an additional two short papers were accepted for this track.

Three eminent researchers presented invited talks at the symposium. Professor Rik Eshuis, a member of the Department of Industrial Engineering and Innovation Science, Eindhoven University of Technology, delivered an invited talk entitled, "Modeling Decision-Intensive Process with Declarative Business Artifacts." He presented the challenges and potential solutions on the use of declarative business artifacts in supporting decision-making. Dr. Ingo Weber of Data61, CSIRO delivered an invited talk entitled, "Blockchain and Services—Exploring the Links." In his talk, he explored the connections between services and blockchain from four different facets, and presented some principles for designing SOA services and microservices that can be applied to smart contract design. Dr. Hoa Khanh Dam, a member of the Decision Systems Lab at the School of Computing and Information Technology, University of Wollongong, delivered an invited talk entitled "Artificial Intelligence for Software Engineering," and discussed the potential use of artificial intelligence in software development and project management from different perspectives, which includes action recommendations and decision-making.

We would like to thank the Program Committee members and the external reviewers for their thorough reviews and discussions of the submitted papers. We express our gratitude to other symposium committees and staff at the Macquarie University, Sydney, Australia, and University of Wollongong, Wollongong, Australia, for their attentive preparations for the two parts of the symposium. We are thankful to the authors of the submissions, the keynote speakers, the presenters, and all the other symposium participants because the symposium could not have been held without their contributions and interest. Last but not least, we are grateful for the support of the Service Science Society Australia.

We very much hope you enjoy reading the papers in this volume.

February 2019   Ho-Pun Lam
                                                                                 Sajib Mistry

Organization

General Chairs

Amin Behesti   Macquarie University, Australia
Hai Dong   RMIT University, Australia
Mustafa Hashmi   Data61, CSIRO, Australia

Program Chairs

Ho-Pun Lam   Data61, CSIRO, Australia
Sajib Mistry   University of Sydney, Australia
Karthikeyan Ponnalagu   Bosch, India

Publicity Chair

Carlos Rodriguez   University of New South Wales, Australia

Industry Chairs

Jay Daniel   University of Derby, UK
Lina Yao   University of New South Wales, Australia

Publication Chair

Metta Santiputri   University of Wollongong, Australia

Web Chair

Osama Misbah   University of Wollongong, Australia

Program Committee

Abhik Banerjee   Swinburne University of Technology, Australia
Amin Behesti   Macquarie University, Australia
Amit Borundiya   Bosch India, India
Hai Dong   RMIT University, Australia
Michael Fellmann   University of Rostock, Germany
Azadeh Ghari Neiat   The University of Sydney, Australia
Aditya Ghose   University of Wollongong, Australia
Mustafa Hashmi   Data61, CSIRO, Australia

Huai Liu	Victoria University, Australia
Senthil Pandian	Sethu Institute of Technology, India
Laurianne Sitbon	Queensland University of Technology, Australia

Additional Reviewers

Mohammed Bahutair
Sheik Mohammad Mostakim Fattah
Bing Huang
Abdallah Lakhdari
Fabienne Lambusch
Vidhya Murali
Babar Shahzaad

Contents

Keynote Papers

Modeling Decision-Intensive Processes with Declarative Business Artifacts

Rik Eshuis[✉]

School of Industrial Engineering, Eindhoven University of Technology,
Eindhoven, The Netherlands
h.eshuis@tue.nl

Abstract. Modern business processes often need to support knowledge workers that are responsible for making decisions about real-world business entities such as orders and quotes. Such decision-intensive processes are driven by data and require flexibility in their execution. Business artifacts model data and process aspects of business entities in a holistic way and are therefore well-suited to model data-driven processes. Declarative process models support flexible process executions. Therefore, declarative business artifacts are a promising ingredient to support decision-intensive processes. However, there are several challenges that need to be overcome in order to support real-world decision-intensive processes with declarative business artifacts. This position paper discusses key challenges and discusses preliminary solutions to overcome them and turn declarative business artifacts into a mature modeling language for decision-intensive processes.

1 Introduction

A decision-intensive process is a "business process whose conduct and execution is heavily dependent upon knowledge workers in a variety of roles performing various decision making tasks that interconnect to drive critical organizational outcomes" [8]. The current abundance of data about business processes and their environments, for instance data about past cases or about the current status of resources, supports the decision making of knowledge workers in these processes. This way, the desired organizational outcomes, i.e. business goals, can be reached.

Decision-intensive processes are "genuinely knowledge, information and data centric and require substantial flexibility at design and run time" [36]. Decision-intensive process (DiPs) are therefore strongly related to knowledge-intensive processes (KiPs) [11], since decision making by experts is one of the key features of a KiP. Moreover, several properties of KiPs, such as collaboration-oriented, unpredictable and emergent [11], also apply to DiPs, which require multiple roles and are organic in nature [8].

DiPs can be viewed on the spectrum of structured vs. unstructured processes [11]. Structured processes are routine work, so highly predictable with little exceptions. Unstructured processes are much less predictable, due to uncertainty in the environment which impacts process executions. Therefore, they

© Springer Nature Switzerland AG 2019
H.-P. Lam and S. Mistry (Eds.): ASSRI 2018, LNBIP 367, pp. 3–12, 2019.
https://doi.org/10.1007/978-3-030-32242-7_1

require more flexibility than structured processes. Structured processes are supported by workflow management systems, unstructured processes by groupware systems, while semi-structured processes are typically supported by case management systems [26]. DiPs cover this entire spectrum of structured-unstructured processes, though they are often semi-structured.

Business artifacts [24] have been proposed to model DiPs [36]. A business artifact is a key business entity. Work done in a business process is performed in the context of business artifacts like Order or Product. Business artifacts are specified with an integrated data and lifecycle model [21,24]. Business artifacts therefore express the information context in which decisions are made.

Even though declarative business artifacts are a promising approach to support DiPs, there are several challenges that need to be overcome to actually support real-world DiPs with declarative business artifacts. This position paper discusses two key challenges, engineering DiPs with declarative business artifacts and integrating decision support for DiPs into declarative business artifacts, and discusses preliminary solutions to overcome those challenges.

The remainder of this paper is organized as follows. Section 2 classifies different modeling languages for DiPs, one of which are declarative business artifacts. Section 3 discusses challenges in engineering DiPs and discusses potential solutions based on declarative business artifacts. Section 4 discusses challenges in supporting decision making within DiPs using declarative business artifacts. Finally, Sect. 5 contains the conclusions.

2   Modeling Languages for Decision-Intensive Processes

There are several business process modeling languages for DiPs (Fig. 1). The standard languages for modeling business processes are Business Process Model and Notation (BPMN) [7] and Business Process Execution Language (BPEL) [6]. These languages use a procedural style, focusing on the ordering of activities. They resemble flowcharts, where boxes denote activities and arrows represent sequencing constraints between activities. Data is accessed inside the activities and can be tested in branching decisions that determine the routing of process instances.

Procedural, activity-centric process modeling languages have two main limitations. First, many activities are actually creating or manipulating data, but these languages do not organize the activities around data; instead, data is hidden inside the activities. In other words, these languages treat data as a second class citizen next to activities.

Second, the procedural languages use strict sequencing constraints on activities, typically denoted with arrows, that are specified at design time. This means ordering constraints are specified in advance, independent of the case being processed. Whereas for many process instances the next activity to be performed depends on the availability of case data or events that occurred, either external or internal. Supporting such processes requires flexibility on the ordering of activities that cannot be expressed very well in procedural-style process models.

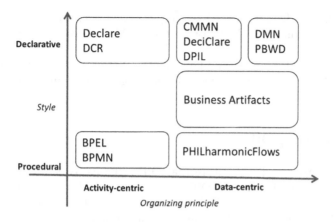

Fig. 1. Spectrum of decision-intensive process modeling languages

In the Business Process Management (BPM) literature, both limitations have been tackled. The first limitation is addressed by data-centric process modeling approaches such as PhilHarmonicFlows [22], business artifacts [3,24] and several derivatives [17,37], and Product-based Workflow Design [28]. PhilHarmonicFlows [22] and business artifacts [3,17,37] use procedural state machines to define ordering constraints. Product-based Workflow Design [28] generates procedural workflow models from the structure of the information product that the process should produce.

The second limitation is addressed by declarative process modeling languages [18] such as Declare [25] and DCR graphs [20]. These languages are activity-centric but use rules to specify the ordering between activities [18]. Declare and DCR graphs use temporal rules that constrain the possible transitions in the state space. Implicitly, those rules define the possible process executions [18]. Declare has been extended into DeciClare [23], which supports the data and resource perspective of processes. For the data perspective, DeciClare uses Decision Model and Notation (DMN) [10], which can be considered a DiP modeling language in itself, since it declaratively specifies information requirements constraints on business decisions. Similar to DeciClare, the Declarative Process Intermediate Language (DPIL) [31] is a declarative process language that supports multiple process modeling perspectives.

Finally, a few proces modeling approaches have addressed both limitations simultaneously, by blending declarative and data-centric process modeling. A declarative version of business artifacts, called Guard-Stage-Milestone (GSM) schemas, has been defined [21]. A milestone is a business objective, a stage an atomic unit of work to reach a milestones, and a guard a condition that specifies when a stage can be opened. To specify changes in activation of stages and milestones, GSM schemas use Event-Condition-Action rules, which define actions to take (activate or inactivate stage or milestone) when events occur and conditions hold. Such rules make them different from the other declarative languages such as Declare and DCR graphs. The standard Case Management Model and Notation (CMMN) [5] of the Object Management Group is based on GSM schemas.

Having sketched the modeling language context of declarative business artifacts, we highlight in the sequel concrete challenges in applying them to support DiPs.

3   Engineering DiPs

There is consensus in the literature that DiPs, just as KiPs, are unpredictable and emerging [8,11]. This means DiPs are unique, though they can be similar. A challenge is how to engineer DiPs in an efficient and reliable way. Without such an approach, engineering DiPs is time consuming and the resulting DiPs have poor quality. To develop a sound engineering approach for DiPs with declarative business artifacts, questions regarding the modeling concepts, the modeling approach and variability need to be addressed.

3.1   DiP Modeling Concepts

A major engineering challenge is motivated by the variety of modeling languages for DiPs, which use somewhat different modeling concepts. Activity-centric languages like DCR graphs [20] and Declare [25] have many different types of rules to specify ordering constraints between activities. On the other hand, their states only consist of the events, typically completion events of activities, that have been executed, can be executed, and need to be executed in the future. Data is typically not considered, though some data extensions of Declare and DCR graphs exist, e.g. [9,33]. In sum, DCR graphs and Declare have fat rules, thin states.

Declarative business artifacts, on the other hand, use only Event-Condition-Action rules that specify how an artifact changes state in its lifecycle. However, states are valuations of attributes of artifacts, which includes both data attributes and attributes representing the life cycle state. Consequently, states of business artifacts are more rich than DCR and Declare states. Thus, declarative business artifacts have thin rules, thick states.

An open question is how to relate both groups of DiP languages. The rules used in Declare and DCR graphs are integrity rules while declarative business artifacts use reaction rules [35]. A mapping from DCR graph to GSM life cycles of declarative business artifacts has been defined [13], implicitly relating integrity rules to reaction rules, but the reverse mapping has not yet been considered. The mapping enables the use of DCR rules in business artifacts.

A broader, more general question is for which kind of DiP which DiP language is most suitable. So far, all researchers use their own DiP language, but there has not yet been an extensive empirical evaluation on which DiP modeling language is most suitable for a particular real-world business scenario.

3.2   DiP Design Approach

Several approaches for designing declarative business artifacts have been proposed. Bhattacharya et al. [4] propose to first discover business artifacts, next specify their data and life cycle stages, and then to specify both the data and life cycle in more detail, for instance by using ER diagrams for the data part and ECA rules for the life cycle part.

Eshuis and Van Gorp [15] propose to first identify the key business artifacts and model in an imperative way the default behavior of these interacting business artifacts. This default behavior is transformed into a skeleton declarative business artifact model, that can be further refined to include behavior for exceptional circumstances.

There is no research on design methodologies for declarative, activity-centric modeling approaches like Declare [25] and DCR graphs [20]. Since temporal relations can only be specified if the involved activities are known, the natural design approach is to first define the activities, then the temporal relations.

While all these design approaches are sequential, in practice they can be used in an iterative, incremental way, by validating and refining the current DiP model and extending it with new behavior.

Given this diversity in designing DiP models with declarative business artifacts and other DiP notations, an open question is which approach works best for which situation. In other words, guidelines on how to properly design a DiP model are lacking. Another interesting research topic is to investigate the effect of using an agile design methodology on languages like Declare and DCR graphs on the one hand and business artifacts on the other hand. In other words, do activity-centric or data-centric modeling notions benefit most from an agile design methodology? Or is the problem domain more of an influence then the modeling notation?

3.3   Variability

Bromberg [8] claims that DiPs are repeated and repeatable, while DiCiccio et al. [11] state that KiPs are unique and non-repeatable. While on the surface these two statements seem to contradict each other, they can be viewed as two alternative perspectives on DiPs. While each DiP is unique, there are common parts that are can be reused in different DiPs.

This raises the challenge how to engineer DiPs from repeatable parts such that reliability, efficiency, and maintainability is ensured. A similar challenge is faced in software product line engineering, where reuse of software parts across different software products needs to be managed [27] properly.

The resulting variability management concepts have been applied to Business Process Management as well, but mostly for procedural, activity-centric process models [1,29]. For declarative, activity-centric modeling languages, variability support has been developed by encoding all variants in a single model [32].

For declarative business artifacts, a more modular variability management approach has been defined [12]. This approach specifies reusable parts of a DiPs

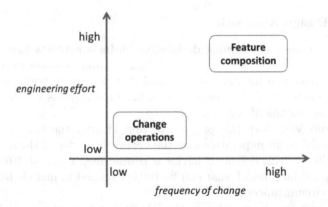

Fig. 2. Comparing variability management approaches for declarative business artifacts

as features which refine a base model and uses feature composition to derive DiP variants [12]. Each feature can be viewed as a function that modifies a base model; this way, feature composition resembles function composition [2].

Another approach is to based on change (insert and delete) operations on a DiP model, for instance defined in terms of GSM schemas [16]. The BPM variability management approach Provop [19] uses change operations to manage variability in procedural process models. By replacing the Provop change operations with GSM change operations, an alternative variability management approach is defined.

To understand the commonalities and differences between both variability management approaches, it is interesting to explore in a bit more detail their expected usability (see Fig. 2). On the surface, engineering features is more costly, since features of the appropriate granularity need to be carefully defined. On the other hand, once the features have been defined, composing them is more easy than defining change operations. If a DiP has many variants, i.e., changes frequently, a feature-oriented approach pays off. A change-operation approach seems more suited if a few ad hoc changes are expected. Which approach is in practice more suitable for which context is a topic for future research.

4   Decision Support

Knowledge workers performing DiPs need to perform decisions to drive DiPs forward. We first discuss how decision making can be integrated in DiPs. Next, we explain how human decision making can be supported in DiPs. The support is developed in terms of declarative business artifacts, notably Guard-Stage-Milestone schemas [21].

4.1   Integrating Decision Making

More and more data is being produced that can be used for decision making in DiPs. For instance, in the financial industry many business processes have become digitized, leading to rich data about clients and financial products that can be used for decision making. In the high tech industry, many processes can be improved if the data generated by machines and products is put to use. Maintenance processes for example can be optimized by learning from usage data generated by assets and historical maintenance data.

This means knowledge workers performing a DiP should be supported in using data to decide how to progress a DiP. While disciplines like Operations Research (OR) and Data Science (DS) study decision problems in isolation, in a DIP these decision problems are interconnected. Often, a DiP includes information gathering tasks that prepare subsequent decision making.

A DiP model can be viewed as a map for such decision problems. Figure 3 illustrates this for the DiP of handling a maintenance request of a train unit [34]. In this process, there are several decision points for knowledge workers, which could be supported using an OR technique like Markov Decision Processes (MDPs).

Note that this goes a step further than using the Decision Model and Notation (DMN) standard [10]. A DMN model uses decision rules, which define statically what the decision outcomes are for various inputs. These decision rules are either derived from expert knowledge or from a sophisticated decision analysis, for which typically an OR or DS decision modeling technique is applied. In the latter case, the decision rules are heuristics that summarize the outcome of the analysis. In that case, the decision analysis is done offline. In contrast, the integrated decision making for DiPs proposed in Fig. 3 supports real-time, online decision analysis.

An open challenge is how to use the predicted outcome of a DiP to drive the execution in the current state, for instance by recommending a step to be performed by the knowledge worker. This requires a careful connection between a DiP and an underlying decision model, such as an MDP.

4.2   Modeling Human Reasoning

Business artifacts contain business rules that specify conditions under which actions are taken [21]. These rules assume clear-cut boundaries between different states of the world. For instance, a rule may test for a client age to be younger than or equal to 40. However, in reality the variables in the rules may have some degree of uncertainty or may not be described precisely. This is caused by either having insufficient data or lacking concrete definitions of the considered concepts.

To deal with such uncertainty and imprecision, fuzzy modeling can be applied to declarative business artifacts [14]. Fuzzy models handle uncertainty in qualitative rather than a quantitative (probabilistic) way, and mimic the imprecise way of human reasoning [30]. Using fuzzy logic, knowledge experts can express their knowledge using linguistic labels. For instance, rather than stating in a rule that a client is young if his age is 40 or lower, business artifacts with fuzzy rules allow to express to which degree a client is young, middle aged or old [14].

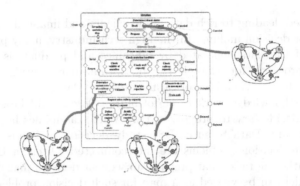

Fig. 3. Guard-Stage-Milestone schema of Train Maintenance Request with decision points governed by Markov Decision Processes [34]

Applying fuzzy logic to the artifact life cycle concepts (stage and milestone) is still an open challenge. Also, integrating models mimicking human reasoning with OR and DS models such as MDPs is an open issue.

5   Conclusion

This position paper has surveyed the use of declarative business artifacts for decision-intensive processes (DiPs), putting them in the context of other declarative and data-centric languages for modeling DiPs. Declarative business artifacts are well suited to model DiPs since they provide the information context for decision making and support flexible process executions.

The paper focused on how to engineer DiPs with declarative business artifacts and how to integrate decision support for DiPs into declarative business artifacts. While preliminary solutions in both areas have been proposed, several open challenges still need to addressed to grow declarative business artifacts into a fully mature modeling technique for DiPs.

References

1. Ayora, C., Torres, V., Weber, B., Reichert, M., Pelechano, V.: VIVACE: a framework for the systematic evaluation of variability support in process-aware information systems. Inf. Softw. Technol. **57**, 248–276 (2015)
2. Batory, D.S., Sarvela, J.N., Rauschmayer, A.: Scaling step-wise refinement. IEEE Trans. Softw. Eng. **30**(6), 355–371 (2004)
3. Bhattacharya, K., Caswell, N.S., Kumaran, S., Nigam, A., Wu, F.Y.: Artifact-centered operational modeling: lessons from customer engagements. IBM Syst. J. **46**(4), 703–721 (2007)
4. Bhattacharya, K., Hull, R., Su, J.: A data-centric design methodology for business processes. In: Handbook of Research on Business Process Modeling, chap. 23, pp. 503–531 (2009)

5. BizAgi and others. Case Management Model and Notation (CMMN), v1.1. OMG Document Number formal/2016-12-01, Object Management Group (2016)
6. Web Services Business Process Execution Language (BPEL), Version 2.0 (2007). http://docs.oasis-open.org/wsbpel/2.0/wsbpel-v2.0.html
7. Business Process Model and Notation (BPMN), Version 2.0 (2011). http://www.omg.org/spec/BPMN/2.0/PDF
8. Bromberg, D.: BPM for knowledge workers inside decision intensive processes (DIPs): knowledge, practice, context, and characteristics. BPTrends, February 2007
9. Burattin, A., Maggi, F.M., Sperduti, A.: Conformance checking based on multi-perspective declarative process models. Expert Syst. Appl. **65**, 194–211 (2016)
10. Decision Management Solutions and others. Decision Model and Notation (DMN), v1.2. OMG Document Number formal/19-01-05, Object Management Group (2019)
11. Di Ciccio, C., Marrella, A., Russo, A.: Knowledge-intensive processes: characteristics, requirements and analysis of contemporary approaches. J. Data Semant. **4**(1), 29–57 (2015)
12. Eshuis, R.: Feature-oriented composition of declarative artifact-centric process models. In: Weske, M., Montali, M., Weber, I., vom Brocke, J. (eds.) BPM 2018. LNCS, vol. 11080, pp. 66–82. Springer, Cham (2018). https://doi.org/10.1007/978-3-319-98648-7_5
13. Eshuis, R., Debois, S., Slaats, T., Hildebrandt, T.: Deriving consistent GSM schemas from DCR graphs. In: Sheng, Q.Z., Stroulia, E., Tata, S., Bhiri, S. (eds.) ICSOC 2016. LNCS, vol. 9936, pp. 467–482. Springer, Cham (2016). https://doi.org/10.1007/978-3-319-46295-0_29
14. Eshuis, R., Firat, M.: Modeling uncertainty in declarative artifact-centric process models. In: Daniel, F., Sheng, Q.Z., Motahari, H. (eds.) BPM 2018. LNBIP, vol. 342, pp. 281–293. Springer, Cham (2019). https://doi.org/10.1007/978-3-030-11641-5_22
15. Eshuis, R., Gorp, P.V.: Synthesizing data-centric models from business process models. Computing **98**(4), 345–373 (2016)
16. Eshuis, R., Hull, R., Yi, M.: Reasoning about property preservation in adaptive case management. ACM Trans. Internet Technol. **19**(1), 12:1–12:21 (2019)
17. Estañol, M., Sancho, M., Teniente, E.: Ensuring the semantic correctness of a BAUML artifact-centric BPM. Inf. Softw. Technol. **93**, 147–162 (2018)
18. Goedertier, S., Vanthienen, J., Caron, F.: Declarative business process modelling: principles and modelling languages. Enterprise IS **9**(2), 161–185 (2015)
19. Hallerbach, A., Bauer, T., Reichert, M.: Capturing variability in business process models: the provop approach. J. Softw. Maint. **22**(6–7), 519–546 (2010)
20. Hildebrandt, T.T., Mukkamala, R.R.: Declarative event-based workflow as distributed dynamic condition response graphs. In: Honda, K., Mycroft, A. (eds.) Proceedings Third Workshop on Programming Language Approaches to Concurrency and communication-cEntric Software, PLACES 2010, Paphos, Cyprus, 21 March 2010. EPTCS, vol. 69, pp. 59–73 (2010)
21. Hull, R., et al.: Introducing the guard-stage-milestone approach for specifying business entity lifecycles. In: Bravetti, M., Bultan, T. (eds.) WS-FM 2010. LNCS, vol. 6551, pp. 1–24. Springer, Heidelberg (2011). https://doi.org/10.1007/978-3-642-19589-1_1
22. Künzle, V., Reichert, M.: Philharmonicflows: towards a framework for object-aware process management. J. Softw. Maint. **23**(4), 205–244 (2011)

23. Mertens, S., Gailly, F., Poels, G.: Towards a decision-aware declarative process modeling language for knowledge-intensive processes. Expert Syst. Appl. **87**, 316–334 (2017)

24. Nigam, A., Caswell, N.S.: Business artifacts: an approach to operational specification. IBM Syst. J. **42**(3), 428–445 (2003)

25. Pesic, M., Schonenberg, H., van der Aalst, W.M.P.: DECLARE: full support for loosely-structured processes. In: Proceedings of the 11th IEEE International Enterprise Distributed Object Computing Conference, pp. 287–300. IEEE Computer Society, Washington, DC (2007)

26. Pillaerds, J., Eshuis, R.: Assessing suitability of adaptive case management. In: Ramos, I., Tuunainen, V., Krcmar, H. (eds.) 25th European Conference on Information Systems, ECIS 2017, Guimarães, Portugal, 5–10 June 2017, p. 37 (2017)

27. Pohl, K., Böckle, G., van der Linden, F.: Software Product Line Engineering - Foundations, Principles, and Techniques. Springer, Heidelberg (2005). https://doi.org/10.1007/3-540-28901-1

28. Reijers, H.A., Limam, S., van der Aalst, W.M.P.: Product-based workflow design. J. Manag. Inf. Syst. **20**(1), 229–262 (2003)

29. Rosa, M.L., van der Aalst, W.M.P., Dumas, M., Milani, F.: Business process variability modeling: a survey. ACM Comput. Surv. **50**(1), 2:1–2:45 (2017)

30. Ross, T.J.: Fuzzy Logic with Engineering Applications. Wiley, Hoboken (2010)

31. Schönig, S., Zeising, M.: The DPIL framework: tool support for agile and resource-aware business processes. In: Daniel, F., Zugal, S. (eds.) Proceedings of the BPM Demo Session 2015 Co-located with the 13th International Conference on Business Process Management (BPM 2015), Innsbruck, Austria, 2 September 2015. CEUR Workshop Proceedings, vol. 1418, pp. 125–129. CEUR-WS.org (2015)

32. Schunselaar, D.M.M., Maggi, F.M., Sidorova, N., van der Aalst, W.M.P.: Configurable declare: designing customisable flexible process models. In: Proceedings of the OTM 2012, pp. 20–37 (2012)

33. Slaats, T., Mukkamala, R.R., Hildebrandt, T., Marquard, M.: Exformatics declarative case management workflows as DCR graphs. In: Daniel, F., Wang, J., Weber, B. (eds.) BPM 2013. LNCS, vol. 8094, pp. 339–354. Springer, Heidelberg (2013). https://doi.org/10.1007/978-3-642-40176-3_28

34. Smit, E.: Modeling rolling stock maintenance logistics with business artifacts: a case study at Dutch Railways. Master's thesis, Eindhoven University of Technology, The Netherlands (2018)

35. Taveter, K., Wagner, G.: Agent-oriented enterprise modeling based on business rules. In: S.Kunii, H., Jajodia, S., Sølvberg, A. (eds.) ER 2001. LNCS, vol. 2224, pp. 527–540. Springer, Heidelberg (2001). https://doi.org/10.1007/3-540-45581-7_39

36. Vaculin, R., Hull, R., Heath, T., Cochran, C., Nigam, A., Sukaviriya, P.: Declarative business artifact centric modeling of decision and knowledge intensive business processes. In: 2011 IEEE EDOC, pp. 151–160. IEEE (2011)

37. Yongchareon, S., Liu, C., Yu, J., Zhao, X.: A view framework for modeling and change validation of artifact-centric inter-organizational business processes. Inf. Syst. **47**, 51–81 (2015)

Blockchain and Services – Exploring the Links
Keynote Paper

Ingo Weber[✉]

Data61, CSIRO and School of CSE, UNSW, Sydney, Australia
ingo.weber@data61.csiro.au

Abstract. Blockchain is a novel distributed ledger technology which has attracted a wide range of interests for building the next generation of applications. The broad range of blockchain applications is made possible by so-called *smart contracts*, which transform a blockchain system into a general compute platform. As a new paradigm and technology platform in the integration space, this bears the question to which degree there is a connection to services, and in how far lessons learned on services can be applied to Blockchain.

In the talk, I explored four different facets of this topic, as follows. First, application-level service interfaces for interaction with blockchain-based applications enable easy integration with existing infrastructure. Second, service composition can be achieved through smart contracts, and enable different approaches to orchestrations and choreographies. Third, Blockchain-aaS offerings cover infrastructure operation, but the idea presents further possibilities. And finally, some principles for designing SOA services and microservices can be applied to smart contract design.

Keywords: Blockchain · Smart contracts · Software architecture · Software engineering · Business process management

1 Introduction

Blockchain is a novel distributed ledger technology, which has attracted a wide range of interests for building the next generation of applications in diverse areas such as supply chain transparency and safety, accounting, utilities, and the sharing economy. As a concept, blockchain can be defined as "[an append-only store of transactions which is distributed across many machines] that is structured into a linked list of blocks. Each block contains an ordered set of transactions." [18, Chap. 1] The broad range of applications of blockchain is made possible by so-called *smart contracts*, i.e., deterministic "programs deployed as data in the blockchain ledger and executed in transactions on the blockchain." [18, Chap. 1] Smart contracts transform a blockchain system into a general compute platform, with interesting properties like immutability and neutrality.

© Springer Nature Switzerland AG 2019
H.-P. Lam and S. Mistry (Eds.): ASSRI 2018, LNBIP 367, pp. 13–21, 2019.
https://doi.org/10.1007/978-3-030-32242-7_2

For this new paradigm and technology platform, we investigated its impact on software architecture and engineering practices. Our starting point for this investigation was the question *what do architects and engineers need to know about blockchain to make good use of it?* In this keynote, I covered the main insights from this work. As such, the keynote also offered a summary of our recent book [18] on this topic.

More specifically, the keynote gave an outline on the following topics (with references to our research on the topics given for the interested reader):

- a background on blockchain concepts and technology
- the functions blockchain can provide within a software system [18, Chap. 5]
- the options of blockchain systems and their configurations [19]
- trade-offs of non-functional properties, such as cost [10,11], performance [20], or availability [15]
- software design patterns for blockchain-based applications [17].

Blockchain offering a new paradigm and technology platform in the integration space, this bears the question to which degree there is a connection to services, and in how far lessons learned on services can be applied to Blockchain. In the talk, I also explored four different facets of this topic, as follows. First, application-level service interfaces for interaction with blockchain-based applications enable easy integration with existing infrastructure, as discussed in Sect. 2. Second, service composition can be achieved through smart contracts, and enable different approaches to orchestrations and choreographies – see Sect. 3. Third, Blockchain-aaS offerings cover infrastructure operation, but can go beyond that as discussed in Sect. 4. And finally, some principles for designing SOA services and microservices can be applied to smart contract design – see in Sect. 5.[1]

2 Integrating Blockchain-Based Applications with Services

Blockchains operate as closed-world systems, i.e., smart contracts can only access (some of the) data that is stored on blockchain. To interact with smart contracts, a client either needs to operate a node that is directly connected to the blockchain, or rely on such a node operated by someone else (which might introduce undesirable levels of risk or dependency). Interaction with smart contracts can, by default, not take the form of typical Web service interactions; instead, clients often do the following. To *write to* a smart contract, they create and broadcast a blockchain transaction for each method call. To *read from* a smart contract, they read the contract's variable values (e.g., through a local call to a suitable smart contract method) and/or its event logs. To see updates, clients can monitor these variable values and logs.

---

[1] Slides of the talk are available at https://www.slideshare.net/IngoWeber2/blockchain-and-services-exploring-the-links.
Note that a small subset of this paper has been included in an extended abstract.

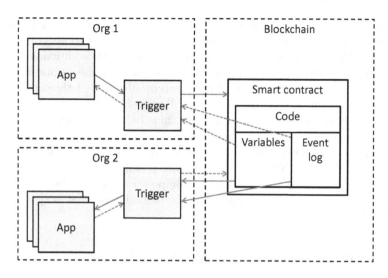

Fig. 1. Trigger component as a bridge between off-chain applications and blockchain

Off-chain applications largely speak the language of Web services, i.e., REST, SOAP-WSDL, JSON RPC or similar. Therefore, a recurring problem when building blockchain applications is how to bridge between the two worlds. A solution we have employed a number of times is to add a so-called *trigger* component as bridge between applications and smart contracts. This component, originally introduced in [16], operates in both directions, i.e., reading from and writing to blockchain. Strictly speaking, the method should apply even when not using smart contracts; but we here focus on the case where smart contracts are used.

The operation of triggers is shown in Fig. 1. In the case shown, applications of two organisations (*Org 1* and *Org 2*) use a smart contract on blockchain to coordinate and interact. One direction of data flow is shown with solid arrows, the other with dashed arrows. Following the solid arrows: if an application of *Org 1* wants to write to the smart contract, it invokes a Web service interface of its trigger component, which in turn creates a blockchain transaction to call a method of the smart contract. In the shown case, the trigger component of *Org 2* observes the update from the event log or variable values of the smart contract, and in turn invokes a Web service exposed by another of *Org 2*'s applications. This application can respond in a similar fashion, as indicated by the dashed arrows. It should be noted that there is no need for the two organisations to coordinate their use of trigger components. The coordination and agreement needs to be about the smart contract's data and functionality, and the purpose of trigger components is to facilitate the integration with other components that use conventional Web service protocols. Numerous alternatives to triggers exist, e.g., by adding blockchain capabilities directly to the enterprise applications.

While the figure shows the interaction of two organisations, it is easy to generalise from this view to many organisations, and to various communication patterns. This style of communication certainly incurs additional overhead in comparison to direct service integration between the applications of organisations: more components, longer latency, potentially limited throughput, and possibly limited control over the blockchain. However, it also has different properties, such as easier scaling to more organisations (where each application needs to integrate only with one blockchain/smart contract, as opposed to integrating with many other enterprise applications), immutability and non-repudiation of writes, global observability, and many other possibilities that come with the use of smart contracts. This includes also composition logic as discussed below, which is executed on a neutral platform – the blockchain – that is typically not controlled by a single entity.

3   Service Composition Using Smart Contracts

Blockchain and smart contracts also offer a new way to enable collaborative business processes and implement web services composition across organizations, by serving as a neutral, independently auditable compute platform [6]. This can be supported by the technology in a number of ways. Specifically, one method is to translate composition models to smart contract code [4,16] using tools such as Caterpillar [5] or Lorikeet [13]. An alternative method is flexible process tracking [8], using the blockchain as a mechanism to track process control via tokens. The focus in the latter case is on tracking handover activities between organisations or individuals, secured by multiple cryptographic signatures.

Web service composition can take the form of an orchestration or a choreography. Both styles of composition have been explored in the context of blockchain, among others in the papers listed above. But blockchain itself stretches the boundaries of those notions – for instance, by enabling choreographies to contain active code that is not executed at either party, but instead on the neutral substrate of the blockchain, an option that was not present in choreography modelling beforehand. These topics deserve further investigation. In a recent research commentary, we broadly discussed the challenges and opportunities for cross-organizational business process implementation using blockchain [6].

4   Blockchain-as-a-Service

Blockchain is a relatively new technology with steep learning curve. According to a survey by Gartner [9], "23% of [relevant surveyed] CIOs said that blockchain requires the most new skills to implement of any technology area, while 18% said that blockchain skills are the most difficult to find." Blockchain-as-a-Service (BaaS) offerings can bootstrap that learning phase to a degree, through pre-made templates or tools for management, development, monitoring, etc. However, it is important not all nodes of a blockchain are running on machines of the same BaaS provider: blockchain introduces decentralisation, but being entirely reliant on a single provider introduces a form of centralisation on a different level, and might negatively impact benefits obtained from using blockchain.

In some currently unpublished research, we investigate the idea of a *unified blockchain as a service* (uBaas) platform, which is vendor and technology platform-agnostic. The main functionalities include deployment as a service, both for blockchain systems and smart contracts, and design patterns as a service. The latter functionality exposes common services for data management and smart contract design, which allow implementing known design patterns to better leverage the unique properties of blockchain (i.e., immutability, data integrity, and transparency) and address the limitations (i.e., privacy and scalability). The patterns are based on the collection presented in [17].

Technology and vendor lock-in might be severe concerns in the future, and much work needs to be done to facilitate the integration of applications across blockchains. Significant efforts are spent on protocols and tools that cross these boundaries. It might be possible to refer to well-known service composition approaches and paradigms as guides for research in this direction.

5   Service Design Principles and Smart Contracts

Before delving into the details of relating service design principles and smart contracts, it is worthwhile discussing microservices, because their design principles deviate from traditional SOA services.

While SOA services can be substantial in scope and complexity, the concept of building smaller services, referred to as *microservices*, has gained popularity in recent years. For instance, microservice architecture is a fitting architectural style for DevOps [1]. Microservice architecture is in wide-spread use now, especially for new development projects. Each service provides small amount of functionality, and the total system functionality comes from composing multiple services – but typically without relying on WS* methods of service composition, which is rather done in code.

There is some similarity of SOA services and microservices with smart contracts. Smart contract code can be compared to a Java Class, and a deployed smart contract is similar to Java Object in that its variables have concrete values, etc. However, a deployed smart contract has some specific properties: it has a defined interface (although it may be unknown); there is a standard way to invoke it; and it is callable by anyone who can send transactions to the blockchain on which the contract is deployed. These properties are shared with Web services. Therefore, some design principles from services could apply to smart contracts.

In Tables 1 and 2, I list the service design principles for SOA services and microservices, and discuss to which degree they might apply to smart contracts. Table 1 lists the Service-Orientation Design Principles from [3], with summary explanations from [14]. The principles of microservice design in Table 2 are mostly derived from [7,12]. In the time between giving the talk and writing this paper, Daniel and Guida wrote an article that explores a comparable angle, although their comparison is through the lens of five categories: service/contract

Table 1. Fit of SOA service design principles to smart contracts

SOA service design principle	Fit to SC	Rationale
Standardized Service Contract: the public interfaces of a services make use of contract design standards. (Contract: WSDL in WS*)	Aspirational	Not present as yet, but would be useful
Service Loose Coupling: to impose low burdens on service consumers (coupling as degree of dependency)	Yes	Should be done for smart contracts as well
Service Abstraction: "to hide as much of the underlying details of a service as possible"	Yes	Abstraction is a fitting design principle for smart contracts, and the design of their public interface deserves careful attention
Service Reusability: services contain agnostic logic and "can be positioned as reusable enterprise resources"	Sometimes	Might apply to some smart contracts, but not often a core concern
Service Autonomy: to provide reliable and consistent results, a service has to have strong control over its underlying environment	Yes	Smart contract control is strong, but limited in scope
Service Statelessness: services should be "designed to remain stateful only when required"	Rarely	Typical contracts carry state, although sometimes it is useful to push state out
Service Discoverability: "services are supplemented with communicative meta data by which they can be effectively discovered and interpreted"	Aspirational	Not present as yet, but would be useful
Service Composability: "services are effective composition participants, regardless of the size and complexity of the composition"	Sometimes	Might apply to some smart contracts, but not often a core concern
Fundamental requirement – interoperability of services: "...stating that services must be interoperable is just about as evident as stating that services must exist"	Rarely	Enabling smart contracts to interoperate directly is rarely a core concern; libraries and common services are of course exceptions

type, interaction style, interaction protocol, data format, and descriptor [2]. They too come to the conclusion that smart contract design would benefit from reuse facilities of services, such as discoverability.

Further to the discussion about abstraction in the tables, architects do need to understand, however, that smart contract (binary) code is visible to other users on most blockchain platforms. As such, implementation details can only be "hidden" in the design sense, not in the security sense – malicious users could re-engineer smart contracts, or attempt attacks (though local calls that are not broadcast) without the knowledge of anyone in the blockchain network.

Table 2. Fit of microservice design principles to smart contracts

Microservice design principle	Fit to SC	Rationale
Small, focused functionality	Yes	Each smart contract should be focused on doing few things, but doing those well
Split of responsibility	Yes	Smart contracts often have limited scope, for which they are fully responsible
Full-stack	Sometimes	Depending on the context, full-stack or split contracts might be the better choice
Independently updatable without downtime	Sometimes	Updates can be independent; but reliance on the *inability* of anyone to update without agreement/governance is one source of trust in smart contracts
Stateless	Rarely	Typically contracts carry state (see Table 1)

As can be seen from the tables, many design principles apply in at least some of the cases. Some are aspirational, in that current practice does not follow these principles, but changing the practice would be beneficial in the smart contract context.

Blockchains and smart contracts could also be used in other, interesting ways. For instance, stateless (or even serverless) services could use smart contracts on blockchain as persistence layer. Such an architecture would especially benefit scenarios with high or highly distributed read and low-frequency write profiles.

6   Summary

Architecting and developing applications on Blockchain is challenging. Our research includes works on Software Architecture for blockchain-based applications, empirical and formal research on blockchains, and model-driven development of smart contracts.

Regarding the links between services and blockchain, this paper and the keynote discussed four main aspects: First, for the integration of blockchain-based applications with off-chain applications, which often use service interfaces, we proposed using a trigger component. Second, service composition can be achieved using smart contracts as neutral mediators, choreography monitors, or other means. Our work in this area often starts with models of cross-organisational business processes for expressing service compositions. Third, Blockchain-as-a-Service can be beneficial for bootstrapping blockchain deployments. And fourth, there are some similarities between smart contracts, and some of the well-studied design principles for SOA services and microservices apply.

In this space, there are still many open research questions. This paper presented some early and some more mature ideas, and I hope these will motivate researchers to work in this very interesting field.

Acknowledgements. My thanks for feedback and insightful discussions go to the audience at the symposium, as well as my colleagues Mark Staples, Hugo O'Connor, Hye-young Paik, Dilum Bandara, and Liming Zhu.

References

1. Bass, L., Weber, I., Zhu, L.: DevOps: A Software Architect's Perspective. Addison-Wesley Professional, Boston (2015). https://doi.org/10.1007/978-0-134-04984-7
2. Daniel, F., Guida, L.: A service-oriented perspective on blockchain smart contracts. IEEE Internet Comput. **23**(1), 46–53 (2019). https://doi.org/10.1109/MIC.2018.2890624
3. Erl, T.: SOA Principles of Service Design. Prentice Hall, Upper Saddle River (2007). http://serviceorientation.com/serviceorientation
4. García-Bañuelos, L., Ponomarev, A., Dumas, M., Weber, I.: Optimized execution of business processes on blockchain. In: Carmona, J., Engels, G., Kumar, A. (eds.) BPM 2017. LNCS, vol. 10445, pp. 130–146. Springer, Cham (2017). https://doi.org/10.1007/978-3-319-65000-5_8
5. López-Pintado, O., García-Bañuelos, L., Dumas, M., Weber, I.: Caterpillar: a blockchain-based business process management system. In: BPM 2017: International Conference on Business Process Management, Demo Track, Barcelona, Spain, September 2017
6. Mendling, J., et al.: Blockchains for business process management - challenges and opportunities. ACM Trans. Manag. Inf. Syst. (TMIS) **9**(1), 4:1–4:16 (2018). https://doi.org/10.1145/3183367
7. Newman, S.: Building Microservices. O'Reilly Media, Sebastopol (2015)
8. Prybila, C., Schulte, S., Hochreiner, C., Weber, I.: Runtime verification for business processes utilizing the Bitcoin blockchain. Future Gener. Comput. Syst. (FGCS) (2017). https://doi.org/10.1016/j.future.2017.08.024
9. Release, G.P.: Gartner survey reveals the scarcity of current blockchain deployments, May 2018. https://www.gartner.com/newsroom/id/3873790. Accessed 4 May 2018
10. Rimba, P., Tran, A.B., Weber, I., Staples, M., Ponomarev, A., Xu, X.: Comparing blockchain and cloud services for business process execution. In: ICSA 2017: IEEE International Conference on Software Architecture, short paper, Gothenburg, Sweden, April 2017
11. Rimba, P., Tran, A.B., Weber, I., Staples, M., Ponomarev, A., Xu, X.: Quantifying the cost of distrust: comparing blockchain and cloud services for business process execution. Inf. Syst. Front. (2018)
12. Subramanian, S.: Microservices design principles. DZone, July 2015. https://dzone.com/articles/microservices-design-principles. Accessed 28 Mar 2019
13. Tran, A.B., Lu, Q., Weber, I.: Lorikeet: a model-driven engineering tool for blockchain-based business process execution and asset management. In: BPM 2018: International Conference on Business Process Management, Demo Track, September 2018
14. Weber, I.: Semantic methods for execution-level business process modeling. Ph.D. thesis, Universität Karlsruhe (TH), November 2009. Springer, LNBIP, vol. 40. https://doi.org/10.1007/978-3-642-05085-5
15. Weber, I., et al.: On availability for blockchain-based systems. In: SRDS 2017: IEEE International Symposium on Reliable Distributed Systems, Hong Kong, China, pp. 64–73, September 2017

16. Weber, I., Xu, X., Riveret, R., Governatori, G., Ponomarev, A., Mendling, J.: Untrusted business process monitoring and execution using blockchain. In: La Rosa, M., Loos, P., Pastor, O. (eds.) BPM 2016. LNCS, vol. 9850, pp. 329–347. Springer, Cham (2016). https://doi.org/10.1007/978-3-319-45348-4_19

17. Xu, X., Pautasso, C., Zhu, L., Lu, Q., Weber, I.: A pattern language for blockchain-based applications. In: EuroPLoP 2018: European Conference on Pattern Languages of Programs, Kloster Irsee, Germany, July 2018

18. Xu, X., Weber, I., Staples, M.: Architecture for Blockchain Applications. Springer, Cham (2019). https://doi.org/10.1007/978-3-030-03035-3

19. Xu, X., et al.: A taxonomy of blockchain-based systems for architecture design. In: ICSA 2017: IEEE International Conference on Software Architecture, Gothenburg, Sweden, April 2017

20. Yasaweerasinghelage, R., Staples, M., Weber, I.: Predicting latency of blockchain-based systems using architectural modelling and simulation. In: ICSA 2017: IEEE International Conference on Software Architecture, short paper, Gothenburg, Sweden, April 2017

Empowering Software Engineering
with Artificial Intelligence

Hoa Khanh Dam[(⊠)]

University of Wollongong, Wollongong, Australia
hoa@uow.edu.au

Abstract. A huge amount of data is constantly generated from the development, maintenance and operation of software products. Buried under this Big Data is insight and patterns that are valuable to the management and development of software projects. The rise of Artificial Intelligence (AI) empowers us to develop next-generation analytics methods to transform software engineering in both quality and productivity. This paper outlines a vision where cutting-edge AI machine learning techniques can be leveraged to develop new data-driven, automated methods for software effort estimation, code patch formulation and risk prediction, all of which are in the context of modern software development settings.

1 Introduction

Software systems have become a critical component of our society as people's daily life depends more and more on the functioning of software applications. Software has increased significantly in size and complexity, making the development of high-quality software products in a productive manner becomes highly challenging. For many years, software projects often suffer late delivery and cost overrun problems. For example, a study conducted by Mckinsey and the University of Oxford in 2012 on 5,400 large scale IT projects revealed that software projects often run 66% exceeding the budget and 33% overtime [1]. Another study by Flyvbjerg and Budzier [2] produced similar findings: one in six of the 1,471 software projects has a budget overrun of 200% and a schedule overrun of almost 70%. Hence, the software industry has been constantly looking for ways to improve software quality, accelerate productivity and increase project success rates. One emerging solution is to provide effective automated support in various software development activities.

The pervasiveness of software products in all areas of society has resulted in millions of software projects (e.g. over 17 million active projects on GitHub) and a massive amount of data about their development, operation and maintenance. Humans are however unable to process such a massive amount of data to obtain insight and patterns that are valuable for software development. Major breakthroughs in recent years in Artificial Intelligence (e.g. deep learning algorithms) enable us to develop machine learners which are capable of harvesting valuable

© Springer Nature Switzerland AG 2019
H.-P. Lam and S. Mistry (Eds.): ASSRI 2018, LNBIP 367, pp. 22–32, 2019.
https://doi.org/10.1007/978-3-030-32242-7_3

insights buried under these Big Data, learning project patterns and training themselves to perform various software engineering supporting tasks. We envision that those AI-powered techniques will significantly improve the theory and practice of software engineering, enabling us to build better software and build software faster, addressing both *quality* and *productivity* needs.

Modern software development is driven by incremental changes made to a software to implement a new functionality, fix a bug, or improve its performance or security. Each change request is often described as an *issue*, and resolving it often requires writing code patches to modify the software's source code. In this paper, we outline a vision for a suite of AI-powered solutions for *predictive analytics* (planning) and *prescriptive analytics* (development) in issue resolution and delivery, specifically:

- **AI-powered techniques for software effort estimation.** Effort estimation is a critical part of software project management, particularly for planning and monitoring a software project. Inaccurate effort estimation may have substantial impact on the success of software projects. Underestimation may result in budget and time overruns, while overestimation may reduce the competitiveness of an organization. Modern agile software development requires highly accurate prediction models which support project managers, software engineers and other decision makers by recommending an estimated effort for a given issue. Effort estimation thus need to take as input not just only the nature of an issue (e.g. issue description) but also the current context (e.g. the existing codebase, the source files likely impacted, the developers involved, and the dependencies with other issues). AI machine learners are able to learn a deep representation of these input information and also learn from historical estimates to predict effort of new issues. This will deliver more significantly accuracy in effort estimation.

- **AI-powered techniques for code patch formulation.** Resolving issues, either for fixing bugs, repairing a security vulnerability, modifying existing functionalities or implementing new functionalities, for a software system remains a central concern in software engineering. Indeed, the development of the widely-used Mozilla Firefox browser has been based on continuously resolving over 1.5 million bugs reported until 2017. A median of 124 issues were created every day in the Firefox project[1]. Due to the significant grow in size and complexity, modern software applications contain many defects. And due to cost and deadline pressures, many software products are shipped with a long list of known but uncorrected defects. Consequences of this unfortunate situation may lead to software failures. AI holds out the promise of providing significant automated support for human developers in resolving issues. AI machine learners are potentially capable of learning from millions of successful code patches written by human developers in open source software repositories. Using this knowledge, AI machinery will then automatically generate a useful template for software developers to complete a full code patch.

---

[1] https://bugzilla.mozilla.org.

– **AI-powered techniques for risk prediction and mitigation**. Predicting future risks is highly challenging due to the inherent uncertainty, temporal dependencies, and especially the dynamic nature of software. This is exactly the area where AI analytics can contribute most, by learning from potentially large datasets and automatically forming a deep understanding of the software, the process of building and maintaining it, and its stakeholders. Such an understanding along with relevant memory of past experience will facilitate automated support for risk prediction and interventions. AI models are needed to predict the delivery performance (both completion time and quantum of work performed) of a team at any given time when they are working towards a release milestone. AI machine learners with its ability to learn from prior iterations to predict the performance of future releases, represents an important advance in the ability to effectively use the incremental model of software development.

In the remaining parts of the paper, we will discuss the challenges and opportunities in meeting the above vision. We then outline a number of approaches which are built on our progress to date.

2   Challenges and Opportunities

Modern software development follows an incremental and iterative approach. A project has a number of iterations, in each of which, a team of software engineers designs, implements, tests and delivers a distinct product increment, e.g. a release. Each release requires the resolution of a number of *issues*. For example, the well-known Web browser, Mozilla Firefox project, currently has over 300 releases and 1.5 million issues since its initial release in 2002. These issue reports were written in natural language, describing a request for implementing a *new functionality* (e.g. bookmark a website), fixing a *bug* (e.g. crash when accessing a certain website), or improving the *security* (e.g. preventing vulnerabilities for phishing scams). Figure 1 shows release *5.14.0* of Bamboo[2], a continuous integration software developed by Atlassian. This release requires the resolution of 42 issues. An issue has a textual description and some additional metadata such as type, priority, status, and so on (see Fig. 2 for an issue report for a bug found in version 5.2 of Bamboo).

Software engineers use these information to resolve an issue, which usually results in writing code patches to modify the software's source code. Writing a code patch is a highly skilled and challenging task, which requires a *deep understanding* of a complex software such as Firefox whose size is around 20 millions lines of source code. Hence, hidden in these releases, issue reports, written code patches and source code are 15 years of valuable, deep insight and experience about how Firefox was developed and evolved. Analyzing this Big Data therefore enables us to learn the nature of these issues, the actual effort and time spent to resolve them, and the resulted changes made to Firefox's source code. It also

---

[2] https://www.atlassian.com/software/bamboo.

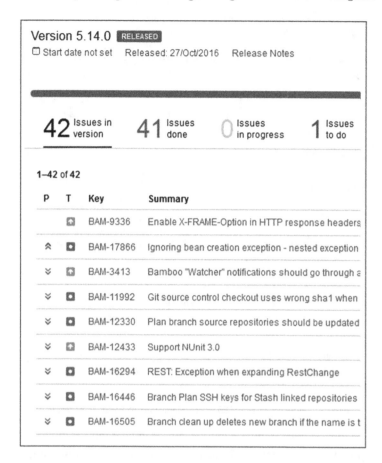

Fig. 1. Release *5.14.0* of project Bamboo at Atlassian

reveals which risks actually occurred (e.g. releases were delayed or missing key functionalities as planned) and the causes of those risks.

It is impossible for humans to process such a massive amount of data and come up with complex, albeit useful, insights. Hence, despite valuable advances made in the past decades, support for project managers, developers and other stakeholders in the following areas is still limited:

– **Estimating the effort of resolving an issue**. Most of the existing work (e.g. [3,4]) in effort estimation focus on estimating the effort required for developing a complete software system (waterfall-like), rather than for a single issue at a time (agile-like). There is thus a serious lack of automated support for estimating issues. Software teams often rely on their subjective assessment to estimate the effort of resolving an issue. This may results in inaccuracy and inconsistencies between estimates. In fact, half of the agile teams studied in [5] provided more than 25% inaccurate estimates.

Fig. 2. Issue *BAM-14425* of project Bamboo at Atlassian

- **Code patch formulation.** Writing a code patch for resolving an issue (either for fixing a security bug or implementing a new functionality) is a time-consuming and challenging task. It may involve a team of highly skilled developers who have to diagnose the issue, understand its root cause, craft the patch to resolve, and validate the patch with regression tests and code reviews. State-of-the-art techniques (e.g. [6,7]) in automatic patch generation mostly follow the prominent generate-and-validate approach: applying modifications to a software's code to generate a space of candidate patches, then searching the generated patch space to find correct patches. Due to a potentially vast search space, this approach is not tractable in practice, especially for large software systems and complex issues. Despite decades of research effort, these techniques only work with simple fixes for small programs with hundreds of lines of code.
- **Risk prediction and mitigation in iterative software projects.** Software practitioners often rely on high-level guidance (e.g. Boehm's "top 10 list of software risk items" or SEI's risk management framework and expert knowledge) to predicting risks in their projects. Although these best practices are useful, making them applicable to a specific situation in a project is typically difficult. Some projects have to rely on external experts to assess risks

specific to the projects. This approach however suffers from subjectiveness. There have been some work (e.g. [8]) addressing risk prediction and mitigation from an empirical perspective. However, they only focused on predicting risks at the project level. Modern software teams however require insightful and actionable information about the current existence of risks at the level of releases and iterations (e.g. delay risks). At these levels, they would be able to work out concrete counter-measures to deal with the risks.

The recent rise of Artificial Intelligence (AI) is potentially a game changer in addressing the above gaps. Machine learning is one well-known form of AI which enables a machine (computer) to perform a task by learning from human experience through historical data (instead of depending on human instructions). Deep learning is a family of machine learning algorithms that allow software to train itself to perform tasks by exposing multilayered neural networks to vast amounts of data. Deep learning has recently delivered many fundamental breakthroughs in computer vision, speech recognition, and natural language processing [9]. Hence, we aim to develop AI machine learners that are capable of harvesting valuable insights buried under the big data about software projects and train themselves to provide automated support for software practitioners in the above tasks. We will now discuss our approach and outline the research work to meet this aim.

3 Approach and Work in Progress

Software can be seen as an evolving organism: how it evolves depends heavily on what has previously been done to it. Hence, an effective approach for automation and prediction is building a data-driven model which sufficiently captures how a software has evolved for a long period of time (e.g. in the case of Firefox, 15 years of evolution), and use it to make future predictions.

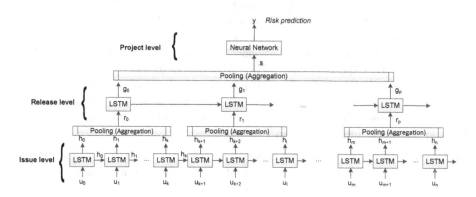

Fig. 3. DeepSoft architecture [10]

One approach is built upon the *DeepSoft* framework [10] (see Fig. 3), which is partly inspired by human memory. DeepSoft is built upon the powerful deep learning architecture called Long Short Term Memory (LSTM) [11]. LSTM is capable of learning long-term temporal dependencies that occur in the evolution of a software. LSTM has demonstrated ground-breaking results in many applications such as natural language processing [12] and speech recognition [13]. As can be seen in Fig. 3, DeepSoft is a compositional architecture. Output from a module (e.g. an LSTM unit) in DeepSoft can be used as input for the next module (e.g. another LSTM unit). DeepSoft carries the full notion of deep learning. It is *end-to-end* prediction model and features are automatically learned from raw data. This reduces the significant effort of manual feature engineering. DeepSoft is capable of analyzing historical software data (e.g. releases, issue reports and source code), learning a long history of past experience and inferring the current "health" state of a software project. It then uses this knowledge to predict future risks and recommend actionable interventions (e.g. code patches).

3.1 Effort Estimation

A prediction system takes as input three important piece of information surrounding an issue: (i) its textual description, additional metadata (e.g. priority, type, etc.), and its relationships to other issues; (ii) the entire existing codebase and the potential affected code; and (iii) the dynamics of teams of software engineers. Thus, we need to compute vector representations for these inputs, which are then used as features to predict the story points of each issue. It is important to note that these features should be automatically learned from raw data, hence removing us from manually engineering the features.

A Deep Representation of Issues: Since the description of an issue is in natural language, there are a number of possibilities we could explore here. Traditional NLP techniques (e.g. Bag of Words) produce very high dimensional and sparse vector representations. By contrast, the latest advances in deep learning-based NLP techniques [14] such as word2vec, paragraph2vec, Long Short-Term Memory (used in Google Translate), or Convolutional Neural Networks (used in Facebook's DeepText engine) are able to generate dense vector representations that produce superior results on various NLP tasks. Our recent work [15] has demonstrated that the Long Short-Term Memory architecture can be leveraged to model software issues for effort estimation, but only used issue description. The issue's dependencies should also be modeled as well as other information we will discuss below. These representations can be combined and then extended to include additional metadata of an issue.

A Deep Representation of Code: A meaningful vector representation for the existing codebase requires modeling of source code. Code elements such as tokens, methods, and classes are embedded into vectors. A few options can be explored here. A code token can be seen as one of the following ways: (a) as a sequence of characters, (b) as an atomic unit, or (c) as a member of a more abstract unit, such as elements in an Abstract Syntax Trees (AST) or Control Flow Graphs. For the first two cases, code is treated in a sequential manner as natural languages where we will build on our prior work [16] on establishing a language model of source code based on the deep learning-based Long Short Term Memory (LSTM) architecture, and using it for vulnerability prediction [17]. For case (c), we can build on our earlier work [18] in using a tree-based LSTM model to automatically learn both syntactic and structural information of the code to generate useful vulnerability-predicting features. A major challenge remains to capture the complex interaction between various code composites such as methods, classes, modules, components, inheritances, call graphs and data dependencies. Capturing all of these require a new graph-based model that can preserve long-range dependencies. We will advance our existing work on graphs modeling [19] and memory-augmented neural nets [20] to develop a new model that capture such complexities.

Identifying Potential Affected Code. We will develop a model which is able to recommend, for a given issue, the most relevant source code files. The model will utilise deep representations of issues and the existing code base. We can then build a machine-learned retrieval model which is able to learn from historical code patches, and returns the most relevant source code files for new issues. Existing research in developing AI machine learners for bug localization can be leveraged here.

Team Modelling. Issue-based estimates are often team specific (e.g. story point estimates are relative values and specific to teams). Hence, an accurate estimation machinery must consider the modeling of the capability and dynamics of software teams. An effective representation of a team requires modeling of its members (e.g. developers). A developer can be represented through the work product they have produced such as the code they wrote. We thus need an AI machinery to extract all the representations of the artifacts related to a developer, and learn to aggregate them to form a vector representation of the developer. Representations of different software artifacts (in both unstructured and structured forms) also need to be aggregated. In addition, features representing work and social dependencies between team members, extracted from communication logs (e.g. comments or discussions on work items), should also be aggregated to form a rich model of the team and its individual members. In our previous work, we have developed several feature aggregation techniques [21] specifically for software artifacts (e.g. iterations and issues). Those aggregation methods can be extended to learn features for representing team members.

3.2 Code Patch Formulation

We can consider this as a machine translation problem: given an issue's description in natural language (source language), we aim to translate it into a code patch written in a programming language (target language). In the first step, the generated code patch would be in the form of a partial template containing a sequence of programming constructs (e.g. API calls). We can adapt state-of-the-art deep learning-based machine translation model such as RNN Encoder-Decoder [22] for code path generation. Given a corpus of $<issue, patch>$ pairs, we train the language model that encodes each sequence of words (annotation) into a fixed-length context vector and decodes a patch template based on the context vector. Then, in response to a new issue's description, it generates a patch template by consulting the language model. Earlier work (e.g. [23]) has demonstrated the initial promise of using a sequence-to-sequence translation model (seq2seq) for fixing bugs. They however operate at the code token level and are thus unable to capture the rich structural properties of code. We have successfully used Neural Machine Translation (NMT) for code transformation [24] and have had preliminary success in developing graph-based deep neural networks [19]. We will build on these experiences to develop new models for code transformation where the source and target representation are tree-based or graph-based.

One potential challenge is that labelled pairs of issue and corresponding patches could be limited. Hence, we will need to extend the NMT models to deal with limited training data. One approach is using adversarial learning with Generative Adversarial Networks (GANs) [25]. The NMT model will be the generator and we will train the discriminator to differentiate between NMT-generated outputs and real examples of expected output.

3.3   Delivery Risk Prediction Models

We will build a risk prediction model based upon DeepSoft [10]. In its basic form, the model has several layers (see Fig. 3) which represent the progression of a software at three levels: issue, release and project. The bottom layer has a series of repeating modules of LSTM units. Each unit takes an input u_t, representing an issue being resolved at time t, and the output h_{t-1} from the previous unit, to compute the output h_t. Hence, h_t captures the summary information from all previous inputs $u_0, u_1, ..., u_{t-1}$. The input u_t represents both the nature of an issue (denoting as vector x_t), its resolution in terms of code patches p_t, and the elapsed time Δ_t between this issue and the previous one, i.e. $u_t = [x_t, p_t, \Delta_t]$.

To deliver a release, a team needs to resolve a number of issues which were scheduled for that release. In the previous step, we have modeled the issue dynamics using LSTM (see to the issue level in Fig. 3). In the next step, we aggregate the issue representation to derive a representation for the release. The aggregation operator is commonly known as pooling. There are different pooling techniques such as mean-pooling which takes the sum of the output vectors of all the issues in the release divided by the number of issues to derive a vector representing a release (i.e. r_i in Fig. 3). In our previous work, we have employed a number of aggregation techniques [21] to derive features representing an iteration and use them to predict the delivery capability in that iteration. Further complex pooling techniques may capture the attention to recency such as assigining more weight to recent issues than outdated ones. The next layer of LSTMs takes as input a sequence of releases $r_0, r_1, ..., r_p$ and produces a corresponding sequence of states $g_0, g_1, ..., g_p$. These vectors are again aggregated into a single vector s which is the representation of the whole project. Vector s is input into a neural network which is trained to predict future risk events. This framework thus enables risk prediction at both the release and project level.

4 Conclusions

AI has the potential to disrupt modern software development, enabling us to build higher quality software with higher productivity. The invention of novel AI data-driven solutions will significantly improve the theory and practice of software engineering. In this paper, we have highlighted some of the recent work in applying AI into software engineering. We have also outlined an AI-powered approach to automate effort estimation, code patch formulation and risk predictions in modern software development settings. Our focus in this paper is on machine learning, but it is important to note that other AI branches such as evolutionary computing, knowledge representation, and agent technology can also be applied to solve software engineering problems.

References

1. Michael, B., Blumberg, S., Laartz, J.: Delivering large-scale IT projects on time, on budget, and on value. Technical report (2012)
2. Flyvbjerg, B., Budzier, A.: Why your IT project may be riskier than you think. Harvard Bus. Rev. **89**(9), 601–603 (2011)
3. Panda, A., Satapathy, S.M., Rath, S.K.: Empirical validation of neural network models for agile software effort estimation based on story points. Procedia Comput. Sci. **57**, 772–781 (2015)
4. Kocaguneli, E., Menzies, T., Keung, J.W.: On the value of ensemble effort estimation. IEEE Trans. Softw. Eng. **38**(6), 1403–1416 (2012)
5. Usman, M., Mendes, E., Weidt, F., Britto, R.: Effort estimation in agile software development: a systematic literature review. In: Proceedings of the 10th International Conference on Predictive Models in Software Engineering (PROMISE), pp. 82–91 (2014)
6. Nguyen, H.D.T., Qi, D., Roychoudhury, A., Chandra, S.: Semfix: program repair via semantic analysis. In: Proceedings of the 2013 International Conference on Software Engineering, ICSE 2013, pp. 772–781. IEEE Press, Piscataway (2013)
7. Long, F., Rinard, M.: Staged program repair with condition synthesis. In: Proceedings of the 2015 10th Joint Meeting on Foundations of Software Engineering, ESEC/FSE 2015, pp. 166–178. ACM, New York (2015)
8. Hu, Y., Zhang, X., Ngai, E., Cai, R., Liu, M.: Software project risk analysis using Bayesian networks with causality constraints. Decis. Support Syst. **56**, 439–449 (2013)
9. LeCun, Y., Bengio, Y., Hinton, G.: Deep learning. Nature **521**(7553), 436–444 (2015)
10. Dam, H.K., Tran, T., Grundy, J., Ghose, A.: Deepsoft: a vision for a deep model of software. In: Proceedings of the 2016 24th ACM SIGSOFT International Symposium on Foundations of Software Engineering, FSE 2016, pp. 944–947. ACM, New York (2016)
11. Hochreiter, S., Schmidhuber, J.: Long short-term memory. Neural Comput. **9**(8), 1735–1780 (1997)
12. Sundermeyer, M., Schlüter, R., Ney, H.: LSTM neural networks for language modeling. In: INTERSPEECH, pp. 194–197 (2012)

13. Graves, A., Mohamed, A.R., Hinton, G.: Speech recognition with deep recurrent neural networks. In: IEEE International Conference on Acoustics, Speech and Signal Processing (ICASSP), pp. 6645–6649. IEEE (2013)
14. Manning, C.D.: Computational linguistics and deep learning. Comput. Linguist. **41**(4), 701–707 (2016)
15. Choetkiertikul, M., Dam, H.K., Tran, T., Pham, T., Ghose, A., Menzies, T.: A deep learning model for estimating story points. IEEE Trans. Softw. Eng. (2018)
16. Dam, H.K., Tran, T., Pham, T.: A deep language model for software code. In: Workshop on Naturalness of Software, Co-located with the 24th ACM SIGSOFT International Symposium on the Foundations of Software Engineering (FSE) (2016)
17. Dam, H.K., Tran, T., Pham, T., Ng, S.W., Grundy, J., Ghose, A.: Automatic feature learning for predicting vulnerable software components. IEEE Trans. Softw. Eng. (2018)
18. Dam, H.K., et al.: A deep tree-based model for software defect prediction. CoRR - under review at the 16th International Conference on Mining Software Repositories (MSR 2019) abs/1802.00921 (2018)
19. Pham, T., Tran, T., Venkatesh, S.: Graph memory networks for molecular activity prediction. International Conference on Learning Representations (ICLR) abs/1801.02622 (2018)
20. Le, H., Tran, T., Venkatesh, S.: Learning to remember more with less memorization. International Conference on Learning Representations (ICLR) abs/1901.01347 (2019)
21. Choetkiertikul, M., Dam, H.K., Tran, T., Ghose, A., Grundy, J.: Predicting delivery capability in iterative software development. IEEE Trans. Softw. Eng. **44**(6), 551–573 (2018)
22. Sutskever, I., Vinyals, O., Le, Q.V.: Sequence to sequence learning with neural networks. In: Advances in Neural Information Processing Systems, pp. 3104–3112 (2014)
23. Gupta, R., Pal, S., Kanade, A., Shevade, S.: Deepfix: fixing common C language errors by deep learning. In: Proceedings of the Thirty-First AAAI Conference on Artificial Intelligence, San Francisco, California, USA, 4–9 February 2017, pp. 1345–1351. AAAI Press (2017)
24. Alhefdhi, A., Dam, H.K., Hata, H., Ghose, A.: Generating pseudo-code from source code using deep learning. In: 25th Australasian Software Engineering Conference, ASWEC 2018, Adelaide, Australia, 26–30 November 2018, pp. 21–25. IEEE Computer Society (2018)
25. Goodfellow, I., et al.: Generative adversarial nets. In: Advances in Neural Information Processing Systems, pp. 2672–2680 (2014)

Research Track

Preference Feedback for Driving
in an Unfamiliar Traffic Regulation

Hasan J. Alyamani[1(⊠)], Annika Hinze[2], Stephen Smith[1],
and Manolya Kavakli[1]

[1] Macquarie University, Sydney, Australia
hasan.j.alyamani@gmail.com
[2] The University of Waikato, Hamilton, New Zealand

Abstract. Driving in an unfamiliar traffic regulation is associated with difficulties in adjusting with the new conditions and rules. Providing feedback in a
proper way can help drivers overcome such difficulties. This paper aims to
explore the most preferred feedback modality, feedback presenting time, and
frequency of presenting feedback when turning left at a roundabout when
driving in an unfamiliar traffic regulation, namely, a keep-left traffic regulation.
Driving in a roundabout includes navigation, speed, and signal indication.
Thirty-five participants who were not familiar with an Australian traffic regulation (i.e. keep-left and a right-hand driving vehicle) answered the online
survey. We found that visual feedback is the most preferred modality in all
driving tasks related to driving at a roundabout. Also, concurrent feedback is the
most preferred feedback presenting time. There is no a particular preferred
frequency to present the feedback. Our findings would help design the feedback
system to assist the driver in such a driving condition.

Keywords: Feedback modality · An unfamiliar traffic regulation · Roundabout

1 Introduction

International drivers who are familiar with a keep-right traffic regulation, which uses a
left-hand driving vehicle, might face difficulties while driving under an unfamiliar
traffic regulation (UFTR). In this research, a UFTR refers to a keep-left traffic regulation which uses a right-hand driving vehicle. A UFTR represents the driving rules in
some countries, such as New Zealand and Australia. When it comes to driving under
UFTR, driving can be more rigorous and might increase vehicle accidents, especially at
roundabouts and intersections [17].

In general, driving tasks such as approaching, entering or exiting roundabouts
mainly require a set of complex skills including perceptual, cognitive and motor skills
[27]. Perceptual skills are responsible for capturing surroundings using audio, visual
and tactile channels. Then, the cognitive skills process the captured information to find
out the proper required reactions. Finally, the motor skills apply those reactions.
Therefore, not capturing important information or capturing irrelevant information
influences both the cognitive and the motor stage.

© Springer Nature Switzerland AG 2019
H.-P. Lam and S. Mistry (Eds.): ASSRI 2018, LNBIP 367, pp. 35–49, 2019.
https://doi.org/10.1007/978-3-030-32242-7_4

In driving, relevant information to the task, instructions or feedback can be provided to drivers by driving assistance systems. However, providing unsuitable feedback modality or presenting feedback in an inappropriate time results in a detriment in driving performance [10, 12, 25] or an increase in the driver's cognitive load [23, 26].

In this paper, we will identify the preference feedback modality and feedback presenting time, and the frequency of presenting feedback when driving under a UFTR. That will help us design the most preferable feedback system for turn-left roundabouts.

2 Background: Augmented Feedback

Augmented feedback is the technology that integrates computer-generated objects with the real/virtual-world environment to improve the performance of a certain task [23]. The feedback is generally provided as visual, audio or tactile signals to enrich the user's sense of surroundings. In addition, the feedback can be presented concurrently with or terminally after performing the target task. Overall, augmented feedback reveals promising results with various applications including driving.

2.1 Feedback Modality

Feedback modality can be either unimodal or multimodal. Unimodal feedback could be visual (e.g.: [5, 24]), auditory (e.g. [4, 20, 29]) or haptic (e.g. [6]) - that is, one feedback format at one time. On the other hand, multimodal feedback is a combination of two or three presentation formats presented at once, simultaneity. It might be audiovisual (e.g. [28]), visuohaptic (e.g. ([25]), audiohaptic (e.g. [12]), or audiovisuohaptic feedback (e.g. [16]).

The visual and auditory feedback stimulates the driver's visual and audio channel, respectively, where the haptic feedback stimulates the driver's sense of touch to collect information regarding the current or the near future surroundings. In driving, visual feedback might come as an image [24, 28] or a text [22]. Auditory feedback might be employed as messages, either short [4] or long [29] or beeping [20]. Haptic feedback may be configured to vibrate the driver's seat [11], steering wheel [12], gas/acceleration pedal [15], the driver's seatbelt [22] or using an additional and special belt [6]. In general, visual feedback is more efficient to improve the spatial aspects of the motor task whereas auditory and haptic feedback shows an improvement in the temporal aspects of the target motor task [23].

In avoiding collisions scenarios, such as vehicle following task, haptic feedback results in a shorter reaction time than using visual feedback [22]. Using only audio feedback also helps the driver to avoid the hazard in a short time [8]. In the tasks that require controlling the speed, providing auditory feedback reduces the speed [8]. Azzi et al. [3] state that haptic feedback has no significant advantage over visual feedback when the feedback provided in eco-driving task as the drivers show similar eco-performance. In a navigation task, drivers prefer auditory feedback of route information over visual ones as auditory feedback helps the drivers to easily remember the route information [10]. The haptic feedback provided in a navigation system reduces the drivers' workload over using the visual feedback [25]. The visual feedback is helpful when it applies with auditory feedback (i.e. audiovisual feedback) to clarify or elaborate the same information presented by the audio feedback. However, providing audiohaptic feedback in a noisy and distracted driving environment helps the driver to make less navigation errors over providing only auditory feedback [12]. In comparison of providing only visual and other multimodal feedback, [7] cites that providing audiovisual and visuohaptic feedback is advantageous compared to providing only visual feedback in general tasks. However, in a high cognitive load environment and a complex task, such as driving, visuohaptic helps to decrease the driver's cognitive load. Also, visuohaptic feedback is more favoured over using only visual or haptic feedback in order to reduce the reaction time [25].

2.2 Feedback Presenting Time and Frequency

Feedback is divided based on presentation time into concurrent and terminal feedback. Concurrent feedback is presented at the same time as motor task execution or situational changes (e.g.: [6]). Terminal feedback, on the other hand, is presented after the motor task execution. For example, the system collects data regarding some driving tasks, such as manoeuvres, speed, and lane-changing and afterward provides visual feedback representing the history of the driving performance in a web-based application [13]. Moreover, it is possible to use the feedback, either concurrent or terminal, more frequently when driving in unfamiliar environments then less frequently when the drivers get more familiar with the environments [11, 14]. In this case, the feedback is known as concurrent/terminal bandwidth feedback.

3 Related Work

3.1 Driving in an Unfamiliar Traffic Regulation

Driving in an unfamiliar traffic regulation is a stressful task and thus it might lead to a vehicle accident. As a result, various studies focus on the driver's behavior, needs and driving performance to assist drivers in such a condition. For instance, [10] investigated the driver's behavior and performance when driving with auditory investigational instructions on unfamiliar roads using a multi-disciplinary approach. They found that drivers prefer the auditory route information when driving in unfamiliar roads in order to remember the direction of the target destination. Saito et al. [21] explore the differences of performing lane-keeping using both a familiar and unfamiliar vehicle configuration (i.e. right-hand driving vehicle and left-hand driving vehicle, respectively) in a familiar traffic regulation. They found that using an unfamiliar vehicle configuration leads to an increase in lane departure.

Alyamani and Kavakli [1] assess the changing between lanes of a dual-lane roads in driving conditions the drivers are not familiar with (i.e. a keep-left traffic regulation and a right-hand driving vehicle). Overall, the drivers show low performance at roundabouts and intersections, particularly before, inside and after roundabouts and intersections although the area of roundabouts and intersections are relatively small.

As a result, [2] studies the driving performance and driver's behavior of unfamiliar drivers with a keep-left traffic regulation, particularly when turning left or right, or going straight ahead at roundabouts and intersections. Drivers make lots of errors, including using an improper lane to enter and exit roundabouts/intersections, not using the signal indicator properly, speeding and driving in a wrong direction around the roundabout. Accordingly, Alyamani et al. [2] recommend designing a feedback system that presents the relevant information for driving at roundabouts. However, to the best of our knowledge, there are no studies so far that focus on the preferable feedback presentation mechanism when driving under UFTR, particularly at roundabouts.

3.2   Feedback Systems at Roundabouts/Intersections

We address some related studies that focus on presenting feedback to the driver at roundabouts as well as intersections. Despite our main focus of this paper being on roundabouts, studies about intersections are included as roundabouts are a configuration/ type of intersection.

Boll et al. [6] introduces a new method of presenting navigation information in a keep-right driving regulation. They display haptic information at different intersection configurations, including roundabouts. They use a special waist belt with a number of vibration points to display the haptic information. Each point is activated in accordance with the needed information. For example, all vibrated points are activated one by one in an anticlockwise direction to indicate the roundabout ahead. When the driver is inside the roundabout and preparing to leave it, only the right point is vibrated. The system managed to help the driver to reach the roundabout from the proper lane. However, the driver should learn the meaning of each haptic feedback and understand it well prior to actually using it in order to gain the benefits of using the system.

Ege et al. [12] introduce an audiohaptic feedback system to support drivers in a navigation task, particularly at roundabouts and intersections in a keep-right regulation. The auditory feedback is produced from the standard GPS while the haptic feedback produced by two vibration motors attached to the left and right of the steering wheel. The multimodal feedback is triggered in different intersection and roundabout driving scenarios. In case of approaching a roundabout, both vibration motors with a voice command "Approaching a roundabout" are activated. "Turn right" associated with continuous vibrations placed on the right side of the steering wheel is activated when the driver should turn right from the roundabout. When the driver should go straight-ahead from a roundabout, the system only provides an auditory feedback "Go ahead" without any vibrations at all. However, the driver must keep both hands on the steering wheel to receive both auditory and haptic feedback together. The driver should be well trained and fully understand the vibration commands to correctly respond to those commands.

Change et al. [9] tested different navigation and speed feedback modalities to help the driver safely reach the target destination. A set of three arrows (i.e. turning right, turning left and going forward) visually represent the target direction. The speed limit sign is provided when speeding. Short auditory feedback (i.e. "Turn right", "Turn left", or "Go straight") is played to notify the driver of the required direction of the upcoming section of the road. Another short auditory feedback (i.e. "the speed limit is 80 km/h") is played when the vehicle exceeds the speed limit. To provide haptic feedback, a set of vibration points are installed in the bolsters, back support and seat pan of the driver's seat. The vibration points on the right bolster are activated when turning right is required and the vibration points on the left bolster are activated when turning left is required. The vibration points on the set pan are working to inform the driver to go forward. The vibrations on the back support are vibrated when the vehicle's speed is too fast. However, the system does not provide information regarding the proper lane the driver should be in.

Rossi et al. [20] designed a feedback system to warn the drivers of excessive speed when reaching a 4-exit-roundabout in a keep-right regulation. The system detects the upcoming roundabout and the vehicle's speed. Then the system builds a communication between them, in terms of the distance remaining to reach the roundabout and the vehicle's current rate of speed. When the driver reaches a certain distance with high speed, for example, a continuous warning (i.e. beeping) is sounded. Beeping is a common method in vehicles to indicate the tasks related to speed which makes it easier for the driver to predict the meaning behind this warning. Nevertheless, the warning does not completely provide sufficient information to the driver to drive at the roundabout, especially when driving under an unfamiliar traffic regulation. In addition to speed, the driver should know some other important information (e.g. the proper lane to enter and leave the roundabout as well as the proper direction of driving within the roundabout).

Zhang et al. [29] employed a collision warning system in a keep-right regulation. The system sends directional and non-directional auditory warning information to the driver in scenarios containing unexpected hazard events at a signalized cross-intersection. The system is triggered when a vehicle is approaching the intersection during a green light while another vehicle crosses the intersection in the red phase. The system will warn the oncoming vehicle, which has the right to cross the intersection, of the danger. The warnings used in the system are clear auditory long directional or non-directional information (i.e. "please watch out for the vehicle running the red light on your right" or "please watch out for the vehicle running the red light", respectively) and then the driver responds to avoid the possible collision. According to Zhang et al. [29], directional information gives the driver adequate time to make proper preparation (i.e. more moderate braking) for potential collision. However, the system is not influenced by driving in the correct entering and exiting lane, driving on the correct side of the road, and signaling. Moreover, the system does not include scenarios when the driver is not familiar with the traffic configuration.

Zhang et al. [28] designed a feedback system that provides either visual or audiovisual information when approaching a poor visibility cross-intersection under a keep-left regulation. The visual information is presented statically (i.e. a traffic light presented above an intersection image) or dynamically (i.e. a vehicle presented above an image of intersection). Similarly, the auditory information has two types: static information (i.e. "Attention! Traffic signal ahead") and dynamic information (i.e. "Attention! Stopping vehicles ahead"). The dynamic information is more effective to assist the driver to avoid a dangerous driving situation. Additionally, the visual and audiovisual information has the same effect on driving safely at the intersection. However, the system helps the driver to reduce speed when reaching a red-traffic light intersection but does not help the driver follow the required reactions to drive at intersections in an unfamiliar traffic regulation.

Tran et al. [24] studied driving performance at intersections when driving under keep-right regulation. They looked particularly at signalized turn-left intersections. In such driving scenarios under this regulation, the driver does not have the right to turn left and thus the driver must cross the path of a vehicle coming from the opposite direction. The driver therefore must correctly judge the velocity and time gap of the oncoming vehicle. The feedback system visualizes a three-second projected path of the oncoming vehicle on 3D Head-Up Display in the driver's main field of view. The system displays a red path to the driver to indicate a dangerous crossing or a green path to indicate a safe crossing. Using this method can increase the driver's awareness of an approaching intersection and project the future reaction. That can help the driver to turn left at the intersection with more caution. The provided path helps the driver to operate on the correct side of the road, and correctly and properly enter and exit from intersections/roundabout. In addition, the system helps the driver decrease their speed or completely stop the vehicle prior to turning at a roundabout/intersection although the projected path does not really show speed information. The only important information the system does not provide is using the signal indicator to indicate the target turn. The system works only when another vehicle is attempting to cross the impending intersection. This sort of information might always be important for drivers who are not familiar with a certain traffic regulation.

4 Method

4.1 Feedback Prototype

Driving safe at roundabouts in NSW, Australia requires drivers to follow a certain procedure [19]. The procedure lies on three instructions as follows:

A. Drive on a proper lane, when approaching, entering and exiting the roundabout, considering entering roundabouts from a correct direction (i.e. clockwise around the roundabout island).
B. Completely stop the vehicle or slow it down.
C. Indicate when entering and leaving roundabout.

According to Alyamani et al. [2], drivers unfamiliar with Australian traffic regulation had difficulties at roundabouts and instructions. Accordingly, we proposed a design for visual, auditory and haptic feedback (see Table 1). The visual feedback representing the first instruction used a similar method used by [24]. The path represented the lane the driver must drive on when approaching, entering and exiting roundabouts. The visual feedback of the second instruction was a well-known and common road sign displaying the road speed limit. The third instruction was visually designed to remind the driver to indicate entering and leaving the roundabout. The feedback presented a steering wheel with two icons representing the placement of wiper and signal indicators. The designed auditory feedback of the first and third instruction was short as the audio feedback did not lead to a significant interference to a simulation-driving task [10]. In addition, the feedback was directional auditory feedback to direct the driver to drive within the correct lane, inform the driver of the target direction and let the driver know of the location of the signal indicator. Directional information gave the driver sufficient time to make proper preparation [29]. For the second instruction, speeding, we designed warning auditory feedback (i.e. beeping). This feedback was used in [20] to control the vehicle speed. The haptic feedback for the first instruction was a combination of the haptic feedback provided in [13] and a modified version of the haptic feedback provided in [6]. The left side of a vibration steering wheel was vibrated in the case of a turn-left roundabout ahead. A special seatbelt supported with vibration points was activated one by one in a clockwise direction to indicate the correct direction around the roundabout. In the case of exiting the roundabout, the vibration point placed on the left was activated to inform the driver of the target exit. The vibrations on the back support of the driver's seat could be used to warn the driver about exceeding the speed limit, like [9]. Due to lack of studies of designing haptic feedback for using the signal indicator, we propose three general possible vibration feedbacks (i.e. steering, seat and seat belt vibration) used to design other information from the literature.

4.2 Questionnaire Design and Procedure

The online survey was designed mainly to extract the information about drivers' preferences with a feedback system that aims to assist international drivers, particularly, when they turn left at roundabouts in a UFTR. Feedback systems can be designed in different modalities and presenting times. It is, consequently, important to undertake an initial assessment to identify whether the drivers have specific preferences in terms of how certain feedback is presented and when the feedback should be presented. We investigated this issue using a questionnaire consisting of three items.

Prior to starting the questionnaire, information regarding driving at roundabouts in Australia was addressed, in case the participant was not familiar with such driving rules. The questionnaire started with collecting demographic information, such as age, gender, handedness and driving experience in both keep-left and keep-right traffic regulation. A short clip of a vehicle driving on a keep-left traffic regulation was played prior to answering the items on the questionnaire in order to give the participants a better sense of driving in Australia, especially those who were unfamiliar with Australian traffic rules.

The participants then moved on to answer the other questions. We provided the participants with Table 1 and the list of roundabout driving instructions mentioned earlier in this section, and coded as instruction A, instruction B and instruction C. In this paper, we focused on three items. The participants were given the chance to comment on their experience with each question.

Table 1. Designed/proposed feedback of each modality for each instruction the driver should follow when driving in a roundabout in a keep-left traffic regulation

Instruction	Visual	Auditory	Haptic
A		"Use the left lane" "Use clockwise direction" "Use the left lane"	Vibrations on the left-side of a vibration steering wheel. Vibrations on the seatbelt in a clockwise direction. Vibrations on the left-side of the seatbelt to leave the roundabout.
B		"Beep! Beep!"	Vibrations on the back support of the driver's seat.
C		"Use the indicator placed on the right side"	Steering, seat or seat belt vibration

Item 1: Indicate the preferred feedback modality for each roundabout driving instruction; it had three questions.

Q1: Using the provided table and driving instructions, rate each feedback modality [visual, auditory, haptic, audiovisual, visuohaptic, audiohaptic, and audiovisuohaptic] of instruction (A) in order to avoid making a driving error or causing an accident.

Q2: Using the provided table and driving instructions, rate each feedback modality [visual, auditory, haptic, audiovisual, visuohaptic, audiohaptic, and audiovisuohaptic] of instruction (B) in order to avoid making a driving error or causing an accident.

Q3: Using the provided table and driving instructions, rate each feedback modality [visual, auditory, haptic, audiovisual, visuohaptic, audiohaptic, and audiovisuohaptic] of instruction (C) in order to avoid making a driving error or causing an accident.

Item 2: Rate the usefulness of presenting the instructions at the following times:
- At the time of making a driving error while driving in the roundabout.
- Only receive a summary of your driving errors at the roundabout when you finish driving (not while driving).

Item 3: Rate the usefulness of presenting the instructions at the following times:
- Every time you are driving at a roundabout, including familiar and unfamiliar driving conditions.
- Every time you are driving at a roundabout in unfamiliar driving environments.

- More frequently in case of driving at a roundabout in an unfamiliar driving environment and then less frequently once you get familiar with the driving environment.

4.3   Participants

We demonstrated the online surveys with 35 participants aged 19-52 (mean: 28.63, SD: 6.571) to select the preference feedback modality and presenting time. The participants took part in a simulated empirical experiment [1, 2] to explore the driving performance of international drivers when driving in a UFTR. The participants were reached by email and the link for the online survey was attached to the email. All selected participants were from keep-right countries and all of them were not familiar with a keep-left traffic regulation.

4.4   Data Analysis

The study used a within-subject design with one independent variable in each question. In questions for item 1, the independent variable is the feedback modality with seven levels representing the possible feedback modalities. Item 2 had an independent variable with two levels representing the possible presenting times while the independent variable of item 3 had three levels representing the possible frequency of presenting the feedback. The dependent variable of each question is the rating value (i.e. 5-point Likert scale). The participants' answers were grouped and then a mean rating score was calculated for each question. According to [18], to compare the mean scores for ordinal data, we should use non-parametric tests. As we had two variables in each question and the independent variable had 2 levels or more, the Friedman and Wilcoxon tests were used.

5   Results

The ratings of participants to the preference modality of each feedback are summarized on Table 2.

5.1   Preference Feedback Modality

Feedback Modality for Instruction A. The mean of the ranks in visual, auditory, haptic, audiovisual, visuohaptic, audiohaptic, and audiovisuohaptic were 4.71, 3.80, 3.20, 4.31, 3.66, 3.29 and 3.60 respectively (see Table 2). Based on the Friedman test, there was a statistically significant difference in preference feedback modality of feedback A, $\chi^2(6) = 58.507$, $p < .001$. That indicates some modalities were more preferable than other modalities. Twenty-one orthogonal contrasts were performed using Wilcoxon tests with the Bonferroni correction (comparison-wise alpha = .007). The contrasts between visual and other modalities were found significant: visual and auditory ($Z = -3.568$, $p < .001$), visual and haptic ($Z = -4.047$, $p < .001$), visual and audiovisual (Z = −2.442, p = .015), visual and visuohaptic (Z = −3.677, p < .001), visual and audiohaptic (Z = −4.442, p < .001) and visual and audiovisuohaptic (Z = −3.447, p = .001).

Feedback Modality for Instruction B. The mean of the ranks in visual, auditory, haptic, audiovisual, visuohaptic, audiohaptic, and audiovisuohaptic were 4.31, 4.11, 3.69, 4.14, 3.77, 3.63 and 3.66 respectively. For feedback B, there was a significant difference among the distributions of the seven feedback modalities based on Friedman's test, $\chi^2(6) = 14.080$, p = .029, which means some modalities were more preferable than other modalities. The pairwise comparisons using Wilcoxons tests with a Bonferroni correction applied, resulting in a significance level set at p < .007 show that participants preferred visual modality over some other modalities: video over haptic (Z = −3.209, p = .001), visual over audiohaptic (Z = −3.219, p = .001), and visual over audiovisuohaptic (Z = −2.907, p = .004). There were no significant differences between visual and auditory (Z = −1.495, p = .135), visual and audiovisual (Z = −.876, p = .381) or between visual over visuohaptic (Z = −2.834, p = .005).

Feedback Modality for Instruction C. The mean of the ranks in visual, auditory, haptic, audiovisual, visuohaptic, audiohaptic, and audiovisuohaptic were 4.23, 3.74, 3.63, 3.54, 3.69, 3.29 and 3.54, respectively. A Friedman test indicated that feedback modalities were rated differently for feedback C, $\chi^2(6) = 16.649$, p = .011. Post hoc analysis with Wilcoxon signed-rank tests was conducted with a Bonferroni correction applied, resulting in a significance level set at p < .007. The test indicated that the median visual ranks were statistically significantly higher than the median of the majority of other modalities: visual higher than auditory (Z = −2.062, p = .039), visual higher than haptic (Z = −2.158, p = .031), visual higher than audiovisual (Z = −2.230, p = .026), visual higher than audiohaptic (Z = −3.140, p = .002), and visual higher than audiovisuohaptic (Z = −2.381, p = .017). However, the median visual ranks were not significantly higher than the median of visuohaptic (Z = −1.904, p = .057).

Table 2. A summary of results for questions of item 1.

Feedback	Mean scores of each modality							Friedman test	
	V	A	H	AV	VH	AH	VAH	X	P
A	4.71 (.622)	3.80 (1.279)	3.20 (1.511)	4.31 (.796)	3.66 (1.392)	3.29 (1.341)	3.60 (1.355)	58.507	.000
B	4.31 (.993)	4.11 (1.051)	3.69 (1.301)	4.14 (1.004)	3.77 (1.352)	3.63 (1.374)	3.66 (1.392)	14.080	.029
C	4.23 (1.140)	3.74 (1.358)	3.63 (1.457)	3.54 (1.482)	3.69 (1.451)	3.29 (1.506)	3.54 (1.358)	16.649	.011

5.2   Feedback Presenting Time

The mean of the ranks in feedback presenting method (i.e. concurrently with the performance or terminally when finishing the performance) were 10.13 and 9.50, respectively. Wilcoxon signed-rank tests with the Bonferroni correction (comparison-wise alpha = .025) of paired comparisons indicated that the participants significantly preferred presenting the feedback concurrently with their performance than terminally when they finished their performance ($Z = -2.349$, p = 0.19).

5.3   Frequency of Presenting Feedback

The mean ranks of presenting the feedback whenever the driver drives in a familiar and an unfamiliar regulation was 1.77. The mean ranks of presenting the feedback only when the driver drives at a roundabout in an unfamiliar driving regulation was 2.03. The mean rank of presenting the feedback more frequently when driving in an unfamiliar regulation and then less frequently after becoming familiar with the driving regulation was 2.20. A Friedman test was used to compare the preference frequency of presenting feedback in terms of getting familiar with an Australian driving regulation. The test indicated that there was no statistically significant difference in preference frequency of presenting feedback, $\chi^2(2) = 4.957$, p < .084. This indicates that participants did not prefer any particular frequency of presenting feedback over other frequencies.

6   Evaluation of Results

Considering the results of the survey with 35 participants, we derived several factors in regard to designing a feedback system for an unfamiliar traffic regulation.

6.1   Feedback Modality for Driving in a Roundabout

In general, our study is characterized by three factors: (1) it is a subjective assessment, (2) it focuses on driving in an unfamiliar regulation and (3) it investigates seven different feedback modalities. Our results showed significant differences in terms of preference modality among the seven feedback modalities for three instructions related to driving in roundabouts in Australia. The modalities are visual, auditory, haptic, audiovisual, visuohaptic, audiohaptic and audiovisuohaptic feedback. The instructions are designated A, B and C which are related to navigation, speed and signal indication tasks, respectively. In presenting instruction A, visual feedback had the highest mean rank (4.71). Participants significantly prefer it over other modalities. Therefore, only visual modality is the most preferred feedback modality to present instruction A (see Table 3) although audiovisual and auditory feedback are recommended in [25] and [10], respectively when driving in a familiar regulation. The reason behind this conflict might be the focus of the study. The case of our study focuses on driving in a UFTR. That might affect the way the driver thinks about feedback modality. For instance, the driver in such an unfamiliar condition is looking for simplicity. One participant commented, "*I feel that a simple feedback is better and does not disturb me*". Despite the fact that providing the haptic feedback during a navigation task being useful to reduce the driver's workload [25], our results implicate that such haptic feedback might confuse the driver of the required performed action during the navigation task. When answering Q1, one participant said that, *"using haptic feedback does not tell me what should I do"*. Navigation task in driving under UFTR scenario should include the required driving lane and the direction around the roundabout.

In presenting the information related to speed, visual feedback had the highest mean rank (4.31). Nevertheless, the preference of using visual feedback was not more significant than audiovisual, auditory and visuohaptic when presenting instruction B. That means visual, audiovisual, auditory and visuohaptic represent the most preferred modalities in presenting instruction B. These results somehow are aligned with the results of [3]. They compare visual and haptic feedback when controlling the vehicle speed is required. They cited that there is no significant difference between visual and haptic feedback. In our results, diversity of selecting the preference modality in speeding task might be due to the task itself. The speeding task in both keep-left and keep-right regulations is similar and the driver is used to feedback related to this task.

Table 3. The order of the most preferred modality based on the mean rank

Instruction	Modality preferences (based on ranking from survey)
A (navigation)	V > AV > A > VH > VAH > AH > H
B (speed)	V > AV > A > VH > H > VAH > AH
C (signal indication)	V > A > VH > H > AV > VAH > AH

In presenting instruction C, visual feedback had the highest mean rank (4.23). Participants significantly prefer it amongst other modalities. However, the preference of using visual feedback was not more significant than visuohaptic. Hence, visual and visuohaptic feedback are the most preferred feedback to present instruction C. Participants of our study had different opinions when employing haptic feedback in a signal indication task. A participant commented that, *"I would not understand the instruction if it is only haptic"*. Another participant suggested that, *"If the stalk vibrates when I have to use then it would be very helpful way to remind me of its place and to use it"*. More studies focusing on haptic feedback are required, particularly in terms of technology affordance.

6.2   Feedback Presenting Time

Our results showed significant differences in terms of preference between two presenting times. Concurrent feedback was significantly the most preferred feedback for driving in an unfamiliar traffic regulation. That might justify the need for a feedback system in this driving condition. Providing feedback when the driver finishes the task might be not useful as the driver needs more immediate feedback to inform him/her about the required and correct reaction. One participant commented on terminal feedback, *"I feel like there is no matter of the system if I have already made a mistake"*.

6.3 Feedback Frequency

There were no significant differences amongst the three possible frequencies the feedback should appear at ($Z = 4.957$, $p = .084$). As a result, any frequency method of presenting the feedback is acceptable to the driver when driving in a UFTR. These results conflict with [12, 15] who recommend starting with concurrent feedback at the stage of unfamiliarity of performing the task, and then decrease the frequency of presenting the feedback when the task is getting familiar. This conflict in results might be due to the design of the study. Our results depended on subjective assessment instead of objective assessment. A practical study is needed to objectively collect and analyze the data.

6.4 Limitations

Some limitations of the current study may impact the results of the study and our understanding of the results. Overall, our results came from a subjective assessment, which might differ from objective assessments. Also, our study covers only a specific driving scenario, turning left from a roundabout. Covering other scenarios at roundabouts, such as turning right and going forward at roundabouts would generalize our feedback presentation mechanism. Moreover, our study does not evaluate the usability of each feedback. Testing the usability would help us to provide the drivers with the most understandable and clear information.

7 Conclusion

In this paper, we presented the results of a quantitative study that subjectively investigated the most preferred feedback presentation mechanism when driving in a UFTR. We focused on providing feedback when turning left at roundabouts. That would help us to design the feedback system to assist the driver in such a driving condition.

Thirty-five participants who were not familiar with an Australian traffic regulation (i.e. keep-left and a right-hand driving vehicle) answered the online survey. The survey had few questions regarding the goal of our study and the survey covered the instructions the driver must follow to drive in Australia. The instructions implicated investigation, speeding, and signal indication tasks. We found that visual feedback is the most preferred feedback for investigation tasks. For speeding, visual, audiovisual, auditory and visuohaptic were the most preferred feedback. Visual and visuohaptic were the most preferred feedback for signal indication task. Moreover, concurrent feedback was the most preferred presenting time. There were no significant differences among the frequencies of presenting the feedback.

We plan to extend our work to cover the following points:

- Conduct an experiment to objectively find out the most effective feedback modality, feedback presenting time and frequency of presenting time and compare it with the results of this study.

- Test the most preferred feedback presentation mechanism of this study on other driving scenarios at roundabouts.
- Evaluate the usability of designed feedback.

Acknowledgements. This study has been sponsored by King Abdulaziz University through a PhD scholarship to the first author.

References

1. Alyamani, H., Kavakli, M.: Situational awareness and systems for driver-assistance. In: Proceedings of the 50th Hawaii International Conference on System Sciences (2017)
2. Alyamani, H.J., Alsharfan, M., Kavakli-Thorne, M., Jahani, H.: Towards a Driving Training System to Support Cognitive Flexibility (2017)
3. Azzi, S., Reymond, G., Mérienne, F., Kemeny, A.: Eco-driving performance assessment with in-car visual and haptic feedback assistance. J. Comput. Inf. Sci. Eng. 11(4), 041005 (2011)
4. Baldwin, C.L., May, J.F.: Loudness interacts with semantics in auditory warnings to impact rear-end collisions. Transp. Res. Part F: Traffic Psychol. Behav. 14(1), 36–42 (2011)
5. Becic, E., Manser, M.: Cooperative Intersection Collision Avoidance System–Stop Sign Assist (2013)
6. Boll, S., Asif, A., Heuten, W.: Feel your route: a tactile display for car navigation. IEEE Pervasive Comput. 10(3), 35–42 (2011)
7. Burke, J.L., et al.: Comparing the effects of visual-auditory and visual-tactile feedback on user performance: a meta-analysis. In: Proceedings of the 8th International Conference on Multimodal Interfaces, pp. 108–117. ACM (2006)
8. Chang, S.-H., Lin, C.-Y., Hsu, C.-C., Fung, C.-P., Hwang, J.-R.: The effect of a collision warning system on the driving performance of young drivers at intersections. Transp. Res. Part F: Traffic Psychol. Behav. 12(5), 371–380 (2009)
9. Chang, W., Hwang, W., Ji, Y.G.: Haptic seat interfaces for driver information and warning systems. Int. J. Hum.-Comput. Interact. 27(12), 1119–1132 (2011)
10. Dalton, P., Agarwal, P., Fraenkel, N., Baichoo, J., Masry, A.: Driving with navigational instructions: investigating user behaviour and performance. Accid. Anal. Prev. 50, 298–303 (2013)
11. de Groot, S., de Winter, J.C., García, J.M.L., Mulder, M., Wieringa, P.A.: The effect of concurrent bandwidth feedback on learning the lane-keeping task in a driving simulator. Hum. Factors J. Hum. Factors Ergon. Soc. 53(1), 50–62 (2011)
12. Ege, E.S., Cetin, F., Basdogan, C.: Vibrotactile feedback in steering wheel reduces navigation errors during GPS-guided car driving. In: 2011 IEEE World Haptics Conference (WHC), pp. 345–348. IEEE (2011)
13. Farah, H., et al.: Can providing feedback on driving behavior and training on parental vigilant care affect male teen drivers and their parents? Accid. Anal. Prev. 69, 62–70 (2014)
14. Forbes, N.: Online Survey of in-Vehicle Navigation System Users. University of Nottingham (2006). http://www.mrl.nott.ac.uk/~nlf/
15. Jamson, A., Hibberd, D.L., Merat, N.: The design of haptic gas pedal feedback to support eco-driving. In: Proceedings of the Seventh International Driving Symposium on Human Factors in Driver Assessment, Training, and Vehicle Design: University of Iowa, pp. 264–270 (2013)

16. Kim, S., Hong, J.-H., Li, Kevin A., Forlizzi, J., Dey, Anind K.: Route guidance modality for elder driver navigation. In: Kay, J., Lukowicz, P., Tokuda, H., Olivier, P., Krüger, A. (eds.) Pervasive 2012. LNCS, vol. 7319, pp. 179–196. Springer, Heidelberg (2012). https://doi.org/10.1007/978-3-642-31205-2_12

17. Ministry of Transport. Overseas Driver Crashes (Including Matched Crash and Visitor Arrival Data), Wellington, New Zealand (2015)

18. Morgan, G.A., Barrett, K.C., Leech, N.L.: IBM SPSS for Intermediate Statistics: Use and Interpretation, 2nd edn (2005)

19. NSW Roads and Maritime Services. Road Users' Handbook (2015)

20. Rossi, R., Gastaldi, M., Biondi, F., Mulatti, C.: Warning sound to affect perceived speed in approaching roundabouts: experiments with a driving simulator. Procedia-Soc. Behav. Sci. **87**, 269–278 (2013)

21. Saito, S., Murata, Y., Takayama, T., Sato, N.: An international driving simulator: recognizing the sense of a car body by the simulator. In: 2012 26th International Conference on Advanced Information Networking and Applications Workshops (WAINA), pp. 254–260. IEEE (2012)

22. Scott, J., Gray, R.: A comparison of tactile, visual, and auditory warnings for rear-end collision prevention in simulated driving. Hum. Factors **50**(2), 264–275 (2008)

23. Sigrist, R., Rauter, G., Riener, R., Wolf, P.: Augmented visual, auditory, haptic, and multimodal feedback in motor learning: a review. Psychon. Bull. Rev. **20**(1), 21–53 (2013)

24. Tran, C., Bark, K., Ng-Thow-Hing, V.: A left-turn driving aid using projected oncoming vehicle paths with augmented reality. In: Proceedings of the 5th International Conference on Automotive User Interfaces and Interactive Vehicular Applications, pp. 300–307. ACM (2013)

25. Van Erp, J.B., Van Veen, H.A.: Vibrotactile in-vehicle navigation system. Transp. Res. Part F: Traffic Psychol. Behav. **7**(4), 247–256 (2004)

26. Van Leeuwen, P., De Groot, S., Happee, R., De Winter, J.: Effects of concurrent continuous visual feedback on learning the lane keeping task. In: Proceedings of the 6th International Driving Symposium on Human Factors in Driver Assessment, Training and Vehicle Design, pp. 482–488 (2011)

27. Yale, S.H., Hansotia, P., Knapp, D., Ehrfurth, J.: Neurologic conditions: assessing medical fitness to drive. Clin. Med. Res. **1**(3), 177–188 (2003)

28. Zhang, J., Suto, K., Fujiwara, A.: Effects of in-vehicle warning information on drivers' decelerating and accelerating behaviors near an arch-shaped intersection. Accid. Anal. Prev. **41**(5), 948–958 (2009)

29. Zhang, Y., Yan, X., Yang, Z.: Discrimination of effects between directional and nondirectional information of auditory warning on driving behavior. Discrete Dyn. Nat. Soc. 1–7 (2015)

Indoor Positioning Knowledge Model for Privacy Preserving Context-Awareness

Abhik Banerjee, Amit Parasmal Borundiya(✉), Himadri Sikhar Khargharia,
Karthikeyan Ponnalagu, Lakshmi Rao Bhatnagar, Ragavendra Prabhakar,
and Vijendran Gopalan Venkoparao

Robert Bosch Engineering and Business Solutions, Bangalore, Karnataka, India
{Abhik.Banerjee,Amit.Borundiya,HimadriSikhar.Khargharia,
Karthikeyan.Ponnalagu,Lakshmi.S,Ragavendra.Prabhakar,
Gopalanvijendran.Venkoparao}@in.bosch.com

Abstract. Context-aware recommendation systems seek to provide relevant recommendation content for users by deriving preferences not just through past behavior but also based on instantaneous context information. Such responsiveness is especially crucial for offline retail setups such as supermarkets and malls, wherein user decisions map directly to how they navigate within the venue. A key area of concern for such systems is management of the tradeoff between relevance of recommendation content and privacy guarantees. In this paper, we propose a system which enables dynamic service composition of context information with recommendation content, while enabling privacy configuration. We focus on the use of indoor positioning as contextual information for indoor environments such as physical retail. Central to the proposed system is a knowledge model that integrates indoor location information with that of positioning schematics as well as relationships among locations. Specifically, we show how incorporation of the ontology model with algorithms for detection of indoor location and location semantics allows for robust configuration of not just recommendation content but also privacy policies that govern the granularity of information shared for generating context-aware recommendations. This integrated knowledge model can enable various context-based offerings in the offline or physical realm, thus bridging gap between the physical as well as digital world.

Keywords: Indoor positioning · Context-Awareness · Privacy preservation

1 Introduction

Context aware recommender systems make use of contextual information to derive recommendations for the user, in order to ensure that they are more relevant for achieving the user objective [1,3]. Location is a key context parameter for applications that seek to react to contextual cues arising from the physical environment and enables to provide appropriate recommendations. Previous

© Springer Nature Switzerland AG 2019
H.-P. Lam and S. Mistry (Eds.): ASSRI 2018, LNBIP 367, pp. 50–64, 2019.
https://doi.org/10.1007/978-3-030-32242-7_5

research has elaborated on the role of context aware recommendations for in-store retail and how it can be performed through location tagging of product data. Given the breadth and diversity of retail scenarios, recommendations could be exposed to a customer in various forms depending on the form of customer interaction. For instance, recommendations to a user doing weekly grocery shopping could be in the form of automatic update of shopping list. On the other hand, a customer at an apparel store could be presented with dynamic discounts and offers to influence his/her buying decision.

For recommendations to be relevant, there needs to be a clear mapping with the context parameters that they target. In case of retail, this implies that it should be possible to associate recommendation content with the customer's shopping intent [13]. Awareness of instantaneous consumer behavior has been looked at as key context parameter [9,15,17,18,22,23] for physical retail. This is particularly crucial for environments such as supermarkets and malls as, in a similar vein as recommendations for online portals [21] make use of real-time behavior, physical shopping behavior is often determined through consumer behavior as observed through their movement and browsing patterns. As a result, the eventual shopping decision is dependent on not just historical purchase behavior but is also driven by customer activities leading to spontaneous decisions. Such information is characterized by their dynamicity and pervasiveness, requiring context aware systems to be reactive to a variety of information while ensuring privacy guarantees. Previous literature has explored addressing privacy preservation for context aware systems through policy definition that negotiate the tradeoff between information granularity and service richness [4,5,11].

Two aspects of existing systems limit their ability to leverage activity based context awareness fully. Firstly, the indoor positioning algorithm operates at a fixed level of granularity independent of the privacy policy configuration. As a result, the position determination continues to work in the same manner which could be redundant even if privacy guarantees are met. Secondly, the granularity levels they address are limited to the construction semantics available from floor plans [12,14]. This limits the extensibility of the context aware recommendations as it does not allow scope for leveraging dynamic interactions between users and indoor spaces. For instance, a supermarket is likely to have static sections defined such as *Meat*, *Vegetables*, etc. and subsequent sub-sections. However, a user's movement around the same store could be based on other factors such as shopping for a house party, which would be the ideal context for generation of recommendation content.

The discussion in this paper is motivated by two objectives. First, we aim to enable determination of user activity based on indoor positioning information obtained at various levels of granularity. Second, we aim to enable positioning granularity to be determined in conjunction with user-defined rules for privacy configuration as well as recommendation content.

In this paper, we propose *Hip-Car*, which is an indoor positioning system (IPS) that leverages location relationships for enabling context aware recommendations and achieve privacy preservation in physical retail environments such as supermarkets, shopping malls, etc. The proposed system incorporates a knowledge model which is characterized by

(a) Ability to capture both hierarchical and location relationships.
(b) Integration of indoor positioning algorithm constructs. This includes the technology used for indoor positioning, such as Wi-Fi, BLE, etc. as well as associated data points, e.g. list of BSSIDs and corresponding fingerprint data.
(c) Tagging of recommendation content at individual location hierarchy levels

A key aspect is that the location relationships and hierarchy are not limited to static information from floor plans but could be implicit relationships. For the example mentioned before, implicit relationships could be generated for locations within the same section of a store or even across neighboring sections. We show that such a model can be used to define privacy policies as well as dynamic recommendation content.

2   Related Work

2.1   Context Aware Systems for Retail

Context-aware recommender systems have sought to use contextual information to improve relevancy of recommendation content. The contextual information typically considered includes location, time and user activity, as well as context derived through these. A majority of existing systems, though, focus on coarse-grained context such as geographical locations or generic activity such as shopping, traveling, etc. Determination of fine-grained user activity has been a focus of context aware systems for physical retail such as supermarkets in order to gain precise insights about consumer shopping behavior [20,22]. Existing literature has looked to detect shopper activities such as browsing stores as well as individual items by making use of data from various sources such as Wi-Fi Channel State Information (CSI) [23], RFID [18] and combination of sensors from wearable devices [15,16]. Further, other literature has looked to interpret shopping intent of users based on their movement behavior within stores, which in turn could be interpreted from indoor positioning information [9,17].

2.2   Privacy Preservation for Context Aware Systems

Privacy is defined as, "the claim of individuals, groups, or institutions to determine for themselves when, how and to what extent information about them is communicated to other" [2]. Mobile devices have become inseparable from humans and the ever increasing features and sensors within the devices have lead to development of variety of use cases with/without installing additional hardware. Indoor Positioning Services is one such example where a smart phone can be used to determine individual position in the indoor environment by sensing the WiFi, BLE etc. Based on where the final comparison of final RSS fingerprint happens we can classify as Server-Side or Client-Side [11]. The Server-Side is more vulnerable for privacy breach as the user movement in form of signals are constantly transmitted out of the mobile devices for further processing. The advent of fine-grained context information as described has meant a greater emphasis on privacy, in order to address the increased privacy risks. Existing literature has looked at using ontology based policies for achieving privacy preservation. Thus, context aware systems could be configured with policies that trade off the granularity of recommendation content with that of contextual information [4,5]. In TVM [11], the authors propose a mechanism in which positioning information at a coarse level is made available to a cloud based positioning system, but precise positioning is done on the smart phone.

2.3   Indoor Spatial Knowledge Models

Indoor spatial models have been the focus of standardization bodies such as IndoorGML [14]. The IndoorGML standard defines a knowledge model for capturing indoor spatial information. Thereby, it includes provisions for defining static and mobile components of an indoor venue. Further, it also allows including references to sensor data such as Wi-Fi and BLE. Existing literature has looked at ways to achieve efficient implementations of IndoorGML. However, a key aspect missing has been interlinking spatial models with indoor positioning system. While the authors of [12] incorporate various measurements for indoor positioning as part of their model, robustness to applying alternative approaches and integration with dynamic context information is not covered.

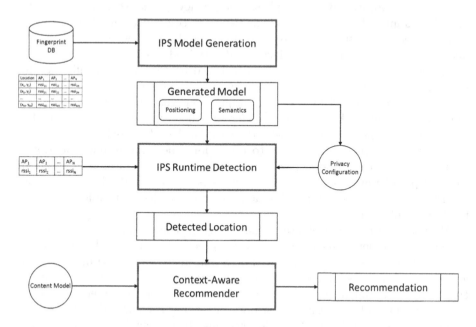

Fig. 1. System architecture depicting interaction between individual components

3 Hierarchical Indoor Positioning for Context Aware Recommendation (Hip-Car)

3.1 System Architecture

We first describe the architecture of the proposed system, outlined in Fig. 1. Since the proposed system is motivated by how indoor positioning integrates with context aware recommendations and privacy policies, we describe the end-to-end interaction among the components. The system comprises of three primary components, which are described below.

The *IPS Model Generation* component operates during the offline generation of the model to be used for indoor positioning. This takes as input a fingerprint database (DB) which comprises of labeled measurements from one or more sensors, with each label corresponding to an individual location. The labels could either be location coordinates or could be point-of-interest (PoI) tags. The generated model comprises of two types of classifiers, the first of which is the *Positioning Classifier* used for runtime detection of user location. The second classifier is termed as the *Semantics Classifier* as it is used to determine the user perception of the detected location. User perception of a location is defined based in terms of (a) location type, (b) relationships with the rest of the indoor space. The ontology model in Sect. 3.2 details how location relationships that can be detected at runtime can be used for privacy configuration as well as integration with content for context aware recommendation.

During the location detection phase, the privacy policies thus configured are provided as input for the *IPS Runtime Detection* component in addition to the real-time sensor measurements obtained on a user device. The detected location information consists of the user location determined based on the *Positioning Classifier*, with the granularity controlled based on the privacy configuration, which in turn is defined based on the *Semantics Classifier*.

Finally, the detected location, in conjunction with the *Content Model*, is used by the *Context Aware Recommender* to deliver appropriate recommendation content to the user. Here, the term *Content Model* is used to account for how content is structured in order to use it for generating recommendations, including references to how specific content instances are located in physical space. A popular example of content structure is the Google Product Taxonomy [7]. Physical retail stores typically maintain product placement information in the form of planograms [19].

We note that the mode of interaction among the components described above depends on the deployment setup. In most practical scenarios, the *IPS Model Generation* is expected to be deployed on a centralized cloud environment with generation of the classifier being done in an offline manner. The location detection component can take place either on a device or on the server. In case of the latter, the real-time sensor measurements being transmitted to the corresponding server and detected location response being sent back to the device. Alternatively, the location detection can take place on the device with the location sent to a server which generates recommendation content. In either of these scenarios, the exposure of the user location presents a significant privacy risk, which can be minimized with appropriate privacy configuration.

For examples discussed later in this paper, we consider physical retail as the deployment of choice. Hence, content instances, in this case, are products. For convenience of explanation, location labels have been considered as PoI tags. For the same reason as well as because of their near universal deployment, the choice of sensor has been taken as Wi-Fi.

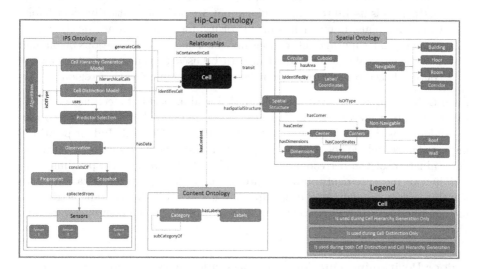

Fig. 2. *Hip-Car* Location Ontology showing the key components of *IPS Ontology, Spatial Ontology, Content Ontology* and *Location Relationships*

3.2   Location Ontology

As outlined before, the key highlight of the ontology model is integration of location semantics with indoor positioning data and algorithms, thereby allowing for concurrent determination of composite user context, which can subsequently be used to enable context aware content such as recommendations.

The proposed *Hip-Car* ontology is shown in Fig. 2, with the key components being *IPS Ontology, Spatial Ontology, Content Ontology* and *Location Relationships*. The core entity of the ontology is defined as *Cell*, which represents a location at any level of granularity. The concept of *Cell* is reused from IndoorGML [14], considering it helps in envisioning hierarchical relationship between spatial representations indoors. *Cells* encapsulate *Cells*. For example, a coarse grained *Cell* may include geographical regions, containing buildings, which, in turn, contain floors and that might include fine grained locations such as an aisle or even parts of an aisle such as entry or exit, with each of these being individual *Cell* instances. A *Cell* could be categorized into one of three categories depending on how it is recognized:

(a) *Static Indoor Semantics:* Indoor constructs such as rooms, passageways, floors, etc. which can be obtained from spatial data representations which could be floor plans or even knowledge models like IndoorGML;

(b) *Indoor Positioning Reference Points:* reference points for which observations have been obtained using one or more sensors. This is typically done only at the highest level of granularity and is defined physically through its co-ordinates or as a Point-of-Interest (POI) label or both;

(c) *Auto Generated Cells:* generation based on observations obtained for other *Cells*. This is useful to define regions that are not automatically identifiable from floor plans but which could be of use for context aware services. For instance, in a supermarket, regions may be defined using locations belonging to adjacent aisles, which could in turn be used to generate context aware content based on user movement between locations of such a region.

Each *Cell* comprises of attributes which, define all aspects of a cell necessary to realize a context aware system. The attributes are divided into three categories: (a) Indoor Positioning (b) Location Relationships (c) Content. Indoor positioning attributes include references to algorithms and *observations* to be used for determination of the corresponding *Cell*. The *observations* corresponding to a *Cell* include measurements obtained through one or more *sensors*. Location Relationship attributes define relationships across *Cells*. Finally, content attributes include references to the content that relates directly to the context aware services.

Indoor Positioning Ontology. Indoor positioning systems make use of readings from multiple technologies such as Wi-Fi, BLE, magnetometer, etc. for distinction of locations. An IPS typically consists of two distinct phases of operation. In the first offline phase, a mapping of readings from one or more technologies to individual physical locations is created. This can be performed either through manual configuration, such as tagging of locations with individual beacons, or by using mapping tools that scan the environment while a user walks around the region. Subsequently, one or more algorithms are used to create a model of the region. We term this as the *Training* phase. In the second online phase of operation which we term as the *Detection* phase, readings obtained at runtime are compared using the model to determine the location at that instant. A detailed overview of indoor positioning systems is out of the scope of this paper, and the reader is referred to the existing literature on the topic [6,8,10].

We define indoor positioning ontology on the basis the high level overview provided above. Each individual *Cell* comprises of four components, namely *Sensors*, *Algorithms*, *Feature Space* and *Observations*. *Sensors* are used to refer to technologies mentioned above. A sensor could, thus, be of type Wi-Fi, magnetometer, BLE, UWB, etc. Each *Cell* comprises of readings obtained from one or more *Sensors* which are stored as *Observations*. The *observations* for a *Cell* correspond to a set of multiple sensor sources. For instance, if Wi-Fi is the type of *sensor*, the *observations* would correspond to multiple access points (APs).

Any set of *observations* is characterized by a *feature space*, which includes the set of sensor sources. Thus, the list of APs would be the feature space for a set of *observations* consisting of only Wi-Fi readings.

The properties described above are provided as inputs to algorithms for the purpose of location determination. A *Cell* can have references to multiple such algorithms as part of the *Algorithms* property. Any algorithm takes as input *observations* and *feature space* and generates a model as output, which is incorporated in the ontology through the *classifier* property. It is important to note here that the feature space used by an algorithm can be any subset of the complete feature space for which observations have been obtained. Thus, for an algorithm operating on Wi-Fi observations, the *feature space* can contain a subset of the APs for which the *observations* have been obtained. The *observations* referenced by an *Algorithm* are related to the relationships defined among *Cells*. In the *Training* phase, the *classifier* referenced by a *Cell* is generated from the observations of the *Cells* contained by it, i.e. the peer cells of the next level of hierarchy. Thus, in the *Detection* phase, the classifier is used to identify the current peer cell. Additionally, new *Cells* can be generated using observations of existing ones. For instance, a group of peer cells could be clustered together to define a *Cell* at the next higher level of hierarchy. Such approaches have been explored in the literature with the objective of identifying zones. Further, these aspects could also be used for interpolation based approaches, in which a few *Cells* are marked with specific tags such as those of Ultra Wide-band (UWB).

Location Relationships. The objective of capturing location relationships in this ontology is to enable recognition of user movement behavior in indoor spaces. We make the observation here that movement behavior in indoor venues, especially public venues such as retail stores, are driven by the exploratory behavioral patterns of users. For instance, a shopper searching for a particular item in a retail store, e.g. a can of juice, is likely to first head to beverages section, and subsequently head to the aisle(s) marked for juices and then browse through various options before deciding on one.

Using the above as a motivation, we define location relationships to be of two types, *hierarchical* and *peer-to-peer*. *Hierarchical* relationships are defined using the *isContainedInCell* property and implies containment relationships among *Cells*. Thus, in the above example, hierarchical relationships exist between the store and various sections, followed by the aisles within each section and finally, locations within an aisle. *Peer-to-peer* relationship exists among *Cells* which are at same level of hierarchy. Thus, all the aisles in a store could be defined as peer *Cells*. Further, a *transit* property is used to define navigability across peer *Cells*.

We note that both hierarchical and peer relationships among locations have been referred to in existing spatial models such as IndoorGML. However, what makes *Hip-Car* unique is the integration with indoor positioning properties described previously, which enables determination of location relationships in conjunction with indoor position determination. Further, it can be observed that such a design allows flexibility in indoor positioning operation. The indoor positioning system works by simply iterating through the ontology and loading references to necessary features. As the *Algorithms* and corresponding classifiers are defined at individual *Cells*, they can be activated in an opportunistic, on-demand fashion. This implies that a *classifier* for different parts of a building could only be activated when the user is detected to have moved in that area, identified through the Cell detection at higher levels of hierarchy. Further, privacy and access control could be configured using the same properties. For instance, the hierarchy levels could be used to configure a desired level of coarseness for location determination, thereby allowing a user to ensure privacy of his/her location information. Similarly, context aware services could be enabled or disabled for individual users depending on the part of the building they are at.

Spatial Semantics. The *Spatial Ontology* captures physical properties for describing a *Cell*. A *Cell* can be identified by both a *label* as well *co-ordinates*. The *label* can be used to refer to the location name such as a specific room. The *co-ordinates* are used to define the exact point on a floor plan at which the *Cell* is located. Given the fact that *Hip-Car* includes provisions for location hierarchy, along with the fact that all indoor positioning systems work within a margin of accuracy, defining a *Cell* using only *co-ordinates* is not likely to be enough. To address these challenges, we incorporate the dimension of a *Cell* to be defined along with it's shape. Thus, *Cells* at lower levels of hierarchy, that contain multiple other *Cells* could be defined to have dimensions encompassing all of them. Consider a typical indoor venue, the location hierarchy ontology starts with a Building. Each Building carries properties like hasDimension, hasFloor, isBuildingType. Each Building has a number of Floors. Each Floor carries properties like hasCell, hasDimension, hasFloorNumbers. Each Floor may have one or number of Cell. A cell may be of type Navigable or NonNavigable.

Content Tagging. Context aware content could be associated for locations at any hierarchy level, thereby enabling context aware services to be generated at any level of location granularity. The property *hasContent* is used to associate content to a *Cell*. The associated content could possess its own structure as per the requirements of the context aware application. In Fig. 3, hierarchical structure of content is shown for a retail area structured as in Fig. 4. Later, in Sect. 4.3, we show how such structures can be integrated to determine user shopping intent and derive relevant recommendations.

4   Context Awareness Through Hip-Car

We now describe how the proposed system can be used to enable context awareness, particularly with respects to the three aspects being focused here, namely context-retrieval, privacy configuration and generation of context aware content.

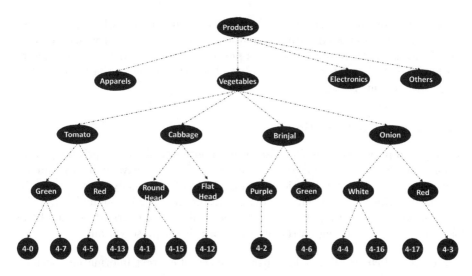

Fig. 3. Hierarchical Content Graph showing various content categories and relationships

4.1 Context Retrieval: Location Queries

Since our discussion is limited to indoor positioning as a context, we present how location querying is performed with the proposed system. As the proposed ontology allows for positioning algorithms and classifiers to be defined at each level of hierarchy, it provisions for flexibility of context-retrieval which can be leveraged for privacy configuration and content retrieval, as will be discussed in subsequent sections.

Algorithm 1. Location Detection

1: **function** LOCATIONQUERY(O, S, l)   ▷ Where O - Observation array, S - Sensor array, l - hierarchy level
2:     Let $L[1 \ldots l]$ be a new array
3:     Let $P[1 \ldots l]$ be a new array
4:     $P[1]$ = set of venues known to the system
5:     **for** $i = 1$ to l **do**
6:         $a = LocationOnt.IPSOnt.getAlgorithm(\text{i})$
7:         $c = LocationOnt.IPSOnt.getClassifier(\text{a})$
8:         $L[i] = runAlgorithm(\text{c, O, S, P[i]})$
9:         $P[i + 1] = getPeers(\text{L[i], i})$
10:     **end for**
11: **end function**

Here, we consider venues to be distinct environments for which positioning models have been created within the system. Determination of which venue a user device is at, therefore, constitutes performing location detection at hierarchy level $l = 1$. Thus, for the location graph shown in Fig. 4, the Supermarket constitutes a venue.

4.2   Privacy Configuration

As discussed previously, the *Hip-Car* location ontology allows for privacy preservation policies based on location granularity. Thus, a privacy policy can be defined which allows for location sharing to be enabled only up to a certain granularity, which in turn could be defined in terms of the hierarchy level or the location resolution. Any policy thus defined could be categorized as one of the following types depending on the objective of privacy preservation:

(a) *Context Privacy:* Defined to ensure privacy of context information, such as user location
(b) *Content Privacy:* Defined to ensure privacy of content delivered based on context information

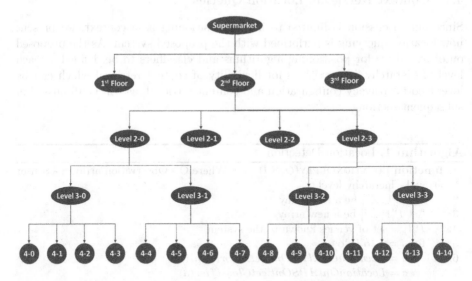

Fig. 4. Location Graph showing location clusters and hierarchical relationships among them

In the following pseudo-code, we illustrate an instance of how *content privacy* can be realized through content querying based on hierarchy level.

Algorithm 2. Privacy Bound Content Query

1: **function** CONTENTQUERY(l)   ▷ Where l - hierarchy level
2:     Let O and S be the observation and sensor arrays respectively, and l_{max} be the maximum hierarchy level
3:     Let $L[1 \ldots l_{max}]$ and $C[1 \ldots l]$ be new arrays
       $L[1 \ldots l_{max}] = \text{LocationQuery}(O, S, l_{max})$
4:     **for** $i = 1$ to l **do**
5:         $C[i] = LocationOnt.hasContent(\text{L}[i])$
6:     **end for**
7: **end function**

In this example, location detection takes place at all hierarchy levels, but content fetch only takes place till the maximum hierarchy level defined. Note that, here the context privacy guarantees are subject to the privacy boundaries on which the *LocationQuery* operation takes place. For a cloud based localization system [11], the operation *LocationQuery* takes place from the smartphone to a cloud server where the location determination takes place based on observations recorded on the smartphone. Alternatively, for an edge based system, the same operation takes place across subsytems on edge device, such as a smartphone.

4.3   Context Aware Content Generation: Recommendation

We discuss how the proposed system can be used to derive contextual recommendations based on user shopping intent interpreted from movement behavior. Deriving user intent for the purpose of deriving relevant recommendation has been explored with regard to both online portals [21] as well as for physical retail, discussed in detail in Sect. 2.1.

We illustrate how context aware recommendations could be generated for a supermarket, by deriving user's shopping intent from movement behavior at specific store locations, such as specific locations within the 'Vegetables' section. Figures 4 and 3 depict the hierarchical location and content graphs respectively which we use for our discussion. In this instance, suppose the indoor positioning system has detected the user being in the location of the Level-4-6 which is located within Level-3-1, which in turn is in Level-2-0. Now as documented in the content ontology, Level-4-6 contains Brinjal-Green, belonging to the subtree marked by the parent-child of vegetables and Brinjals. Within the category Brinjal, Brinjal-Purple is identified as a subcategory which is contained in Level-4-2. Using the user location movement as an indicator of shopping intent, the retailer can provide advertisement based on recommendation with the closest content category. Thus, a customer browsing through an aisle containing brinjal of a certain type, could be redirected to another aisle storing other brinjal variants. The SPARQL Query for the same is given below in Listing 1.1, with *Input − Location* here being Level-4-6:

```
PREFIX rdf: <http://www.w3.org/1999/02/22-rdf-syntax-ns#>
PREFIX owl: <http://www.w3.org/2002/07/owl#>
PREFIX rdfs: <http://www.w3.org/2000/01/rdf-schema#>
PREFIX xsd: <http://www.w3.org/2001/XMLSchema#>
PREFIX hipcar: <http://www.semanticweb.org/ontologies/2017/5/location-ontology#>
Select DISTINCT ?CurrentContentCategoryHierarchy ?SubContentCategory ?ContainedCell where {hipcar:Input-Location
    hipcar:containsContentCategory+ ?CurrentContentCategoryHierarchy.?CurrentContentCategoryHierarchy hipcar:
    subContentCategory ?SubContentCategory.?ContainedCell hipcar:containsContentCategory ?SubContentCategory.?
    ContainedCell hipcar:isTypeCell "true"^^xsd:boolean .}
```

Listing 1.1. SPARQL query

The recommendation comes as Level-4-2 which is of the category Brinjal-Purple part of Brinjal. It exists in Level-3-0, which is also contained within the same area Level-2-0. Thus, an integrated recommendation system as described above can result in recommendation content which is optimized based on user's movement behavior. This, in turn, can result in a profitability for the retail store. For instance, in the above example, the user's estimated intent is that of brinjal, which can be converted into a purchase decision if he/she did not purchase in the first place.

A key point here is that the same query can be applied to any other retail layout to get the desired results, by only replacing the location and content graphs with the relevant ones. In the case of a shopping mall, for example, user movement at a specific areas could be taken as an indicator of the shopping intent. For example, the dining intent of a user at a food court could be inferred based on the time spent browsing individual stalls, and subsequently directed to the closest match. Thus, a user looking at sandwich options could be directed to the nearest alternative food stall with the most similar cuisine.

5   Implementation Overview

The current implementation of the *Hip-Car* system proposed in this paper is in the form of a library which can be integrated into Android and iOS applications. The number of sensors supported varies due to platform restrictions.

For a typical deployment, the library is integrated into two separate apps, one for administrative usage and another to be used by target users. The administrative app primarily focuses on the *Training* phase of IPS operation, whereas the user app is concentrated on the *Detection* phase.

Privacy configurations can be specified for desired granularity of location and content. The location granularity can be set as $h_p^{loc} = l_i^{loc}$ with h_p^{loc} being the location hierarchy to which content query is to be restricted, while $l_i^{loc} \in [0, l_{max}]$. In an actual user app, these location levels could be specified in terms of user perceptible location definitions. For instance, in Fig. 4, a privacy configuration of $h_p^{loc} = 1$ could be presented to the user as "floor" and $h_p^{loc} = 2$ could be presented as a "wing". Content granularity can be specified similarly as above, although the user description of the same would depend on the application scenario.

Currently, the library is being deployed as part of user applications of retail chains in Bangalore, India, with Wi-Fi being the primary sensor choice and fingerprinting being the primary algorithm choice. These choices are primarily driven by ease of deployment and business considerations. For instance, widespread Wi-Fi deployment in existing stores is a key decision factor.[1]

Using the same configuration as above, the system was tested in an indoor office environment, with the detection accuracy at the highest granularity, i.e. l_{max}, being 70–75%, 95% for $l_{max} - 1$ and around 100% for all other levels. Locations at l_{max} were defined as square regions with a side of 2–3 m, with those at $l_{max} - 1$ consisting of 3–4 contiguous l_{max} locations.[2]

6 Conclusion

In this paper, an indoor positioning middleware has been presented which integrates indoor positioning algorithm features with spatial semantics. To the best of our knowledge, this is the first system that achieves such an integration. We show, through examples, how such a system can achieve the combined goals of adaptability to indoor positioning deployment challenges and context awareness based on user movement behavior. In future, we propose to explore integration with contextual content in detail.

References

1. Adomavicius, G., Tuzhilin, A.: Context-aware recommender systems. In: Ricci, F., Rokach, L., Shapira, B., Kantor, P.B. (eds.) Recommender Systems Handbook, pp. 217–253. Springer, Boston, MA (2011). https://doi.org/10.1007/978-0-387-85820-3_7

2. Alan, W.: Privacy and Freedom. Atheneum, New York (1967)

3. Anand, S.S., Mobasher, B.: Contextual recommendation. In: Berendt, B., Hotho, A., Mladenic, D., Semeraro, G. (eds.) WebMine 2006. LNCS (LNAI), vol. 4737, pp. 142–160. Springer, Heidelberg (2007). https://doi.org/10.1007/978-3-540-74951-6_8

4. Celdrán, A.H., Clemente, F.J.G., Pérez, M.G., Pérez, G.M.: SeCoMan: a semantic-aware policy framework for developing privacy-preserving and context-aware smart applications. IEEE Syst. J. **10**(3), 1111–1124 (2016)

5. Celdrán, A.H., Pérez, M.G., Clemente, F.J.G., Pérez, G.M.: Precise: privacy-aware recommender based on context information for cloud service environments. IEEE Commun. Mag. **52**(8), 90–96 (2014)

6. Davidson, P., Piche, R.: A survey of selected indoor positioning methods for smart-phones. IEEE Commun. Surv. Tutorials **19**, 1347–1370 (2016)

7. Google: Google product taxonomy, June 2018. https://www.google.com/basepages/producttype/taxonomy-with-ids.en-US.txt

---

[1] Privacy configurations are not currently part of commercially deployed setups.

[2] The authors are unable to provide further details of the evaluation results at office and retail locations due to privacy and copyright restrictions.

8. He, S., Chan, S.H.G.: Wi-Fi fingerprint-based indoor positioning: recent advances and comparisons. IEEE Commun. Surv. Tutorials **18**(1), 466–490 (2016)
9. Hwang, I., Jang, Y.J.: Process mining to discover shoppers' pathways at a fashion retail store using a WiFi-base indoor positioning system. IEEE Trans. Autom. Sci. Eng. **14**, 1786–1792 (2017)
10. Khalajmehrabadi, A., Gatsis, N., Akopian, D.: Modern WLAN fingerprinting indoor positioning methods and deployment challenges. IEEE Commun. Surv. Tutorials **19**, 1974–2002 (2017)
11. Konstantinidis, A., Chatzimilioudis, G., Zeinalipour-Yazti, D., Mpeis, P., Pelekis, N., Theodoridis, Y.: Privacy-preserving indoor localization on smartphones. IEEE Trans. Knowl. Data Eng. **27**(11), 3042–3055 (2015)
12. Kun, D.P., Varga, E.B., Toth, Z.: Ontology based navigation model of the ilona system. In: 2017 IEEE 15th International Symposium on Applied Machine Intelligence and Informatics (SAMI), pp. 000479–000484. IEEE (2017)
13. Lamche, B., Rödl, Y., Hauptmann, C., Wörndl, W.: Context-aware recommendations for mobile shopping. In: LocalRec@ RecSys, pp. 21–27 (2015)
14. Li, K.J., Lee, J.Y.: Basic concepts of indoor spatial information candidate standard IndoorGML and its applications. J. Korea Spatial Inf. Soc. **21**(3), 1–10 (2013)
15. Radhakrishnan, M., Eswaran, S., Misra, A., Chander, D., Dasgupta, K.: Iris: tapping wearable sensing to capture in-store retail insights on shoppers. In: 2016 IEEE International Conference on Pervasive Computing and Communications (PerCom), pp. 1–8. IEEE (2016)
16. Radhakrishnan, M., Sen, S., Vigneshwaran, S., Misra, A., Balan, R.: Iot+ small data: transforming in-store shopping analytics & services. In: 2016 8th International Conference on Communication Systems and Networks (COMSNETS), pp. 1–6. IEEE (2016)
17. Sen, S., et al.: Accommodating user diversity for in-store shopping behavior recognition. In: Proceedings of the 2014 ACM International Symposium on Wearable Computers, pp. 11–14. ACM (2014)
18. Shangguan, L., Zhou, Z., Zheng, X., Yang, L., Liu, Y., Han, J.: Shopminer: mining customer shopping behavior in physical clothing stores with COTS RFID devices. In: Proceedings of the 13th ACM Conference on Embedded Networked Sensor Systems, pp. 113–125. ACM (2015)
19. Sheehan, A.: Planograms: What they are and how they're used in visual merchandising, June 2018. https://www.shopify.com/retail/planogram-visual-merchandising
20. Tomko, M.: Understanding indoor behavior: where, what, with whom? In: Proceedings of the 26th International Conference on World Wide Web Companion, pp. 1455–1456. International World Wide Web Conferences Steering Committee (2017)
21. Wu, C.Y., Alvino, C.V., Smola, A.J., Basilico, J.: Using navigation to improve recommendations in real-time. In: Proceedings of the 10th ACM Conference on Recommender Systems, RecSys 2016, pp. 341–348. ACM, New York (2016). https://doi.org/10.1145/2959100.2959174
22. Yaeli, A., et al.: Understanding customer behavior using indoor location analysis and visualization. IBM J. Res. Dev. **58**(5/6), 3–1 (2014)
23. Zeng, Y., Pathak, P.H., Mohapatra, P.: Analyzing shopper's behavior through WiFi signals. In: Proceedings of the 2nd Workshop on Workshop on Physical Analytics, pp. 13–18. ACM (2015)

NERSE: Named Entity Recognition in Software Engineering as a Service

M. Veera Prathap Reddy[1,2]([✉]), P. V. R. D. Prasad[2], Manjunath Chikkamath[1], and Sarathchandra Mandadi[1]

[1] Robert Bosch, Bangalore, India
prathapreddymv@gmail.com, {Manjunath.Chikkamath,
Mandadi.Sarathchandra}@in.bosch.com
[2] KL Education Foundation, Vaddeswaram, Andhra Pradesh, India
pvrdprasad@kluniversity.in

Abstract. Named Entity Recognition (NER) is a computational linguistics task that seek to classify every word in a document as falling into different category. NER serves as an important component for many domain specific expert systems. Software engineering is one such domain where very minimum work has been done on identifying entities specific to domain. In this paper, we present NERSE, a tool that enables the user to identify software specific entities. It is developed with machine learning algorithms trained on software specific entity categories using Conditional Random Fields (CRF) and Bidirectional Long Short-Term Memory - Conditional Random Fields (BiLSTM-CRF). NERSE identifies 22 different categories of entities specific to software engineering domain with 0.85% and 0.95% for CRF (source code for Named Entity Recognition Model CRF is available at https://github.com/prathapreddymv/NERSE) and BiLSTM-CRF (source code for Named Entity Recognition Model BiLSTM-CRF is available at https://github.com/prathapreddymv/NERSE) models respectively.

Keywords: CRF · BILSTM-CRF · Natural Language Processing · Software engineering

1 Introduction

The web hosts millions of unstructured data such as scientific papers, question and answers, news articles as well as forum and archived mailing list threads or (micro) blog posts. This information has usually a rich semantic structure, which is clear for the human being, but that remains mostly hidden to computing machinery [1]. In recent years, social media have established themselves as high-value, high-volume content information sources, which organizations are increasingly using for their research [2]. The social media platforms, such as Stack Overflow and Quora, play a significant role in knowledge sharing and acquisition for software developers [3]. The wealth of software engineering knowledge

H.-P. Lam and S. Mistry (Eds.): ASSRI 2018, LNBIP 367, pp. 65–80, 2019.
https://doi.org/10.1007/978-3-030-32242-7_6

in the form of literature is increasing continuously at an exponential phase in these websites. The user-generated content of these websites became an important information resource. Most of the information stored in these websites are in unstructured format. According to a market survey performed by IDC [4], between 2009 and 2020, the amount of digital information will grow by a factor of 44, but the staffing and investment to manage it will grow by a factor of just 1.4. With current trend, the information related to software engineering will grow much faster rate than the normal digital information. Dealing with such a huge mismatch is a great challenge, and one of the proposals to the problem is to develop tools for the search and discovery of information, which includes finding ways to add structure to unstructured data [5].

The socio-technical nature of software engineering social content available on such websites call for innovative forms of information extraction, organization and search [6]. The goal would be to organize the information in a knowledge base about different software specific entities and relationships between entities. Such knowledge base can be represented as a graph, known as "Knowledge Graph" [7]. Search systems can exploit knowledge graph for finding the content that actually discusses a particular software-specific entity and to displaying additional facts and direct information about the central entity in a query [8]. As the first step towards knowledge graphs and entity-centric search systems for software engineering domain, we must be able to recognize mentions of software-specific entities in software engineering social content and classify them into pre-defined categories [6]. Therefore, there is a rising need for effective natural language processing tools to assist in organizing, curating, and retrieving this information. The important goal of NLP is the interface between how the humans communicate (natural language) [9] and what the computer understands (machine language). Natural Language Processing embraces great promise for making computer interfaces that are easier to use for people [10]. Apache OpenNLP, Natural Language Toolkit (NLTK), GATE annotator, Stanford NLP are various open source NLP libraries used in real world application for processing unstructured data [11].

Information Extraction helps to retrieve demanded information from the huge unstructured collection of data [12]. Information extraction is the task of extracting specific kinds of information from documents as opposed to the more general task of "document understanding" which seeks to extract all of the information found in a document. To that end, Named Entity Recognition (NER) is an important first step towards entity-centric search systems for any domain. NER is a computational linguistics task in which we seek to classify every word in a document as falling into different category. The task of recognizing named entities was first considered in Sixth Message Understanding Conference (MUC-6) [13]. At that time, MUC was focusing on Information Extraction tasks. While defining this task, MCU realized that identification of information units such as person, location, organization, monetary values, numeric expressions etc. are essential for information extraction task. Since that time, named entities have been playing an important role of efficiently conducting information extraction process in a large number of generic texts. In this way, an NER system can also serve as an important component for many domain specific expert systems. NER can also be used for standard Natural Language Processing tasks, such as question answering [14], machine translation [15], social media analysis [16], semantic search [17], summarization [18–20], ontology population [21], opinion mining [22] and text clustering [23] specific to any domain.

In the field of software engineering very less literature is available on NER. Ye et al. [6], worked on this by including few higher-level categories of software engineering in recognizing named entities. In this work, we are further deep diving to include software entities at lower granular level, by including more categories related to software engineering in identifying named entities. In this work, we aimed to perform a foundational study of a diverse set of Stack Overflow posts, covering different Object Oriented, Procedural, Scripting, Web development languages etc. to develop a tool which will categorise software specific entities in to predefined categories.

2 Related Work

Rizzo and Troncy [1] developed NERD, a framework that unifies 10 popular named entity extractors available on the web. The algorithms were developed for analyzing atomic information elements which occur in a sentence and identify Named Entity (NE) such as name of people or organizations, locations, time references or quantities. The approach relies on the development of the NERD ontology which provides a common interface for annotating elements, and a web REST API which is used to access the unified output of popular tools. They compared 6 different systems using NERD.

Jung [16] worked on exploiting the conventional NER methods for analyzing a large set of microtexts of which lengths are short. Particularly, the micro texts are streaming online social media, e.g., Twitter. To do so, Jason proposed three properties of contextual association among the microtexts to discover contextual clusters of the micro texts, which can be expected to improve the performance of NER tasks. As a case study, he applied the proposed NER system to Twitter. Experimental results demonstrate the feasibility of the proposed method (around 90.3% of precision) for extracting relevant information in online social network applications.

Wang et al. [24] proposed Bacterial Named Entity Recognition. They used dataset from Genia corpus in the field of biomedical and algorithm used were Condition Random Field and Support Vector Machine (SVM). The Bacterial NER model was trained based upon the dictionary key pair value and CRF algorithm. The paper also discusses constructing feature set of bacterial entities.

Cruzes et al. [25] proposed the paper titled "Automated Information Extraction from Empirical Software Engineering Literature: Is that possible?" defines the idea of information extraction techniques to software engineering domain. This paper has explained text mining and information extraction by three different types. The first type identifies the named entity recognition such as people, organization, and locations. The second type to identify the relationship between entities. The third type extracting fillers for a predetermined set of slots in a particular template relevant to a certain domain.

Das et al. [26] proposed A Two-stage Approach of Named-Entity Recognition for Crime Analysis. Authors used the online newspaper articles to extracts crime reports. The first stage recognizes the basic named entities, such as the name of states, cities, person etc. to count the frequency of occurrence of those entities and rank based upon the occurrence. It helps to find which state leads in crime. The second stage Modus Operandi Features helps to identify more information about crime such as crime type, place of crime, weapons used, etc. Finally, the results were compared with NCRB reports to evaluate.

Ye et al. [6] worked on Software-specific Named Entity Recognition in Software Engineering Social Content, enabling entity-centric applications for software engineering to recognize and classify software-specific entities. This paper defines five broad categories of software entities for a wide range of popular programming languages, platform, and library. The paper, builds S-NER, a semi-supervised machine learning method for NER in software engineering social content, and demonstrate that S-NER significantly outperforms a well-designed rule-based NER system when applied on Stack Overflow posts.

3   A Framework for Tool and Application

Currently available Named Entity Recognition taggers recognize expressions such as People, Product, Organization, and Location [2]. In our work, we are extending Named Entity tagger to recognize common entities related to software domain. This task referred as Named Entity Recognition in Software Engineering (NERSE). We developed a software specific, machine learning based NER model trained on software-specific entity categories, using Conditional Random Fields (CRF) [9] and Bidirectional Long Short-Term Memory - Conditional Random Fields (BiLSTM-CRF) neural network models [27]. The built model predicts the sequence of words in a sentence into their respective categories based on the context it learnt from the training data.

NERSE is a web application, which is responsible for finding textual data into default pre-defined categories. NERSE is trained to recognize software-specific entities in software engineering social content to classify them into pre-defined categories as named entities. The web interface is developed in HTML. The main purpose of this interface is to enable the user to use application for identifying the named entities in software engineering.

NERSE is developed in Linux-Ubuntu OS environment. We used python as our scripting language for back end model building and Flask frame work for back end server integration. Our front-end for user interface was developed using JavaScript language. Users can enter the software related text in the text box provided in GUI and can visually see the entities highlighted and their entity classes in the front-end. The front-end has two tabs with CRF and Bi-LSTM CRF models. The user can switch between these tabs to see and compare the output from both the models. Users can also find the result in the form of JSON output, which can be accessed through APIs. NERSE web page for both the models is shown in Figs. 1 and 2.

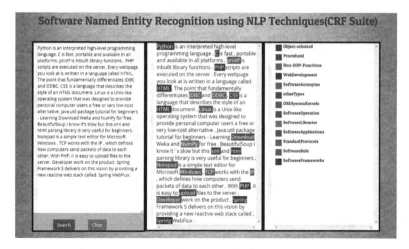

Fig. 1. NER model using CRF

4 NERSE

Existing NER models can identify common entities like Person, Organization, Location, Percentage, Money, Date, and Time in formal or informal texts [6]. However, these entities are not what software developers are concerned within software engineering data. A little work has been done to recognize software-specific entities that developers care. For any NER related work, entity classes must be defined clearly. In software engineering, our first task would be to define domain specific entities. We have identified 22 categories of software entities specific to software engineering. Table 1 shows the Software-specific entity categories which we used in our work. Object oriented category covers different types of known programming languages, such as Python, Java. The web development category includes PHP, HTML. CPU instruction sets category refers to IA-32, x86-64. Hardware architecture includes platforms such as, CHRP, PReP. OOP-packages refers to Java language, and so on. Figure 3 shows the NERSE processing architecture.

We randomly selected posts from Stack Overflow data related to software domain. The dataset consists of 1,50,000 rows including HTML tags and codes. Each cell contains multiple sentences. Table 2, shows the sample data from Stack Overflow Posts, used for NER training.

4.1 Data Preparation and Pre-processing

Data preparation improves the quality of data and consequently helps improve the results. Data preprocessing refers to a set of activities, which we follow to clean the raw data to make it suitable for further processing to the context. Initially, we identified the tags present inside the text (Eg: <p>, </p>, <pre>, </pre>, <h1>, <strong>), then we removed the tags, which have code between

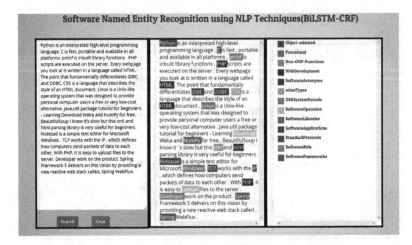

Fig. 2. NER model using Bi-LSTM CRF

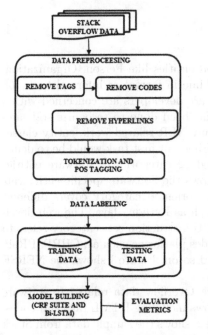

Fig. 3. NERSE processing architecture

Table 1. NERSE entity classes

Entity tag	Examples
1. Object Oriented	Python, Java
2. Procedural	Ada, C
3. Scripting	Oriel
4. Web Development	PHP, HTML
5. Other Types	SQL, XML
6. CPU instruction sets	IA-32,x86-64
7. Hardware architectures	CHRP, PReP
8. Operating systems	system kernels & Android, Ubuntu
9. OOP-packages	Java.Lang
10. OOP-public methods	charAt()
11. Non-OOP-Functions	Scanf, calloc
12. Other-Events	on click event
13. Software tools	Firebug, Weka
14. Software framework	AngularJS, ASP.Net
15. Software libraries	NumPy
16. software applications	WordPad
17. Data formats	.jpg, .png
18. Standard Protocols	HTTP, SMTP
19. Software design patterns	Builder
20. Software acronyms	JDBC, WWW
21. Software Roles	Manager, client
22. Software Operation	Search, download

them, as it makes no sense for an algorithm to learn patterns. Also removed the tags with hyperlinks (Eg: <a href=https://www.gmail.com/ target="blank">) to get the cleaned data. The cleaned data from stack overflow posts is shown in Table 3.

Table 2. Stack overflow data for entity classification

Body
</p> I want to be able to display a normal YouTube video with overlaid annotations, consisting of colored rectangles for each frame.</p>
</p> On one Linux Server running Apache and PHP 5, we got multiple Virtual Hosts with separate log files and everything. </p><p> Overriding this setting in the <code> & lt; Location & gt ;</code> Did I overlook something?
</p> May be this might help: < a href="http://jsefa.sourceforge.net/ quick-tutorial.html" rel="noreferrer"> JSefa </a></p><p> You can read CSV file with this tool and serialize it to XML.</a>

Table 3. Stack overflow data after pre-processing

Body
I want to be able to display a normal YouTube video with overlaid annotations, consisting of colored rectangles for each frame.
On one Linux Server running Apache and PHP 5, we got multiple Virtual Hosts with separate log files and everything. Overriding this setting in the Did I overlook something?
Maybe this might help: You can read CSV file with this tool and serialize it to XML.

4.2 Tokenization

Natural Language Tool Kit provides packages and modules to handle text data such as tokenization, stemming tagging etc. [28]. Tokenization package is used to split set of characters into tokens for further processing. For examples, each word is a token when a sentence is "tokenized" into words. Each sentence can also be a token, if we tokenize the sentences out of a paragraph. Each of the tokens consists of a string of characters without white space [29]. Tokens can be words, numbers, identifiers or punctuations. Table 4 shows the tokenizer output.

Table 4. Data after tokenization

Input data	On one Linux Server running Apache and PHP.
Word tokenizer	['On', 'one', 'Linux', 'Server', 'running', 'Apache', 'and', 'PHP', '.']

4.3 Tagging

Part-of-speech tagging is the base of Natural Language Processing, and is commonly used in information retrieval, text processing and machine translation fields. Words with POS tag as NN (Nouns), NNP (Proper Noun), UB (Verb), JJ(Adjectice) etc. were extracted from the dataset [30]. Table 5 shows the input and output of Word tokenizer and tagging.

Table 5. Data after POS tagging

Input data	On one Linux Server running Apache and PHP.
POS	[('On', 'IN'), ('one', 'CD'), ('Linux', 'NNP'), ('Server', 'NNP'), ('running', 'VBG'), ('Apache', 'NNP'), ('and', 'CC'), ('PHP', 'NNP')]

4.4 Data Labeling

Data Labels contains dictionary key and values. We labeled data based on 22 categories such as Software Role, Software Operation, Software Applications, Software Frameworks, Software Libraries, Software Tools, NonOOPFunctions, OthersEvents, OOPPublic Methods, OOPPackages, OS & System Kernels, CPUInstruction, Hardware architecture, Software acronyms, Software design patterns, Software protocols, Data formats, Other types, Web development, Scripting, Procedural, Object-oriented. For example, Java and PHP are denoted as 'Java Object Oriented', 'PHP': 'Web Development'. Then others were labeled as 'O' (others). Finally, we removed the unwanted sentences, i.e. the sentence with all the words tagged as 'O', because the algorithm will have nothing to learn from such sentences.

4.5 Model Training

The data in the format as shown in Table 6 is fed to the algorithm to train models. The processed data is trained with Conditional Random Fields (CRF) and Bidirectional Long Short-Term Memory-Conditional Random Fields (BiLSTM-CRF) algorithms.

Table 6. Data for training

Input data	On one Linux Server running Apache and PHP
Training data	Sentence #,Word,POS,Tag
	Sentence: 1,On,IN,O
	Sentence: 1,one,CD,O
	Sentence: 1,Linux,NNP,OS& SystemKernels
	Sentence: 1,Server,NNP,O
	Sentence: 1,running,VBG,O
	Sentence: 1,Apache,NNP,O
	Sentence: 1,and,CC,O
	Sentence: 1,PHP,NNP,Web development
	Sentence: 1,.,.,O

NER Using Conditional Random Fields. Conditional Random Fields (CRFs) [31] are undirected graphical models used to calculate the conditional probability of values on designated output nodes given values assigned to other designated input nodes. A conditional random field (CRF) is a type of discriminative probabilistic model used for labeling sequential data such as natural language text. Conditionally trained CRF's can easily include large number of arbitrary non independent features. When applying CRF's to the named entity recognition problem an observation sequence is the token sequence of a sentence or document of text and state sequence is its corresponding label sequence.

In a special case where the output nodes form a linear chain, CRF's make a first-order Markov independence assumption, and can be viewed as conditionally trained probabilistic finite state machines (FSMs). These models are analogous to maximum entropy/conditional log-linear finite state machines, except that they are normalized over entire sequences rather than per-state.

Let $o = <o_1, o_2, ...o_T>$ be some observed input data sequence, such as a sequence of words in text in a document, (the values of n input nodes of the graphical model). Let S be a set of FSM states, each of which is associated with a label, $l \epsilon L$, (such as PROCEDURAL). Let $s = <s_1, s_2, ...s_T>$ be some sequence of states, (the values on T output nodes). By the Hammersley-Clifford theorem, CRFs define the conditional probability of a state sequence given an input sequence to be

$$P_\wedge(S/O) = \frac{1}{Z_o} \exp \sum_{t=1}^{T} \sum_k \lambda_K f_k(S_{l-1}, S_l, o, t)$$

where $f_k(S_{l-1}, S_l, o, t)$ is a feature function whose weight λ_k is to be learned via learning. CRF's define the conditional probability of a label sequence based on total probability over the state sequences,

$$P(1/O) = \sum_{S:1(S)=1} P(S/0)$$

where l(s) is the sequence of labels corresponding to the labels of the states in sequences. Z_o is a normalization factor over all state sequences. To make all conditional probabilities sum up to 1, we must calculate the normalization factor $Z_O = \sum_s \exp \sum_{t=1}^{T} \sum_k \lambda_K f_k(S_{l-1}, S_l, o, t)$. A feature function may, for example, be defined to have value 0 in most cases, and have value 1 if and only if s_{t-1} is state #1 (which may have label OTHER), and s_t is state #2 (which may have label SCRIPTING), and the observation at position t in o is a word appearing in a list of country names. Higher λ weights make their corresponding FSM transitions more likely, so the weight λ_k in this example should be positive.

More generally, feature functions can ask arbitrary questions about the input sequence, including queries about previous words, next words, and conjunctions of all these, and $f_k(.)$ can range $-\infty...+\infty$.

The weights of a CRF, $\wedge - \{\lambda, ...\}$, are set to maximize the conditional log-likelihood of labeled sequences in some training set, $D = \{(o, l)^1, ...(o, l)^j, ...(o, l)^N\}$:

$$L \wedge - \sum_{j=1}^{N} \log(p \wedge (l^j \| o^j)) - \sum_{k} \frac{\lambda_k^2}{2\sigma^2}$$

where the second sum is a Gaussian prior over parameters (with variance σ) that provides smoothing to help cope with sparsity in the training data. When the training labels make the state sequence unambiguous (as they often do in practice), the likelihood function in exponential models such as CRFs is convex, so there are no local maxima, and thus finding the global optimum is guaranteed. It has recently been shown that quasi-Newton methods, such as L-BFGS, are significantly more efficient than traditional iterative scaling and even conjugate gradient [32,33]. This method approximates the second-derivative of the likelihood by keeping a running, finite-sized window of previous first-derivatives. L-BFGS can simply be treated as a black-box optimization procedure, requiring only that one provide the first-derivative of the function to be optimized. Assuming that the training labels on instance j make its state path unambiguous, let s_j denote the path and then the first-derivative of the log-likelihood is

$$\frac{\delta L}{\delta \lambda_K} = (\sum_{j=1}^{N} C_k(s^j, o^j)) - (\sum_{j=1}^{N} \sum_{s} P_\wedge(s|o^j)C_k(s, o^j)) - \frac{\lambda_k}{\sigma^2}$$

where $C_k(S, O)$ is the count for feature k given s and o, equal to $\sum_{t=1}^{T} f_k(S_{l-1}, S_l, o, t)$, the sum of $f_k(S_{l-1}, S_l, o, t)$ values for all positions, t, in the sequence s. The first two terms correspond to the difference between the empirical expected value of feature f_k and the model expected value: $(E[f_k] - E_\wedge[f_k])N$. The last term is the derivative of Gaussian prior.

BI-LSTM-CRF Networks: we combine a Bidirectional LSTM network and a CRF network to form a BILSTM-CRF network. In addition to the past input features and sentence level tag information a BILSTM-CRF model can use the future input features. The extra features can boost tagging accuracy.

Many existing models use generic stochastic Gradient Descent (SGD) forward and backward training procedure. We choose BI-LSTM-CRF to train NER model. While training the model, in every epoch, the training data is divided in to multiple batches and one batch at a time is processed. Each batch contains a list of sentences which is determined by the parameter of batch size. In our experiments, we use batch size of 32 which means to include sentences whose total length is no greater than 75. For every batch, we first run bi-directional LSTM-CRF model forward pass which includes the forward pass for both forward state and backward state of LSTM. As a result, we get the the output score $f_\theta(|x|_1^T)$ for all tags at all positions. We then run CRF layer forward and backward pass to compute gradients for network output and state transition edges. After that, we can back propagate the errors from the output to the input, which includes the backward pass for both forward and backward states of LSTM. Finally we update the network parameters which include the state transition matrix $[A]_{i,j} \forall_{i,j}$ and

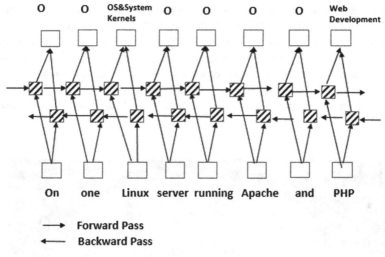

Fig. 4. BI-LSTM-CRF named entity recognition model

the original bidirectional LSTM parameters Θ. The BI-LSTM-CRF architecture for the given sentence is shown in Fig. 4 and algorithm for training BI-LSTM CRF model is shown in Algorithm 1.

for *each epoch* **do**
> **for** *each batch* **do**
>> 1) bidirectional LSTM-CRF model forward pass:;
>> forward pass for forward state LSTM;
>> forward pass for backward state LSTM;
>> 2) CRF layer forward and backward pass;
>> 3) bidirectional LSTM-CRF model backward pass:;
>> backward pass for forward state LSTM;
>> backward pass for backward state LSTM;
>> 4) update parameters
>
> **end**

end

Algorithm 1. Bi-Directional LSTM CRF model Training Procedure

5 Evaluation

We downloaded the data dump of Stack Overflow until Dec, 2017 from Stack Overflow official data dump[1]. Our experiments are designed to demonstrate the need of a software-specific NER system We extracted 64075 posts which include minimum two entities per sentence in the post. The annotated corpus consists of 1,50,000 sentences derived from 64075 Stack Overflow posts. Tokens extracted

---

[1] https://archive.org/details/stackexchange.

after the process of tokenization is 30,37,881. The number of software-specific named entities from all the 22 categories were 3,21,768. The sentences annotated for different categories were thoroughly studied by annotators such that no category is under represented with respect to other category to avoid under-fitting or over-fitting. We used 6 annotators who were having average experience of 5 years in software engineering domain for annotating data. The distribution of entities among different categories from the labelled data set were represented in Fig. 5.

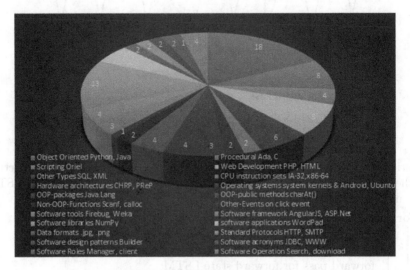

Fig. 5. Percentage of training data for each category

To fully evaluate the model performance, we randomly split the data set into two parts for training and testing respectively, and we gradually increase the percentage of training examples from 60% to 80%. We used 10-fold cross validation by randomly dividing our annotated corpus into 10 equal sized subsets. Of the 10 subsets, one single subset is retained as the testing data, and the remaining 9 subsets are used as training data. We repeat this process 10 times and produce a single estimation by averaging the 10 results obtained. It is very likely that a question and its answers discuss the same set of software entities. Therefore, to avoid model over-fitting, we make sure that the answers to a particular question will not be put in the testing data if the corresponding question is in the training data.

We use precision, recall, and F1 as evaluation metrics. For each category of named entity, precision measures what percentage the output labels are correct. Recall measures what percentage the named entities in the data set are labeled correctly. F1-score is the harmonic mean of precision and recall. Using 10-fold cross validation produces 10 sets of testing results. We calculate the average precision, recall and F1-score as the overall performance. We report phrase-level

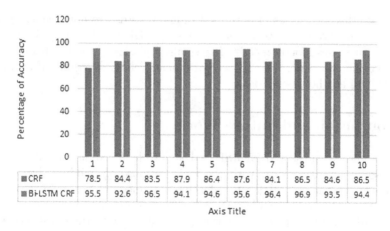

Fig. 6. Cross validation output of NERSE models

precision, recall and F1. This means that if an entity consists of a span of tokens, it is considered correctly labeled if and only if all its tokens are labeled correctly.

For the proposed LSTM-based neural network models, the dimension of each unit output is set to 75. Adam algorithm is used for training the models, its initial learning rate and its iteration number is set to 0.01 and 1000 respectively with parameters $\beta 1 = 0.9$, $\beta 2 = 0.999$ and $\epsilon = 1\text{x}10^{-8}$ For the CRF model, L-1 regularization is used for conducting the maximum likelihood estimation. L-BFGS algorithm is used for training the CRF model, the number of iterations is set to 50 with parameters $\epsilon = 1\text{x}10^{-5}$ and $\delta = 1\text{x}10^{-5}$ respectively. Figure 6 summarizes the F1 scores of the models (namely CRF, BiLSTM-CRF) for each cross validation.

The average of overall results obtained by using CRF and Bi-LSTM CRF models for all 22 different software engineering specific entities were listed in Table 7. We see that the overall F1-score of CRF is 0.85% and Bi-LSTM CRF is 0.95%.

Table 7. Evaluation metrics for NERSE

Models	Precision	Recall	F1-score
CRF	0.87	0.82	0.85
Bi-LSTM CRF	0.96	0.94	0.95

In evaluation of entity category we identify that the precision and recall of CPU Instruction sets, hardware architectures, operating systems, frameworks, software libraries, standard protocols were not ambiguous when compared to naming of other categories of entities. Common words are not frequently used for these entity types. As we increase the size of labeled data from 60 to 80%, we see F1 increases monotonically. The smaller the size of the labeled data, the larger the increase rate. The F1-score becomes relatively stable after we use about 80% of all the labeled data

6   Conclusion and Future Work

In this paper, we presented NERSE, a framework for Named Entity recognition in software engineering, with the main purpose of enabling the software engineers to use the application for identifying named entities in software engineering. The CRF and BiLSTM-CRF algorithms were used to train model. The NERSE predicts the sequence of words in a sentence into their respective categories. In future, named entity categories related to software specific domain can be extended to other domains such as farming, aviation etc. and then relation extraction can be performed between the named entities, which will provide deeper analysis on a specific domain. The future direction would be making use of software named entities in multiple domains to automate the process.

Method presented in this paper can be extended other software entity types like bug reports, tweets etc. We planned to contribute much more training data sets to increase accuracy as well as to build entity centric search systems for software engineering entities.

References

1. Rizzo, G., Troncy, R.: NERD: a framework for unifying named entity recognition and disambiguation extraction tools. In: Proceedings of the 13th Conference of the European Chapter of the Association for Computational Linguistics, Avignon, France, pp. 73–76 (2012)
2. Derczynski, L., et al.: Analysis of named entity recognition and linking for tweets. Proc. Inf. Process. Manag. **51**, 32–49 (2015)
3. Mamykina, L., Manoim, B., Mittal, M., Hripcsak, G., Hartmann, B.: Design lessons from the fastest Q&A site in the west. In: Proceedings of the SIGCHI Conference on Human Factors in Computing Systems, pp. 2857–2866. ACM (2011)
4. Gantz, J., Reinsel, D.: The Digital Universe Decade - Are You Ready?. Sponsored by EMC Corporation May 2010
5. Marrero, M., Urbano, J., Sánchez-Cuadrado, S., Morato, J., Gómez-Berbís, J.M.: Named entity recognition: fallacies, challenges and opportunities. Proc. Comput. Stand. Interfaces **35**, 482–489 (2013)
6. Ye, D., Xing, Z., Foo, C.Y., Ang, Z.Q., Li, J., Kapre, N.: Software-specific named entity recognition in software engineering social content. In: IEEE 23rd International Conference on Software Analysis, Evolution, and Reengineering (SANER), Suita, pp. 90–101 (2016)
7. Meij, E., Balog, K., Odijk, D.: Entity linking and retrieval for semantic search. In: WSDM, pp. 683–684 (2014)

8. Pantel, P., Fuxman, A.: Jigs and Lures: associating web queries with structured entities. In: Proceedings of the 49th Annual Meeting of the Association for Computational Linguistics: Human Language Technologies-Volume 1, pp. 83–92 (2011)
9. Surabhi, M.C.: Natural language processing future. In: Proceedings of International Conference on Optical Imaging Sensor and Security, Coimbatore, Tamil-Nadu, India, 2–3 July 2013
10. Kaur, N., Pushe, V., Kaur, R.: Natural language processing interface for synonym. Proc. Int. J. Comput. Sci. Mobile Comput. **3**(7), 638–642 (2014)
11. Adak, C., Chaudhuri, B.B., Blumenstein, M.: Named entity recognition from unstructured handwritten document images. In: Proceedings of IEEE 12th IAPR Workshop on Document Analysis Systems (2016)
12. Settles, B.: Biomedical named entity recognition using conditional random fields and rich feature sets. In: Proceeding JNLPBA 2004 Proceedings of the International Joint Workshop on Natural Language Processing in Biomedicine and Its Applications, Geneva, Switzerland, pp. 104–107, 28–29 August 2004
13. Grishman, R., Sundheim, B.: Message understanding conference-6: a brief history. In: COLING, vol. 96, pp. 466–471 (1996)
14. Rodrigo, Á., Pérez-Iglesias, J., Peñas, A., Garrido, G., Araujo, L.: Answering questions about European legislation. Expert Syst. Appl. **40**, 5811–5816 (2013)
15. Chen, Y., Zong, C., Su, K.Y.: A joint model to identify and align bilingual named entities. Comput. Linguist. **39**, 229–266 (2013)
16. Jung, J.J.: Online named entity recognition method for microtexts in social networking services: a case study of Twitter. Expert Syst. Appl. **39**, 8066–8070 (2012)
17. Habernal, I., Konopík, M.: SWSNL: semantic web search using natural language. Expert Syst. Appl. **40**, 3649–3664 (2013)
18. Baralis, E., Cagliero, L., Jabeen, S., Fiori, A., Shah, S.: Multi-document summarization based on the Yago ontology. Expert Syst. Appl. **40**, 6976–6984 (2013)
19. Glavas, G., Snajder, J.: Event graphs for information retrieval and multidocument summarization. Expert Syst. Appl. **41**, 6904–6916 (2014)
20. Kabadjov, M., Steinberger, J., Steinberger, R.: Multilingual statistical news summarization. In: Poibeau, T., Saggion, H., Piskorski, J., Yangarber, R. (eds.) Multilingual Information Extraction and Summarization. Theory and Applications of Natural Language Processing, pp. 229–252. Springer, Berlin (2013)
21. Etzioni, O., et al.: Unsupervised named-entity extraction from the web: an experimental study. Artif. Intell. **165**(1), 91–134 (2005)
22. Popescu, A.M., Etzioni, O.: Extracting product features and opinions from reviews. In: Kao, A., Poteet, S.R. (eds.) Natural Language Processing and Text Mining, pp. 9–28. Springer, London (2007). https://doi.org/10.1007/978-1-84628-754-1_2
23. Cao, T.H., Tang, T.M., Chau, C.K.: Text clustering with named entities: a model, experimentation and realization. In: Holmes, D.E., Jain, L.C. (eds.) Data mining: Foundations and Intelligent Paradigms, pp. 267–287. Springer, Berlin (2012)
24. Wang, X., Jiang, X., Liu, M., He, T., Hu, X.: Bacterial named entity recognition based on dictionary and conditional random field. In: Proceedings of IEEE International Conference on Bioinformatics and Biomedicine (BIBM) (2017)
25. Cruzes, D., Mendonça, M., Basili, V., Shull, F., Jino, M.: Automated information extraction from empirical software engineering literature: is that possible? In: Proceeding of IEEE First International Symposium on Empirical Software Engineering and Measurement (2007)
26. Das, P., Das, A.K.: A two-stage approach of named-entity recognition for crime analysis. In: Proceeding of IEEE - 40222 8th ICCCNT 2017, 3–5 July 2017

27. Lin, B.Y., Xu, F., Luo, Z., Zhu, K.: Multi channel BiLSTM CRF model for emerging named entity recognition in social media. In: Proceedings of the 3rd Workshop on Noisy User Generated Text, Copenhagen, Denmark, 7 September, pp. 160–165 (2017)
28. Seshathriaathithyan, S., Sriram, M.V., Prasanna, S., Venkatesan, R.: Affective—hierarchical classification of text—an approach using NLP toolkit. In: Proceedings of 2016 International Conference on Circuit, Power and Computing Technologies (2016)
29. Barcala, F.M., Vilares, J., Alonso, M.A., Grana, J., Vilares, M.: Tokenization and proper noun recognition for information retrieval. In: Proceedings of the 13th International Workshop on Database and Expert Systems Applications (DEXA 2002) (2002)
30. Kanya, N., Ravi, T.: Modelings and techniques in named entity recognition an information extraction task. In: Proceeding of Third International Conference on Sustainable Energy and Intelligent System, 27–29 December (2012)
31. Lafferty, J., McCallum, A., Pereira, F.: Conditional random fields: probabilistic models for segmenting and labeling sequence data. In: Proc. ICML (2001)
32. Malouf, R.: A comparison of algorithms for maximum entropy parameter estimation. In: Sixth Workshop on Computational Language Learning CoNLL (2002)
33. Sha, F., Pereira, F.: Shallow parsing with conditional random fields. In: Proceedings of Human Language Technology, NAACL (2003)

Bit-Vector-Based Spatial Data Compression Scheme for Big Data

Dukshin Oh[1] and Jongwan Kim[2]([⊠])

[1] Department of Management Information Systems, Sahmyook University,
Seoul 01795, Korea
ohds@syu.ac.kr
[2] Smith Liberal Arts College, Sahmyook University, Seoul 01795, Korea
kimj@syu.ac.kr

Abstract. The progress achieved by location-based services has significantly increased the frequency of access to, and improved the usability of, location information. In a mobile environment, spatial data are utilised to provide various services focused on the location information of users. As spatial data represent location information of various objects, cars, hospitals, personal locations and buildings, they require significant storage space as well as methods for rapid searching and transmission to provide services in a timely manner. In this paper, we propose a bit vector-based compression scheme to reduce the storage space requirements and transmission times for large quantities of spatial data. In the proposed scheme, a bit vector represents the minimum bounding rectangle of an R-tree as a location vector of x- and y-axes in quadrant 1 of a two-dimensional graph and stores each axis utilising 1 byte. This has double the compression effect, as compared to that of a conventional compression scheme that performs compression utilising a maximum of 4 bytes. Storage space is reduced to 12.5%, as compared to conventional compression schemes, and the speed of transmission across the network is increased.

Keywords: Spatial data · Spatial data compression · Minimum bounding rectangle · Quantized minimum bounding rectangle · Bit vector

1 Introduction

Driven by advancements in location-based services, there has been a marked increase in various services based on spatial data for providing location information regarding spatial objects over the past decade. Location-based services utilise spatial data to indicate the location of a user or any spatial object, such as a hotel, petrol station, or nearby taxi service. The geographic location information is provided in a two-dimensional space utilising the coordinates of the centre point of a selected object or other coordinates within that object as spatial data. Therefore, the location of any given

This research was supported by Basic Science Research Program through the National Research Foundation of Korea (NRF) funded by the Ministry of Education (NRF-2018R1D1A1B07045642, NRF-2017R1D1A1B03035884).

H.-P. Lam and S. Mistry (Eds.): ASSRI 2018, LNBIP 367, pp. 81–92, 2019.
https://doi.org/10.1007/978-3-030-32242-7_7

object, such as a park, building, petrol station, school or forest, can be expressed by multiple coordinates according to the area occupied by that object. Indicating the location information of an object utilising different coordinates increases the spatial data processing cost at the location server.

Geospatial data constitute location information regarding spatial objects indicated by latitude and longitude values. Given the multitude of shapes of real spatial objects, it is a significant challenge to manage the location of each object and its shape on a location server. Therefore, in a spatial index R-tree, every spatial object with a circular or polygonal shape is represented by a minimum bounding rectangle (MBR). As shown in Fig. 1, an MBR is the smallest rectangle that can envelope a spatial object. The selected object is covered by its MBR and presented as an object occupying the area of that MBR, which is then managed based on the coordinates of its two diagonal corners. Although the MBR contains both the area occupied by the actual object and non-occupied area *r4*, as shown in Fig. 1, it has the advantage of managing all objects in the same rectangular form in a spatial index.

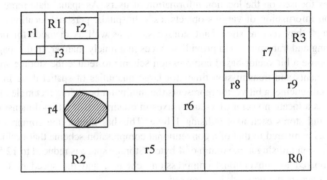

Fig. 1. Approximation of spatial objects and MBRs

On the location server, each coordinate of spatial data occupies four bytes of integer data and the two diagonal corners of the MBR require a storage space of 16 bytes. In location-based services, reducing the size of the coordinates allows faster searching and enables more rapid provision of location information. Therefore, many research efforts have been dedicated to spatial data compression to reduce the size of spatial data.

This paper proposes a novel bit vector-based compression scheme that can double the compression rate of the quantised representation of an MBR (QMBR), which is the most efficient existing scheme. The proposed scheme saves disk storage space and transmission time by compressing MBRs, which contain four coordinates, into a 2-byte bit string.

Even if continuous technological advancements accelerate the processing speed of location servers and mobile devices, spatial data compression will still provide additional performance enhancements by reducing data size. Consequently, spatial data compression further accelerates object detection and location information transmission. A method of compressing spatial data into 2 bytes is proposed here, and the proposed spatial data compression scheme can be applied not only to special objects but also to any geographical or virtual space.

The major contributions of this study can be summarised as follows:

- Saving disk storage space and minimising transmission time by compressing spatial data.
- Saving battery power of mobile devices by reducing spatial data transmission time.
- Accelerating spatial object detection time by increasing the volume of data being read per disk based on smaller storage size compared to conventional schemes.

2   Spatial Index and MBR Compression

The geographic locations of spatial data are expressed by utilising latitude and longitude, which are expressed as two coordinates. In an R-tree, because spatial data are approximated by MBRs, a single spatial data point is expressed by utilising the four coordinates representing an MBR diagonal.

In an R-tree, for indexing spatial data, an MBR is stored in a node as an entry, as shown Fig. 2. A single node occupies 4 KB on disk and when the coordinate is compressed, the number of entries stored in a node increases and the height of the index decreases. For an index with low height, as the search and transmission speed of data in the network increase, the compression requirements become stricter for spatial data in location-based services.

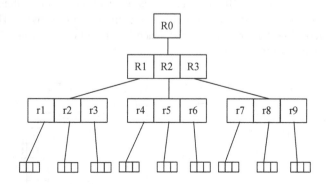

Fig. 2. R-tree index

Conventional spatial data compression schemes can be classified into relative coordinate compression and quantisation [1]. In the former scheme, the coordinates of an MBR are compressed to the minimum possible value based on the relative coordinates of the spatial object calculated from the origin of the space. In the latter scheme, the space is quantised into a grid form and an MBR is compressed on each side by replacing it with the nearest quantisation line. These schemes can yield a relative representation of an MBR (RMBR) [2], hybrid representation of an MBR (HMBR) [2] and QMBR [3], with the spatial coordinates being compressed to 8, 6 and 4 bytes, respectively.

2.1   R-tree

An R-tree indexes spatial data for fast searching [4]. In the indexing process, spatial data of various forms are reconstructed as MBRs. Therefore, a spatial object is identified by two points representing its diagonal location.

Figure 2 shows an index of an R-tree. In an R-tree, the root node $R0$ includes the entire search area and each entry in the internal nodes indicates the node of a lower level. Each node other than the root node has three entries, each of which represents the MBR of a sub-node. A terminal node includes entries for each spatial data and each entry is matched 1:1 to the spatial data.

2.2   Relative Coordinate Compression Scheme

The compression scheme utilising relative coordinates is straightforward. It calculates the difference between the starting point of the search space and each coordinate of an MBR [2]. For example, for the two points a and b in $R1$ in Fig. 3, the relative distance is calculated from the starting point p of $R0$. The coordinate of point b is calculated utilising the same method. Each coordinate of an MBR occupies 16 bytes when utilising integers, but this size is reduced to a maximum of 8 bytes when calculated as the difference from the origin point, p.

HMBR scheme further reduces the size of the coordinates [2]. For $R2$ in Fig. 3, the starting point c is calculated based on the relative distance from the origin point, p. For the end point, d, the relative coordinate is made based on the starting point, c. That is, the conventional RMBR utilises the relative coordinates based on the search area for both points. However, in HMBR, because a relative coordinate is calculated only for the starting point of an MBR, the two points are compressed to 6 bytes. This has the advantage of reducing the size and storage space for spatial data, because 2 bytes are removed in comparison to RMBR.

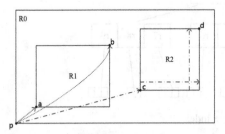
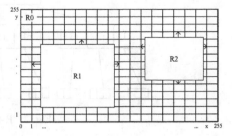

Fig. 3. RMBR, $R1$ and HMBR, $R2$ **Fig. 4.** Quantised representation of MBRs

2.3   Quantization Compression Scheme

Quantisation compression creates a grid-based search space of a certain size and expands each side of an MBR to the closest quantisation lines [3]. The actual coordinates for the two points of an MBR are compressed by replacing them with quantisation line numbers. Figure 4 presents the MBR quantised into 256 units for the entire search space, *R0*. The four sides of *R1* are replaced by the corresponding quantisation lines in the x- and y-axes. As a result, an MBR is expressed in a total of 4 bytes (1 byte for each side) in QMBR. The size of compressed spatial data depends on the quantisation unit. If units are larger than 256, each coordinate will be compressed to more than 1 byte.

3 Bit-Based Compression Scheme

3.1 Two-Dimensional Bit Vector

Quantisation is a frequently utilised technique to identify the locations of spatial objects when searching through spatial data [5]. In this study, the search space is quantised in a manner similar to conventional QMBR. For each side of an MBR, the x-axis is expanded to the closest left and right quantisation lines and the y-axis is expanded to the closest top and bottom quantisation lines. However, each coordinate of an MBR is not replaced with a quantisation line number. A series of x- and y-axes quantised around each quantisation line are converted into pairs of bit vectors.

The quantisation unit defining the quantisation line is described in Definition 1.

Definition 1. Quantisation Unit
Let Q_{unit} be the quantisation unit and Len_{cor} be the maximum length of x- or y-axes in a two-dimensional graph; then, the quantisation unit for one axis is defined as follows:

$$Q_{unit} = \frac{Len_{cor}}{Len_{vec}} (cor = x \, or \, y, Len_{vec} = 8). \tag{1}$$

The quantisation unit is generated differently in each axis because the maximum values of x- and y-axes are based on the search region. A search region is the largest area, which includes all MBRs and it is calculated from MBRs. Quantisation is obtained by dividing the maximum value of each axis by the length of a vector, Len_{vec}, and sets up the quantisation locations from the starting point of each axis based on the number of quantisation units. Q_{unit} determines a quantisation line, which meets with a side of an MBR. For example, if the right side on the x-axis of an MBR is greater than the fifth quantised line, the quantisation location is the sixth quantised line because the side should be extended to the right line. This is decided by the quantisation unit, Q_{unit}.

The following observation explains why the quantization units can be expressed utilizing the bits of an MBR.

Observation 1. Bit Vector of an MBR
In an arbitrary axis, if one side of an MBR meets a quantisation line, the corresponding location is expressed as 1; otherwise, it is expressed as 0. Each axis has a bit string according to the congruence between a side of an MBR and a quantisation line. This determines the size of each side of an MBR, and the area of that MBR can be derived.

Figure 5 presents the bit vector compressions for *R1* and *R2*. First, the two-dimensional graph is expressed by the x- and y-axes to define the search space. Each axis is divided into 8-bit units and the search space is divided into rectangles or squares based on its size. In the quantised space, *R1* is expanded to the closest quantisation line on each side. The left and bottom sides are expanded to the quantisation lines that lie closer to the origin point and the remaining sides are expanded to the closest outside lines. If the location where the quantisation unit of each axis and the side of an MBR meet is set to 1 and locations where they do not meet are set to 0, then the size of the MBR is composed of 16 bits.

For example, in Fig. 5, $q = 8$, which is the quantisation unit of the x- and y-axes. The bit vector of the x-axis for the quantisation line that *R1* meets is [10001000] and the bit vector of the y-axis is [01000100]. Therefore, to express *R1*, a bit vector of 16 bits is utilised. Figure 5 shows how to compress an MBR in a vector area.

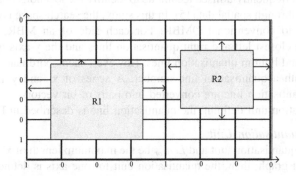

Fig. 5. Bit Vector representation of MBRs

3.2 Bit Vector Compression and Restoration

Figure 6 presents the algorithm for compression of MBRs utilising bit vectors. This algorithm accepts all of the MBRs that form the spatial data as inputs and makes a largest area as the search region that includes all MBRs. Subsequently, it defines a quantisation line (*ql*) that meets the x- and y-axes for each MBR of the search area and sets it to 1 (lines 4–5). For the bit setting, this process is repeated for the x- and y-axes (line 2). After determining the proper bit for each axis, it returns a bit vector of 16 bits for an MBR (line 10).

The two-dimensional data for MBRs compressed into bit vectors are stored in the variable *BitVector* as 16 bits. To restore the compression results to the original quantisation lines, each bit of *BitVector* must be checked to determine which quantisation line it meets. Figure 7 presents the algorithm that restores the original quantisation lines from the compression results stored in *BitVector*. The final results of restoration are the locations of the MBRs, where each location is stored as a text string and *MBRstr* is returned. The process for drawing an MBR based on the restoration results stored in *MBRstr* is straightforward.

```
Algorithm: MBR compression to bit vector
Input: MBRs
Output: Bit vectors BitVector[d] for d=x and y-axes
01: for each MBR in spatial dataset
02:    for each dimension d
03:       for each ql in 0, …, 7
04:          if ql == MBR.line then
05:             BitVector[d][ql] = 1;
06:          endif
07:       loop
08:    loop
09: loop
10: return BitVector
```

Fig. 6. Bit vector compression algorithm

```
Algorithm: MBR unzip from bit vector
Input: Bit vectors
Output: The quantized line numbers with MBRstr
01: for each bit in BitVector[d] for d = x and y-axes
02:    for each ql in 0, …, 7
03:       if BitVector[d][ql] == 1 then
05:          MBRstr += ql;
06:       endif
07:    loop
08: loop
09: return MBRstr for drawing an MBR;
```

Fig. 7. Bit vector decompression algorithm

4 Simulation

Compression of spatial data is required to reduce storage space and network transmission time. Therefore, we performed a simulation with as many spatial data as possible.

For this simulation, the basic assumptions are as follows:

- The search area *R0* is assumed to be identified prior to the simulation. Therefore, the process of identifying the search area by reading all spatial data is not included in the performance evaluation.
- The restoration of MBRs to the original coordinates is outside the scope of this study, and is not included in the performance evaluation.

As it is difficult to compose a large spatial dataset for simulation of a real environment, we utilised virtual spatial data in this simulation. For the virtual dataset, 100,000 MBRs were generated by utilising the data generator DaVisual Code [6], as shown in Fig. 8. The settings for spatial data generation are shown in Table 1.

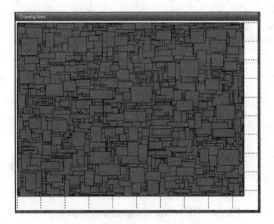

Fig. 8. Synthetic MBRs

Table 1. Settings of spatial data generation

World Settings:	Dimensions [1...3]: 2
	Size [1...100000, 1...100000]: 10000, 10000
Generator Settings:	Boxes created [1...100000]: 100000
	High ranges for the box size [1...99999, 1...99999]: 1000, 1000
	Variable size of boxes: Yes
	Non-zero size of boxes: Yes
	Distribution: Uniform
	Seed [1...65535]: 17494

This study focused on the size and quantity of spatial data, so their distribution was not considered. Although the distribution of spatial data has an influence on the search process, it is not related to the compression of data. Therefore, the number of entries per node in an R-tree, volume occupied on the disk and network transmission time were estimated in our simulation.

The simulation environments are described in Table 2.

Table 2. Simulation environment

Category	Environment
MBRs	100,000
Distribution	Uniform
Entries	Four entries in a node (R-tree)
MTU	1,500 bytes, 1 packet: 1,024 bits
Language	C++
System	Linux(Fedora), RAM 8 GB, Intel Xeon 3.2 GHz

4.1   Space Utilization

In an R-tree, the volume of data stored on the disk is affected by the number of entries included in a node. In this study, compression effects were analysed and insights were derived by mathematically analysing the number of entries that could be stored in a node through compression. There is a restriction in performing this analysis as the construction of a node considers only the entries in which pure MBRs are stored and the additional data comprising the index are not included because they are all the same constant. As one node contains four entries, four MBRs can be stored and each entry is 16 bytes with a single node occupying 64 bytes. In Linux, a block on disk is initialised as 4,096 bytes.

The calculation of storage space for 100,000 spatial data is defined by Eq. (2):

$$Byte_{total} = \left(\frac{D_{set}}{Ent_{node}} \right) \times Size_{node} \tag{2}$$

To calculate the disk volume for 100,000 spatial data, the total spatial data D_{set} are divided by the number of entries per node Ent_{node}. Subsequently, the total volume $Byte_{total}$ is calculated by multiplying the above result by the size of the nodes $Size_{node}$.

From Fig. 9, it can be seen that the total number of bytes is 1,600 KB for unzipped spatial data. To store these data on disk, 391 blocks are required according to Eq. (3). N_{blk} is the number of blocks on the disk and $Unit_{allo}$ is the size of the blocks, which is determined at the time of disk initialisation.

$$N_{blk} = \left\lceil \left(\frac{D_{set}}{Ent_{node}} \right) \times Size_{node} \div Unit_{allo} \right\rceil \tag{3}$$

The compression process utilising the bit vectors is described below. We do not describe the iterative calculation processes or identical equations in detail. A single bit vector is 2 bytes and represents the location where the quantisation units of the x- and y-axes meet. This constitutes the two-dimensional information that defines an MBR. Therefore, each node has a capacity of 8 bytes and is reduced to 12.5% of its size prior to compression. For example, the total volume required for storing 25,000 nodes is 200 KB, which occupies 49 blocks on disk.

Consequently, when the number of spatial data are increased from 100,000 to 1,000,000, the volume after compression is decreased to 12.5% of that before compression, as shown in Fig. 9. Here, the unit of volume is bytes. For example, for the 100,000 spatial data, the volume of the compressed data and number of blocks were eight times smaller than those before compression. The results are identical when the number of data amount to 1,000,000.

4.2   Transmission Cost

For a packet on a network, the maximum transmission unit (MTU) was set to 4,096 bits and compared from 1,024 to 4,096 bits in the simulation. In Figs. 10 and 11, the network transmission times are shown as the average values from 10 simulations with identical data.

This simulation was performed by expanding from a small packet size to a large packet size to analyse the effects on transmission speed when packet size increases as the amount of spatial data increase, which is important because the transmission speed of a small packet is fast. Furthermore, this was done to analyse the following phenomena. When the size of a packet increases, transmission performance is improved because several MBRs are sent in a single transmission. However, when the network is unstable, the transmission performance decreases because retransmission requests increase in TCP/IP.

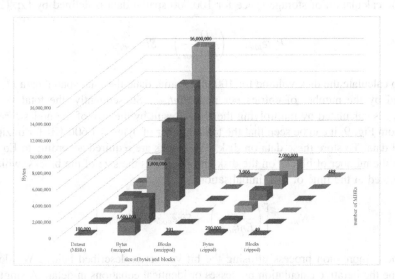

Fig. 9. Comparison of space utilization between compressed and uncompressed MBRs

Figure 10 presents the measurements of network transmission times for the uncompressed 100,000 spatial data. The number of bits of spatial data amount to 12,800,000 bits because an MBR is 16 bytes. With an increase in the MTU, the number of packets decreased and the transmission time gradually increased. The fastest speed was achieved when the MTU was 1,024 because this MTU responds quickly to retransmissions in the event of network errors. In contrast, for an MTU of 4,096, the number of packets decreased and the total transmission speed increased.

Figure 11 presents the measurements of network transmission speed for compressed spatial data. When the MTUs were the same as those prior to compression, the number of packets decreased. As the number of packets decreased, there was a large difference in transmission speed compared to that prior to compression. In the case of compressed spatial data, even when the MTU was large, the transmission speed was approximately twice that prior to compression. This confirmed that, even when delays occur because of retransmission requests in the network, transmission is faster than that prior to compression.

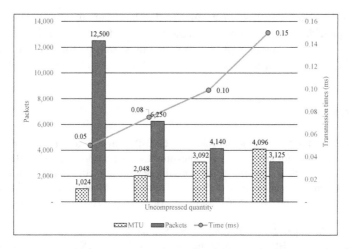

Fig. 10. Network transmission times for uncompressed spatial data

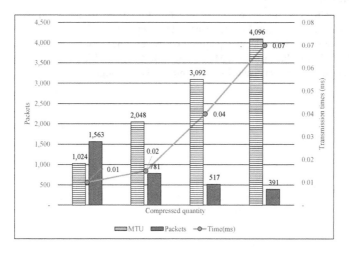

Fig. 11. Network transmission times for compressed spatial data

5 Conclusion

The usage of spatial data is gradually increasing in mobile environments and, regardless of hardware speed, compression of spatial data is required for the reduction of storage space and coordinate transmission time.

In this paper, a compression scheme utilising bit vectors was proposed. The proposed method outperforms the conventional schemes, i.e. RMBR, HMBR and QMBR that compress a 16-byte MBR into 8, 6 and 4 bytes, respectively. Our scheme achieves twice the compression of the conventional compression scheme, QMBR.

The simulation results showed that by compressing spatial data, the storage space usage rate decreases and spatial data can be transmitted more quickly across the network. For location-based services that utilise large amounts of spatial data, the advantages provided by the proposed method are significant and facilitate faster services for users. Future studies will be conducted on search performance and accuracy by comparing R-trees, and restoration of original latitude and longitude values.

References

1. Jongwan, K., Dukshin, O., Keecheon, K.: QMBRi: inverse quantization of minimum bounding rectangles for spatial data compression. Comput. Inform. **32**, 679–696 (2013)
2. Kim, J.-D., Moon, S.-H., Choi, J.-O.: A spatial index using MBR compression and hashing technique for mobile map service. In: Zhou, L., Ooi, B.C., Meng, X. (eds.) DASFAA 2005. LNCS, vol. 3453, pp. 625–636. Springer, Heidelberg (2005). https://doi.org/10.1007/11408079_58
3. Kim, J., Im, S., Kang, S.-W., Hwang, C.-S.: Spatial index compression for location-based services based on a MBR semi-approximation scheme. In: Yu, J.X., Kitsuregawa, M., Leong, H.V. (eds.) WAIM 2006. LNCS, vol. 4016, pp. 26–35. Springer, Heidelberg (2006). https://doi.org/10.1007/11775300_3
4. Guttman, A.: R-trees: a dynamic index structure for spatial searching. In: ACM SIGMOD International Conference on Management of Data, pp. 47–57 (1984)
5. Yeqing, L., Wei, L.: Sub-selective quantization for learning binary codes in large-scale image search. IEEE Trans. Pattern Anal. Mach. Intell. **40**(6), 1526–1532 (2017)
6. Spatial data generator, DaVisual Code1.0. http://isl.cs.unipi.gr

Blockchain in Supply Chain Management: Australian Manufacturer Case Study

Elias Abou Maroun[1]([✉]) [iD], Jay Daniel[2] [iD], Didar Zowghi[1] [iD],
and Amir Talaei-Khoei[3]

[1] Faculty of Engineering and IT, University of Technology Sydney,
Sydney, Australia
Elias.AbouMaroun@student.uts.edu.au,
Didar.Zowghi@uts.edu.au
[2] Derby Business School, University of Derby, Derby, UK
J.Daniel@derby.ac.uk
[3] Department of Information Systems, Ansari College of Business,
University of Nevada, Reno, NV, USA
Atalaeikhoei@unr.edu

Abstract. The recent explosion of interest around Blockchain and capabilities of this technology to track all types of transaction more transparently and securely motivate us to explore the possibilities Blockchain offers across the supply chain. This paper examines whether Blockchain makes a good fit for use in an Australian manufacturer supply chain. To address this, the research uses Technology Acceptance Model (TAM) as a framework from the literature. Blockchain allows us to have permissioned or permission-less distributed ledgers where stakeholders can interact with each other. It details how Blockchain works and the mechanism of hash algorithms which allows for greater security of information. It also focuses on the supply chain management and looks at the intricacies of a manufacturers supply chain. We present a review of the processes in place of an electrical manufacturer and the problems faced in the supply chain. A model is proposed in using public and private Blockchains to overcome these issues. The proposed solution has the potential to bring greater transparency, validity across the supply chain, and improvement of communication between stakeholders involved. We also point out some potential issues that should be considered if adopting Blockchain.

Keywords: Manufacturing supply chain management · Blockchain ·
Distributed ledger

1 Introduction

The amount of data being created and collected is growing at an exponential rate. This growth is primarily due to technology advances in devices which are known as the 'Internet of Things' (IOT) and the significance of computer power and availability of storage resources. Data is evolving and becoming part of everyday human activity, from product goods being sourced, product manufacturing and delivery of products to

H.-P. Lam and S. Mistry (Eds.): ASSRI 2018, LNBIP 367, pp. 93–107, 2019.
https://doi.org/10.1007/978-3-030-32242-7_8

consumers. The increase in data has provided opportunity for new approaches and techniques to create, store, analyse and obtain useful insight from the supply chain.

Supply chains are known to be large, complex and often unpredictable as they include four essential functions: sales, distribution, production, and procurement. They represent all the links that are involved in the sourcing of raw materials, manufacturing of goods, and the distribution of a finished product to the end consumer. Operational management of supply chains requires methods and tools to enable organisations to better understand how unexpected disruptions occur and what impacts they will have on the flow of goods to customer demand. Supply chain visibility provides opportunities for managers not only to plan efficiently but also to react appropriately to the accurate information [1].

Supply chains can span from over hundreds of stages and multiple geographical locations which makes it complex to trace events in the supply chain and investigate any issues. To date, customers have no reliable way to validate the true value and authenticity of a product purchased due to the lack of transparency, tracking, recording and sharing of information. The lack of transparency causes an absence of information from being shared about the manufacturing process of goods, assembly, delivery and certification of materials used that might pose risks and issues in the supply chain. This also poses a risk to fraud occurring in the supply chain such as counterfeiting of products, and the accountability of any illicit activities that may occur. Generally, questions are raised when manufacturing goods such as where are these components coming from? Do they meet the expected standards and are they safe?

Supply chains suffer from inefficiencies in the recording of assets such as pallets, trailers and containers that are continuously moving between supply chain nodes. There are issues in the tracking of purchase orders, receipts, shipment notifications and other trade related documents. The lack of assigning or verification of certain properties of the physical products or the linking of goods to serial numbers, bar codes or digital tags like radio frequency identification (RFID). Current Supply chain systems hold key data relating to each stage of the supply chain, people working in different stages must use the same system to update or complete the data of the process. This localized system typically an enterprise resource system (ERP) are comprised of localized possession of the company data and does not hold the complete stages of the supply chain. The objective is to bridge the gap between the different stages of the supply chain using Blockchain for supply chain management.

The Blockchain technology allows for data to be written in files called Blocks. The Blockchain technology can record transactions of almost any type based on certain conditions that are agreed on by stakeholder which can solve record keeping issues, however, computer professionals remain skeptical about relying on this technology for complex and long-term transactions management. They remain unsure about the preservation ability of the system for trusted digital records. Lemieux [2] and [3] identify threats and vulnerability of Blockchain as control base threats (Control of Blockchain, and Control of record creation outside of Blockchain), attack base threats (Man-in-the-middle attack, SYN Flood attack, Sybil attack, and Audit server attack), system base threats (Timing errors, and Preservation of original records), and process base threats (Change of bit rot to encryption, Collision of hashes, and encryption code Breakage). The Blockchain enables different organisations to collaborate and validate entries in the Blockchain hence giving stakeholders visibility of the overall activities taking place. This paper proposes using Blockchain technology to enable various upstream and downstream parties in supply chain to verify the authenticity of each individual Block and provide transparency across different stages of the supply chain. Various parties in the supply chain first provide input and agree on the content of a Block. Once in place, the Blockchain will include a set of constraints which cannot be violated by any Block.

An Australian electrical manufacturer (AEM) has been chosen to address the issues of traceability, transparency and inefficiencies which are common in supply chain management. The supply chain chosen is also common among the fast-moving consumer goods industry. The remainder of this paper is organised as follows: Sect. 2 the related work is reviewed. The proposed model and case study are discussed in Sects. 3 and 4, respectively. Finally, Sect. 5 provides discussion, conclusion and future work in this area.

2 Literature Review

Recently, more and more applications are being created based on Blockchain technology [4]. Initially, the Blockchain technology was the key technique behind Bitcoin [5]. Bitcoin is a popular form of digital cryptocurrency which was developed in 2008 by "Satoshi Nakamoto". The technology underlying Bitcoin is named Blockchain which acts as the payments layer for Internet. This new form of general computational substrate is a mechanism for updating truth states in distributed computer networks [6]. A recent survey has divided Blockchain-inspired technologies into two [7] fully decentralized permission-less ledgers, (e.g., Bitcoin, Ethereum), and semi-centralized permissioned ledgers (e.g. Ripple). These ledgers are known as 'distributed ledgers'. Lack of studies in the applicability of Blockchain technology motivated researchers to find the possibilities of this technology in other areas. Ølnes [8] investigated the possible application of this technology in electronic governments. To this end, a case of storing academic certificates on the Blockchain was presented to highlight the innovation potential of the new technology for storing and securing vital information. He concluded that although Blockchain is a promising technology for validating many types of persistent documents, still there is a long way to implement this technology in public sector. Nevertheless, the implications and limitations of using such technologies as a software connector had been elaborated as well. Dierksmeier and Seele [9] provided rationale to address the impact of "Blockchain technology" on the nature of financial transactions from a business ethics perspective. They combined different business and society levels such as micro, meso, and macro to propose a framework for assessing current status of cryptocurrencies ethical debates.

2.1 Blockchain

Several studies have attempted to find the performance and impacts of Blockchain in comparison with other systems. Focusing on their scalability limits. Vukolić [10] made a comparison between proof-of-work (PoW)-based Blockchains to those based on

Byzantine fault-tolerant (BFT) state machine. To tackle these limits, they reviewed recent proposed solutions developed for the ultimate Blockchain fabric. Based on the experience in several Blockchain projects, Xu, Pautasso [4] studied the architectural decisions in a system. In the situation whether to employ a decentralized Blockchain as opposed to other software solutions such as a traditional shared data storage.

Lemieux [2] studied to what extent Blockchain technology creates trustworthy digital records by applying a risk-based assessment method to evaluate the implementation of Blockchain technology in land registry system. The results indicated that although Blockchain technology can be used to address issues associated with information integrity in the present and near term [2], the reliability of information and maintaining long-term preservation could not be guaranteed. In 2016, a study was conducted on interdisciplinary fields of Blockchain and the healthcare system to prevent data sharing and improve patients' privacy by enabling them to own, control and share their own data easily and securely. In this regard, an App named Healthcare Data Gateway (HGD) that was designed based on Blockchain architecture has been developed by Yue, Wang [11] with the capability to organize and categorize all kinds of personal healthcare data and secure Multi-Party Computing.

The solution that Blockchain proposes is the use of a timestamp server that takes the hash of a Block of items, timestamps it, and widely publishes the hash [12]. This involves using hash algorithms to find a specific value. The Block is only accepted by users if all transactions in it are valid and the Bitcoins have not been spent previously [12]. Users show their acceptance by using the newly found hash in the "previous hash" section of the next Block they attempt to generate. This adds a new Block to the chain (the Block chain or transaction log). The chain thus contains the entire history of all transactions that have been carried out in the network [12]. The first Block of a Blockchain is called the genesis and has no parent as each Block on the Blockchain is referenced or identified by its hash [13]. A Blocks hash is typically a one-way hashing function used that maps an input to an output. There are different types of hash algorithms which may be used. For example, applying the SHA-1 hash algorithm function to a string "hello Blockchain" will produce the following hash value "bdb9814fb8929bd976a8ba1a4e037992ca7111e0".

Applying a hash function to a string will return a new string and if that string remains the same, the same hash will be produced. Data integrity is optimal as one can verify their hash with a hash key that has been given when downloading a file. This is done by comparing both hash keys as this ensures the file has not been tampered with and every byte of data is exactly the same. The Blockchain, also known as the consensus protocol [14], serves as a public or private ledger for any transactions, and every user is able to connect to the network and send transactions to the Blockchain, verify transactions and create new Blocks. It is a data structure which is used to ensure secure and tamper proof distributed ledgers. Each Blockchain is made up of Blocks which are linked to a previous Block and contain exclusive data and a timestamp.

To form a Blockchain, sequences of bits encrypted as a Block are stored by networked computers (nodes) within a system and are chained together. The veracity of new Blockchain links are established by a decentralized mining process. Before new links are formally added to the Blockchain, a meticulous mathematical hash is derived by competing mining computers to verify their content [12]. When a bitcoin is transferred to the next user, it gets digitally signed with a hash value denoting the precedent transaction and the public key of the next owner. The hash is defined as a chain of signatures. These can be verified by the payee to authenticate the chain of ownership [12]. To become part of the peer-to-peer network, one needs to have a client software that runs on either an own device or on a cloud service [12]. Nodes in the network only accept the first authenticated transaction and reject any subsequent attempts to make any further transactions to stop malicious users from rewriting their history.

2.2   Applications of Blockchain

Most current cloud-based applications rely on a single trusted controlling organisation that manages the network, storage and compute. This approach may be desirable for some applications however in some cases, a decentralized and distributed approach is better suited. For example, Walmart, the world's largest retailer is conducting pilot tests for worldwide supply chain food traceability [15]. The increasing development of the digital economy, the internet of things (IOT) and the growing use of sensors providing information in supply chains is providing Blockchain leverage to streamline and create an efficient supply chain track and trace management system. There are examples of Blockchain technology going beyond the realm of currencies and banking and evolving into industries such as real estate, for land registry systems, digital healthcare record systems [16] and government identification and registry systems [13]. Many businesses have already begun accepting Bitcoin in their payments including PayPal, Apple, and Universal Air Travel Plan (UATP). In addition, firms such as Citi Corp, Goldman Sachs, Barclays, Overstock, and IBM started to pay attention to cryptocurrencies. Governments around the world are creating policies for cryptocurrency, including Brazil, Russia, India, China and South Africa (BRICS). The BRICS business council is also debating the possibility in creating a BRICS cryptocurrency as an alternative to other financial instruments Council [17]. USA has already deployed bitcoin technology for interbank payments and Australia has already began a trial for bank guarantees using Blockchain technology [18]. Interoperability challenges between bitcoin and other ledger assets between multiple Blockchains have been addressed by creating mechanisms such as Pegged Sidechains [19].

2.3   Benefits and Limitations

Processing transactions over a distributed network without a central node functioning as a bank or clearing house reduces the cost of the transactions. Processing transactions using the Blockchain is less costly than the traditional approach Chuen and Deng [20]. However, the validation and verification of data comes with high hardware and energy costs [21]. The business of processing transactions tends to be highly concentrated and can be impacted with waiting for stakeholders executing their due diligence actions. With Blockchains, business transactions can be made to run in parallel potentially unleashing huge efficiency dividends e.g. businesses can unlock capital or value quickly rather than waiting for a transaction to be completed. The transactions volume handled by each payment processor can be increased manyfold but the added coordination costs to overcome network effects need to be considered. The drawback of a single Blockchain is the exponential increase in the cost and time per Block and hence per transaction. However, there is an argument that the technology's primary benefit is security and not efficiency Dirkmaat [22]. The ability to use multiple Blockchains to improve efficiency requires interoperability between different Block-chains. Blockchains need to be able interact with each other as a single Blockchain alone has limited performance [23]. Various studies such as [24], [25] and [26] have established a framework to exchange information between multiple Blockchains. Promising solutions also proposed to address this challenge by storing actual data in sidechains and operating the Blockchain as a control layer rather than as a storage layer [27]. The added benefits of using Blockchain is the reliability, where a single point of failure does not affect the whole operation of the network. The various works reviewed in this study show that Blockchain is a promising technology for a wide area of services.

2.4 Supply Chain Management

Supply chain management comprises of a series of entities, including people, systems, knowledge and processes. In a large supply chain, it is difficult to have an overall picture of all transactions within the chains [28]. This data is typically stored in multiple systems which are only accessible by certain participants in the supply chain. Several papers [27, 29, 30] investigate how supply chain is becoming transformed through Blockchain technology. The digital supply chain integration is becoming increasingly dynamic. Blockchain technology is providing a major advance for supply chains in assisting the delivery of source, process and products. The adoption of Blockchain technology should make the process faster and make transactional records more robust and reliable [30]. Rather than limiting a supply chain to regions, the utilisation of Blockchain will make it possible to have global production chains that are visible remotely. This is in line with what Kietzman [31] observed the current unseen dimensions from the vast network of retailers, distributors, transporters, storage facilities, and suppliers that participate in design, production, delivery and sales will be transparent. Organisations will have a competitive advantage of open, transparent supply chains and sustainable manufacturing. Models have been created for tracking agriculture in the supply chain [32]. This new model demonstrates the concept of circular economy and eliminates many of the disadvantages of the supply chain such as the cost to exchange between different parties in the supply chain. An overview of the proposed application of Blockchain in supply chain is illustrated in our model.

2.5 Technology Acceptance Model (TAM)

The technology acceptance model (TAM) was originally developed through a doctoral dissertation [33] and well cited in a MIS quarterly article [34]. Technology acceptance model is an information systems theory that models the decision-making process by which users may or may not adopt and implement new technology. There are two major considerations in TAM, perceived ease of use and perceived usefulness by the intended user.

Perceived ease of use (PEU) is defined by [34] as "the degree to which a person believes using the system will be free of effort." The perceived usefulness (PU) is defined by [34], as "the extent to which a person believes that using a particular technology will enhance his/her job performance". Technology acceptance models have been used to analyse the acceptance of technology in a variety of domains, from healthcare [35], a physician's choice and acceptance of the use of smartphones. Technology acceptance model has also been helpful in education learning [36], where scholars have examined student and faculty adoption of online learning [37].

3   Proposed Model

The supply chain management involves many internal and external stakeholders which makes Blockchain suitable as it can accept inputs from different parties. The proposed model is for organisations to develop Public and Private Blockchains which are also interoperable. In addition to this, organisations need to ensure governance and business standards are in place in a virtual community. The segregation of data records and their hash value in different ledgers was also proposed [7] in order to protect the personal data and privacy of users.

The first Blockchain proposed in Fig. 1 is "Public Blockchain 1", The Blockchain looks at the procurement from suppliers. Given this Blockchain is public it allows for external stakeholders to enter information such as the sources of the raw materials, the factory of where the components are being produced, the stock availability, minimum order quantities. The supplier of the produced components can also enter any of their purchase order details and the quality assurance and testing which has been performed. Finally, the freight forwarder enters details of the goods being picked up and details of expected timeframes of delivery and any delays experienced.

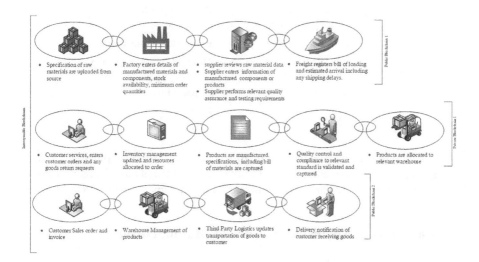

Fig. 1. Overview of proposed concept

The second interoperable Blockchain proposed is "Private Blockchain 1", this Blockchain contains customer orders, inventory and specific product specifications such as the bill of materials required. Once the components or products are received from the supplier, they are entered and the allocation of products to a warehouse is captured. Quality control and compliance records are also added to the Blockchain.

The third Blockchain is a public Blockchain and contains, customer orders, warehouse management such as stock availability, distribution management of the transportation from the warehouse to the customer and delivery confirmation. The use of interoperable public and private Blockchain technology allows for a more transparent supply chain of goods or services. Each Block in the chain provides stakeholders ability to control information through secure, auditable, and immutable record.

The model proposed captures all parties involved in the supply chain management and ensures there are no missed transactions, or errors, or even a transaction is not done with the consent of all the stakeholders involved. All data in the supply chain network is captured on the Blockchain and is available to participants who have the correct authentication. The most crucial area where the Blockchain helps in is the guarantee of validity and accountability of a transaction by the relevant stakeholder. The three Blockchains allow for interoperability hence giving the business the ability to view the entire supply chain. It is up to the discretion of the organisation to allow consumers to view further then the "Public Blockchain 2".

Based on review of the literature and the development of both bitcoin and Blockchain we apply the conceptual TAM model and derived Table 1. This table identifies the major factors that influence users of Blockchain PE and PEU. Most Blockchain applications are still in the development stage, and the characteristics of their PEU would differ depending on the product and application.

Table 1. TAM factors applied to Blockchain

Perceived ease of use (PEU)	Perceived usefulness (PU)
Variable depending on application use	Reduce cost
	Eliminate intermediaries
	Simplify business process
	High transaction security
	Increase trust
	Scalable

The general idea for the existence of Blockchain is to simplify processes, reduce costs and eliminate intermediaries. One of the earliest attempts to do this was use of Blockchain to replace the currently centralized domain name system (DNS) [38].

4 Case Study – Australian Electrical Manufacturer

The case study is an example application scenario where specific details of the supply chain are explained to better clarify the potential for the proposed concept.

Australia's leading electrical manufacture and distributor (AEM) has a wide range of brand portfolios targeting the roadway & infrastructure, commercial & industrial, consumer and retail market segment of the electrical industry. In a very competitive market and with the availability of cheap imports easily accessible via the internet, organisations need to continuously streamline and optimise their processes to remain competitive. AEM is vertically integrated, incorporating, engineering and design, research, manufacturing, global sourcing, importation and distribution. This allows AEM to develop new products and produce prototypes for customer approval. It also gives the flexibility to design variations and bespoke designs from a single unit to thousands of units. The supply chain consists of three warehouses, one located on the west coast of Australia and the other two on the east coast.

The electrical industry has intensely changed in the past 5 years due to the rapid advancements in technology. The lifespan of products has also changed to as low as 6 months, hence the speed to market is crucial. The supply of products is an intricate part of the business as it consists of multiple segments of the electrical industry, currently the flow of information in the supply chain is siloed where information can't be easily shared and accessed. A technique used to try and improve the flow of inventory between the raw material and component suppliers to the manufacturer is a contract to commit. This guarantees payment and provides comfort for international suppliers to purchase the materials required based on the contract. The technique is also used to reduce delays the supplier may face in sourcing raw materials. The Roadway business segment involves luminaries for roads, tunnels and bridges. It is run by contractual agreements with customers that detail what products are required and when. These product demands are added to the forecast based on these agreements. At times, there may be delays in obtaining goods from suppliers however this information is not always relayed back to all stakeholder's due to the intricacies of the supply chain.

ABC analysis also known as selective inventory control is a term used to define inventory into categorisations. The grouping in to three or more categories (A, B and C) is carried out to manage the different stocked keeping units (SKU's) that are not all in equal value or customer order frequency. Special consideration is taken for new and critical items such as components required to manufacture make to order products. There are two types of purchasing instruments which are used, customer demand driven purchasing and system forecasting. Forecasting is based on policies setup in the enterprise resource planning (ERP) system and relies on historical sales; these items may not necessarily have customer demand but are required to meet customer's availability expectations. Customer demand driven orders (Indent Stock) don't consider historical sales, however, the purchasing team do need to contemplate lead times and the suppliers' minimum order quantity. These are generally not considered when a sales representative makes a sale to a customer. The demand unpredictability causes series risks with procurement and can lead to a rapid increase of obsolete stock.

Material Requirements Planning (MRP) is a planning and inventory control system which is contained in the enterprise resource planning (ERP) system. Its aim is to safeguard adequate inventory levels are kept and assure that the required materials needed to manufacture goods are available when needed. Consideration also needs to be taken if stock is ordered and it does not meet the minimum requirement; does the organisation proceed with the sale and purchase excess stock and risk having an overstock which results to additional overheads. The retail segment of the business is also based on projects and project plans of what and when the products are required. As these products are generally one of the last parts that are installed in a project there is a risk of miscommunication in the business, for instance if a project falls behind plan or over budget the product requirements may change and the sales representative does not inform the planning department, products which are no longer required could end up in the warehouse and take up valuable resources and space.

The category team manage product categories and their performance, they set the objectives and targets for the category and devise an overall strategy and specific tactics to achieve the required sales. The team oversees new products for 12 months from the date the product is received. Overall category, forecasting and marketing teams advise the purchasing team of what the business is expecting to sell.

Generally, the top 80% of customer required products are stored in the warehouse and 20% of the products (SKU) is 80% of the business [39]. At times when products ordered by a customer cannot be located in the one warehouse a distribution order is completed to relocate the required product to the one distribution warehouse. However, if a product is not located in either warehouse an inventory sourcing purchase order needs to be raised to the supplier. A common issue faced is whereby sales representatives may not know the lead times required or are reluctant to tell the customer that there is a 10-week lead time and then pressure is put back on to the purchasing and supply chain teams to ensure the product can be sourced with minimal amount of time. Also, if a customer order is cancelled by the sales representative and the distribution order is not this causes the purchasing team to have no visibility of the cancelled order and the purchases may still proceed. This is an issue where the chain of events occurring in Fig. 2 are not connected and transparency of information is not present to all stakeholders.

It is generally easy for the organisation to place an order with the suppliers but extremely difficult once a purchase order has been approved and sent. The organisation is simply locked in at that stage and committed to the purchase of the goods. It is also possible for the purchasing team to miss any cancelled orders made on the distribution orders. Traceability and transparency are the most important in logistics.

The safety stock applicable to certain products will only cover a small amount additional orders, however it will not cover any spikes in sales; therefore, communication between marketing, sales, supply chain and procurement team is crucial. At times the marketing team may run promotions on certain products and this may cause an influx in orders which quickly depletes the safety stock and customer orders are held up in backorder. The previously forecasted purchase order which may be expected to arrive may only cover the backorders and not any new orders. This creates a cycle of where the purchasing team try to catch up to customer orders. It is important to calculate it accurately, because having too much stock will increase the inventory costs and having too little will cause stockouts as inventory will be exhausted. There is a standard calculation which is used for safety stock, however the lead time is also considered and hence the higher the lead time than the higher the safety stock is. A key system issues faced in such an environment is when a product is deemed as "I" (Indent Stock) and has a safety stock. This should flag for an alarm to sound and no safety stock should be purchased. It is ideal to be running a lean supply chain with the aim to

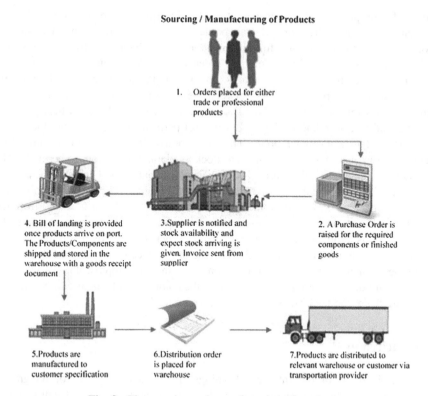

Fig. 2. The sourcing and manufacturing of products

balance customer service goals and the inventory costs. The transparency and accuracy of information is vital to achieve this and ensure no wastage.

The proposed model of using public and private Blockchains optimises the man-ufactures business transactions and trading relationships with its suppliers both locally and globally. A Blockchain on the supply chain can give clear visibility to all parties and allow for decisions and actions to be made quicker. Compared with conventional databases, using public Blockchain costs more to add records. Calculations and experiments have been performed in literature and show that the cost for business process execution on a Blockchain can have a two fold increase than a traditional database on a cloud platform [40]. However, data becomes globally replicated and the Blockchain ecosystem will retain this data indefinitely as long as the Blockchain exists, at no additional cost [41]. The three interoperable Blockchains create a chain of events or transactions that occur between the end customer, manufacturer, and supplier. A Blockchain that can directly interact with the sales team within the business and the suppliers will provide assurance that performance and correct communication is achieved in obtaining stock for the customer when needed. By using the proposed "Public Blockchain 1" the manufacture will have traceability from the source of the raw materials through to the components and the quality assurance and checks which have been performed. In addition to this the supply of goods can be tracked through with the freight provider. This transparent level of information provides a link between the manufacture and the external stakeholders involved all recording and sharing information that can be assigned further down the supply chain. This Blockchain solves the issue of not knowing when a purchase order of goods is arriving and the properties and details of the products that it contains. The use of "Private Blockchain 1" is within the organisation and provides links between the customer order and the final manufactured goods for the customer. This Blockchain creates visibility on where products can be found in a warehouse, the quality control performed and if the products have been allocated to a customer order. This traceability also helps with the inventory management in ensuring there is adequate stock available for an order to be made. The third Blockchain proposed "Public Blockchain 2" is public and links the customer order through to the warehouse and transportation provider. The record keeping and linking of this chain ensures customers receive the order in full, on time and from the correct warehouse. Due to the absence of other available alternatives to solve the communications problem in the supply chain, Blockchain is likely to become an attractive and cost-effective option [23]. The use of the three interoperable Blockchains within the business also provides transparency for the sales representatives who will have visibility on relevant information such as the components being used, the supplier its coming from, the lead times required and stock availability.

5 Conclusion

The general spread of the Internet of Things (IoT) makes the idea of integrating Blockchains in existing transaction supply chains the more significant. It will facilitate the creation of new supply chains to support the spread of sensor technologies. Blockchain can enable various upstream and downstream parties in supply chain to verify the authenticity of a Block of items. For this to happen, the paper describes several opportunities where Blockchain can integrate its use in the flow of the supply chain. This research develops a conceptual model for the adoption and use of Blockchain technology in supply chain, while utilizing the influential factors from TAM. The supply chain demonstrated in the case study is a large part of an organisation and it involves internal and external stakeholders. It is possible that not all parties will participate in this technology, however, the idea is compelling as it enables interoperable public and private deployment of Blockchains in supply chain management. This will allow organisations to leverage a variety of Blockchain applications and solutions to help in the transparency, traceability and authenticity of information. This technology does not necessarily need to be applied to an entire supply chain, it may be added to certain parts to the supply chain management such as the "Public Blockchain 2" used for inventory management. This can improve the record keeping, traceability and accuracy within the manufacturing organisation.

Recently, IBM is experimenting with a system called Adept that permits exchange among billions of interconnected devices using a Blockchain approach. It has developed a semi-autonomous device based on Internet of Things concept integrated with the Blockchain with the collaboration of Samsung. This device is a kind of intelligent washing machine which can manage its own consumables supply like ordering detergent as required, perform its own self-service and maintenance, and even optimize its environment by negotiating with other peer devices in the home or outside. Technology leaders believe that Blockchain will do for transactions what the internet did for information. One potential issue that needs to be considered in the use of Blockchain is that if the first Block in the chain the geneis is created without a trustworthy source and each additional Block thereafter is also agreed on by the Blockchain stakeholders then theoretically this chain of events can be unreliable. Compared to conventional centralised databases and computational platforms, Blockchains can reduce some counterparty and operational risks by providing neutral ground between organisations [42].

In this paper the authors reviewed some of the main characteristics of Blockchain and discussed the benefits and limits. The focus of the paper was placed on the application within the supply chain in an electrical manufacturing business and the influential variables of TAM. A hypothetical vision for a Blockchain supply chain was proposed and an example scenario of the supply chain was explained. The authors fully understand the technical and political challenges ahead. For future studies we will invite domain experts to evaluate the proposed model in a real-world application. There is still much that is unknown about the Blockchain-based systems [42]. Further research is required to improve our knowledge on how to create Blockchain-based systems that work and creating Blockchain-based systems that work as required.

References

1. Ali, M.M., Babai, M.Z., Boylan, J.E., Syntetos, A.A.: Supply chain forecasting when information is not shared. Eur. J. Oper. Res. **260**(3), 984–994 (2017)
2. Lemieux, V.L.: Trusting records: is Blockchain technology the answer? Rec. Manag. J. **26** (2), 110–139 (2016)
3. Luther, W.J.: Bitcoin and the future of digital payments. Independent Rev. **20**(3), 397–404 (2016)
4. Xu, X., et al.: The blockchain as a software connector. In: Proceedings - 2016 13th Working IEEE/IFIP Conference on Software Architecture, WICSA 2016 (2016)
5. Nakamoto, S., Bitcoin: A Peer-to-Peer Electronic Cash System (2009)
6. Swan, M.: Blockchain temporality: smart contract time specifiability with blocktime. In: Alferes, J.J.J., Bertossi, L., Governatori, G., Fodor, P., Roman, D. (eds.) RuleML 2016. LNCS, vol. 9718, pp. 184–196. Springer, Cham (2016). https://doi.org/10.1007/978-3-319-42019-6_12
7. Zyskind, G., Nathan, O., Pentland, A.: Enigma: Decentralized computation platform with guaranteed privacy. arXiv preprint arXiv:1506.03471 (2015)
8. Ølnes, S.: Beyond bitcoin enabling smart government using blockchain technology. In: Scholl, H.J., et al. (eds.) EGOVIS 2016. LNCS, vol. 9820, pp. 253–264. Springer, Cham (2016). https://doi.org/10.1007/978-3-319-44421-5_20
9. Dierksmeier, C., Seele, P.: Cryptocurrencies and business ethics. J. Bus. Ethics **152**, 1–14 (2016)
10. Vukolić, M.: The quest for scalable blockchain fabric: Proof-of-work vs. BFT replication. In: Camenisch, J., Kesdoğan, D. (eds.) iNetSec 2015, vol. 9591, pp. 112–125. Springer, Heidelberg (2016). https://doi.org/10.1007/978-3-319-39028-4_9
11. Yue, X., Wang, H., Jin, D., Li, M., Jiang, W.: Healthcare data gateways: found healthcare intelligence on blockchain with novel privacy risk control. J. Med. Syst. **40**(10), 218 (2016)

12. Yuan, Y., Wang, F.Y.: Blockchain: the state of the art and future trends. Zidonghua Xuebao/Acta Autom. Sinica **42**(4), 481–494 (2016)
13. Christidis, K., Devetsikiotis, M.: Blockchains and smart contracts for the internet of things. IEEE Access **4**, 2292–2303 (2016)
14. Herlihy, M., Moir, M.: Enhancing accountability and trust in distributed ledgers. arXiv preprint arXiv:1606.07490 (2016)
15. Zhao, J.L., Fan, S., Yan, J.: Overview of business innovations and research opportunities in blockchain and introduction to the special issue. Financ. Innov. **2**, 28 (2016)
16. Kar, I.: Estonian citizens will soon have the world's most hack-proof health-care records, Quartz. https://qz.com/628889/this-eastern-european-country-is-moving-its-health-records-to-the-blockchain. Accessed 15 July 2017
17. Council, B.B.: Russia's Central Bank to Develop National Cryptocurrency. http://brics-info.org/. Accessed 06 June 2017
18. Nott, G.: ANZ and Westpac trial blockchain for bank guarantees, (CIO). https://www.cio.com.au/article/621585/anz-westpac-trial-blockchain-bank-guarantees. Accessed 10 July 2017
19. Back, A., et al.: Enabling blockchain innovations with pegged sidechains. https://blockstream.com/sidechains.pdf. Accessed 20 July 2017
20. Chuen, D.L.K., Deng, R.H. (eds.): Handbook of Blockchain, Digital Finance, & Inclusion, Volume 2: ChinaTech, Mobile Security, & Distributed Ledger. Academic Press, Cambridge (2017)
21. PWC, Blockchain - an opportunity for energy producers and consumers? (2016)
22. Dirkmaat, O.: Beyond the Bitcoin Hype: Limitations of Bitcoin and Blockchain Technology. https://trends.ufm.edu/en/article/beyond-bitcoin. Accessed 16 Sept 2017
23. Kan, L., Wei, Y., Muhammad, A.H., Siyuan, W., Linchao, G., Kai, H.: A multiple blockchains architecture on inter-blockchain communication. In: 2018 IEEE International Conference on Software Quality, Reliability and Security Companion (QRS-C), pp. 139–145. IEEE, July 2018
24. Wood, G.: Polkadot: Vision for heterogeneous multi-chain framework. White Paper (2016)
25. Ding, D., Duan, T., Jia, L., Li, K., Li, Z., Sun, Y.: InterChain: A Framework to Support Blockchain Interoperability (2018)
26. Greenspan, G.: MultiChain private blockchain—White paper. http://www.multichain.com/download/MultiChain-White-Paper.pdf. Accessed 05 Aug 2018
27. Andoni, M., et al.: Blockchain technology in the energy sector: a systematic review of challenges and opportunities. Renew. Sustain. Energy Rev. **100**, 143–174 (2019)
28. Haq, I., Monfared, R., Harrison, R., Lee, L., West, A.: A new vision for the automation systems engineering for automotive powertrain assembly. Int. J. Comput. Integr. Manuf. **23**(4), 308–324 (2010)
29. Korpela, K., Hallikas, J., Dahlberg, T.: Digital supply chain transformation toward blockchain integration. In: Proceedings of the 50th Hawaii International Conference on System Sciences, January 2017
30. Apte, S., Petrovsky, N.: Will blockchain technology revolutionize excipient supply chain management? J. Excipients Food Chem. **7**(3), 910 (2016)
31. Kietzman, S.: What is a Supply Chain? http://www.wisegeek.org/what-is-a-supply-chain.htm. Accessed 08 Sept 2017
32. Casado-Vara, R., Prieto, J., De la Prieta, F., Corchado, J.M.: How blockchain improves the supply chain: case study alimentary supply chain. Procedia Comput. Sci. **134**, 393–398 (2018)
33. Davis, F.D.: A technology acceptance model for empirically testing new end-user information systems: theory and results. Doctoral dissertation, MIT (1985)

34. Davis, F.D.: Perceived usefulness, perceived ease of use, and user acceptance of information technology. MIS Q. **13**, 319–340 (1989)
35. Chen, J., Park, Y., Putzer, G.J.: An examination of the components that increase acceptance of smartphones among healthcare professionals. Electron. J. Health Inform. **5**(2), 16 (2010)
36. Abdalla, I.: Evaluating effectiveness of e-blackboard system using TAM framework: a structural analysis approach. Aace J. **15**(3), 279–287 (2007)
37. Liu, I.-F., Chen, M.C., Sun, Y.S., Wible, D., Kuo, C.-H.: Extending the TAM model to explore the factors that affect Intention to Use an Online Learning Community. Comput. Educ. **54**(2), 600–610 (2010)
38. Fotiou, N., Polyzos, G.C.: Decentralized name-based security for content distribution using blockchains. In: 2016 IEEE Conference on Computer Communications Workshops (INFOCOM WKSHPS). IEEE (2016)
39. Coyle, J.J., Langley, C.J., Novack, R.A., Gibson, B.: Supply Chain Management: A Logistics Perspective. Cengage Learning, Boston (2012)
40. Rimba, P., Tran, A.B., Weber, I., Staples, M., Ponomarev, A., Xu, X.: Comparing blockchain and cloud services for business process execution. In: Proceedings - 2017 IEEE International Conference on Software Architecture, ICSA 2017 (2017)
41. Staples, M., et al.: Risks and opportunities for systems using blockchain and smart contracts. Data61. CSIRO, Sydney (2017)
42. Cosmos. https://cosmos.network/docs/resources/whitepaper.html. Accessed 05 July 2017

A Digital Interaction Framework for Managing Knowledge Intensive Business Processes

Madhushi Bandara[1](✉), Fethi A. Rabhi[1], Rouzbeh Meymandpour[2],
and Onur Demirors[1,3]

[1] University of New South Wales, Sydney, Australia
{k.bandara,f.rabhi,o.demirors}@unsw.edu.au
[2] Capsifi, Sydney, Australia
rmeymandpour@capsifi.com
[3] Department of Computer Engineering, Izmir Institute of Technology, Izmir, Turkey

Abstract. Many business processes present in modern enterprises are loosely defined, highly interactive, involve frequent human interventions and coupled with a multitude of abstract entities defined within an enterprise architecture. Further, they demand agility and responsiveness to address the frequently changing business requirements. Traditional business process modelling and knowledge management technologies are not adequate to represent and support those processes. In this paper, we propose a framework for modelling such processes in a service-oriented fashion, extending an ontology-based enterprise architecture modelling platform. Finally, we discuss how our solution can be used as a stepping stone to cater for the management and execution of knowledge-intensive business processes in a broader context.

Keywords: Knowledge intensive business processes
Semantic modelling · Agile · Business process
Service oriented architecture

1 Introduction

During the last decade, we have seen a growing success of applications that support Business Process Management (BPM) practices. These achievements are mostly associated with operational business processes which can be defined as routine, repetitive, standardized and high-volume transactional processes. The intrinsic nature of operational business processes has enabled organisations to define their models using the state of the art modelling notations such as BPMN[1], execute these models on service oriented architectures[2], collect data in traditional database management systems and analyze the results using traditional

---

[1] http://www.bpmn.org.
[2] http://www.opengroup.org/soa/source-book/soa/p1.htm.

© Springer Nature Switzerland AG 2019
H.-P. Lam and S. Mistry (Eds.): ASSRI 2018, LNBIP 367, pp. 108–122, 2019.
https://doi.org/10.1007/978-3-030-32242-7_9

statistical techniques. Although these achievements are extraordinary, they have not scaled up to address the requirements of non-traditional business processes such as Knowledge Intensive Business Processes (KIBPs) [17]. Organisations might be spending most of their resources for operational processes but the competitive advantages are frequently created by KIBPs [17] which are regarded as "people-driven processes" that by nature involve less scripted and even ad-hoc process flows, composed with less structured "smart" decision-making tasks completed by knowledge workers [16].

To address the ad-hoc nature and frequent changing nature of KIBPs, related techniques and tools should support process agility. One obstacle in supporting agile process re-engineering is the gap between organizational level process models and the models built for execution [11,13]. The models built for execution capture the current state of the organizational goals, strategies, and structures, but do not explicitly define them and create the associations between high-level concepts and the execution models. As a result, once the high-level concepts such as strategies and goals change the mapping exercise corresponding to the whole process should be repeated.

The existing technologies discussed in Sect. 2 does not have sufficient capability to capture business or domain knowledge and link them with process models. Further, those modeling approaches are not flexible or malleable to support frequently changing loosely-defined KIBPs.

Baghdadi [3], in his work of modelling business processes for agile enterprises, defines a business process as an artefact that defines a dynamic composition of concrete activities and data, provided as services that add value to customers. We extend that definition with a "Digital Interaction" (DI) construct, which is defined as part of an enterprise architecture model and enables concurrent definition of process and data models. The proposed framework enables the dynamic composition of concrete services, user interactions and underlying knowledge and information concepts and delivers value to the customer. This composition can capture complex interactions involving humans, events or programming entities such as web services.

Following are the main contributions of this paper.

- DI meta-model: An ontology-based knowledge repository to capture elements of a KIBP, integrating domain knowledge, operational artifacts and human interactions.
- DI framework that embeds the propose meta model into an architectural framework, facilitating organizations to manage associations between high-level and execution-level concepts with less effort, re-engineer and deploy them rapidly in response to business changes

We discuss the background of knowledge modelling approaches and business process modelling in Sect. 2. Section 3 presents CAPSICUM framework and its proposed extension to cater for the Digital Interaction construct. Section 4 presents a case study. The paper concludes in Sect. 5 with an discussion of the future work and limitations of the proposed framework.

2 Related Work

2.1 Business Process Modelling

There are two main approaches for business process modelling [3] - graphical modes and rule specifications popular in workflow coordinations. These modeling approaches limit their focus to a specific feature or capability [15]. Yet the dynamic nature of unconventional business processes is not sufficiently addressed in these approaches [3]. Integrating service-oriented architecture provides a certain flexibility for business process modelling and links the execution model to the business level process model. Yet research efforts that focus on the composition of business processes with services such as Cauvet et. al [7] and Stein [23] are limited in their contribution to a static description of an executable business process.

There are studies that address challenges related to non-traditional business processes such as SmartPM [18] which offers a certain flexibility via run-time adaptation of processes with BPMN 2.0 based modeling schema. ArtiFact-GSM [8] proposes an event-driven, declarative and data-centric approach for business process modelling and highlights the importance of information models as business artefacts to address change management. Baghadadi [3] proposes a more agile business process modelling approach where the business process is a state representing its life cycle, with a set of specialized services that will interface business objects.

The main limitation of this line of research is the inadequacy in associating domain knowledge in a flexible manner and the inability to model complex interactions such as event-based and human interactions together with other business artefacts such as services and strategies.

2.2 Knowledge Modelling

We look beyond traditional information modelling techniques and focus on advanced knowledge representation techniques based on semantic modelling and ontologies. The main role of an ontology is to capture the domain knowledge, to evaluate constraints over domain data, to prove the consistency of domain data and to guide solution engineering while developing domain models [2]. It is a powerful tool for modelling and reasoning [1]. A recent study [5] of how semantic models are used for modelling and realizing data analytics processes stands as an evidence of the potential of knowledge modelling for KIBPs.

There are vocabularies such as Semantic Annotations for REST (SA-REST) [22] notation and Web Service Modelling Ontology [12] that capture semantic representations for service implementations and service related knowledge around a business process. Ontologies are proposed for business process management in different research works such as Hepp and Roman [14], and Weber et. al. [24]. Approaches such as PROMPTUM [10] aim to integrate domain ontologies with business processes to provide semantic quality and traceability between domain knowledge and process models. Rao et. al. [20] propose to use ontology-based knowledge maps for process reengineering, demonstrating the level of traceability achieved by an ontology.

Yet they provide limited support for KIBP management, and need to have formalized knowledge representation around KIBPs. Further, existing modeling approaches have limited ability in linking accumulated knowledge with execution-level process model.

2.3   Research Contribution

Literature suggests that existing process modeling approaches do not leverage domain knowledge sufficiently and do not support complex interactions associated with KIBPs. Knowledge modeling is a possible solution for that. Yet the existing technologies lack formal knowledge representation and management strategies to accumulate knowledge and link it with execution-level processes.

According to our experience in studying data analytic process engineering [4,5,19], BPM Ontology integration [9,10] and backed by different literature discussed, we identify a need for new frameworks that could be used by an enterprise to support flexible business processes, with adequate knowledge representation and agility in an integrated way. Instead of developing a framework from scratch, we advocate in this paper an extension of the CAPSICUM enterprise architecture modeling framework [21]. Details for the proposed framework are discussed in the Sect. 3.

3   Proposed Framework

The contribution of this paper is the Digital Interaction framework, based on a semantic meta-model, defined as a dynamic composition of concrete services, set of interactions and underlying information concepts which can be easily converted into execution level code. This is designed as an extension for the CAPSICUM architecture modeling framework and implemented using the Capsifi Jalapeno tool.

This section starts with a motivation scenario to demonstrate the behavior and challenges associated with KIBPs. Then introduction to the CAPSICUM framework is presented, followed by DI meta-model. How it is supported by Jalapeno tool is described in Sect. 3.4.

3.1   Motivation Scenario

We consider a large scale organization that conducts data analytics to support the day-to-day decision making based on information repositories. Each data analytics process can be observed as a KIBP, designed by data scientist to conduct particular objective and repeatedly executed by different users in different contexts. For example, one KIBP will be designed to predict sales of the next quarter, and it will be executed independently in each sales center located in different suburbs.

As Fig. 1 illustrates, information repositories related to this scenario fall into 3 categories: domain-specific knowledge, analytics models and data obtained from different sources. This information changes frequently in response to changes in the external environment and needs to be frequently updated.

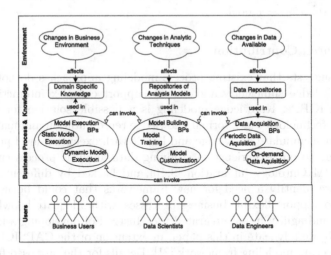

Fig. 1. Overview of case study

As an example KIPB, we are presenting the process of conduction predictive in such environment. Data scientist can import different datasets, apply prede-fined prediction models for a specific time period and generate a report. This is realized using three services (REST APIs) that import datasets from given data sources, execute a predictive model and export results. The process and related knowledge are presented in Fig. 2.

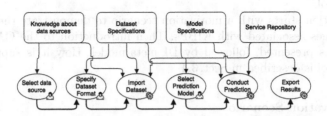

Fig. 2. Example digital interaction 1

To model similar KIBPs in a flexible manner, preserving the knowledge through an information model is the objective of the proposed framework. Web services, user interactions and information models are represented and linked together and when a change occurs in any one part of the model, it should be reflected in other related parts. Finally, our solution should provides the capability to convert the abstract process model into execution-level model.

3.2 CAPSICUM Framework

The CAPSICUM[3] framework proposes an integrated, semantic meta-model for an executable business architecture [21]. Based on an ontological definition, it decomposes various actors and artefacts of the business into a dynamic, canonical model which articulates how constructs such as strategies, goals, business processes, roles and rules interact with and relate to each other. The framework provides a meta model which details what these fundamental constructs are, how they are defined and how they relate to each other. For each organisation, the meta model and the concepts can be instantiated and relevant links can be defined to provide an accurate and dynamic representation of the organisation's business architecture.

The main constructs in the CAPSICUM Framework are encapsulated in logical cells and arranged in four abstraction layers as shown in Fig. 3. The layers are:

- Strategic Purpose (SP) is where high-level concepts of a strategic plan such as strategies, goals, policies, requirements and capabilities are defined and relationships between them are established;
- Business View (BV) represents elements of the architecture and operation of a business such as business processes, roles, rules, conceptual data models and common terms and definitions;
- Technical View (TV) defines platform-independent constructs of technical system designs such as APIs and data types;
- Platform View (PV) documents the implementation details of the technical designs in specific technology platforms.

This layered approach enables organisations to document their business assets at different abstraction levels enabling business architects to focus on the business model of the organisation without getting into the implementation details and the specifics of relevant business processes. The high-level business assets can then be reconciled with the details of technical implementations, supporting systems and applications, underlying data models and APIs. The interconnection between concepts in the CAPSICUM Framework provides great traceability, consistency and transparency across the organisation and enables maintaining the alignment between implemented systems with high-level strategic goals and requirements.

The CAPSICUM framework is the foundation of Capsifi Jalapeno platform[4], a cloud-based enterprise architecture modelling platform backed by a multi-model triple store as the database. Jalapeno provides a dynamic way to define,

---

[3] Stands for Coordinating, Access, Processes, Services and Information in a Common Unified Model.

[4] https://www.capsifi.com.

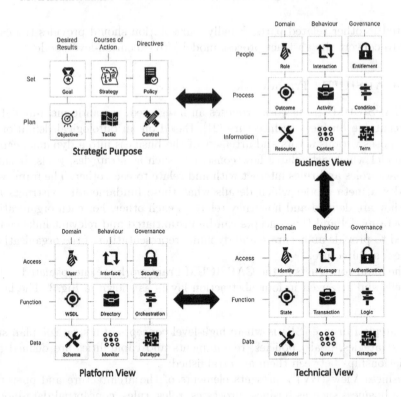

Fig. 3. The four layers of CAPSICUM framework and the cells in each layer (extracted from the Capsifi Jalapeno platform)

analyse and maintain comprehensive business models based on the framework. It offers a variety of views to explore and trace the models from various perspectives as well as ways to export the models in machine-readable formats (RDF, OWL, XSD, JSON).

Validity of the CAPSICUM framework as an effective tool for enterprise architecture modelling is visible through the customers such as Australian regulatory financial supervision authority (APRA), Service NSW and Australian Taxation Office (ATO) as well as many more in the US and Europe who use the platform to catalogue, manage and transform their enterprise business architecture.

Thanks to the underlying semantic technologies (e.g. RDF, OWL, SPARQL) and semantic inferencing capabilities, both the CAPSICUM Framework and the Capsifi Jalapeno platform provide great extensibility. They can be extended with new concepts and relationships and customised to satisfy the specific needs of organisations and to evolve in response to ever-changing business environments. In the following section, we will explain how the CAPSICUM Framework is extended with a meta model for Digital Interaction.

3.3   Digital Interaction Meta-Model

As we are proposing a process model with execution level artefacts, CAPSICUM framework's ontologies at technical view layer were extended to represent Digital Interactions composed of services models, information models, and interaction models. Some concepts from business view layer were also extended to capture the links of execution level and the business level.

Namespaces used for ontology definitions

```
rdfs: <http://www.w3.org/2000/01/rdf-schema#>
rdf: <http://www.w3.org/1999/02/22-rdf-syntax-ns#>
owl: <https://www.w3.org/OWL/>
capsi-bv: <http://capsi.com.au/core/CAPSICUM-BV#>
capsi-tv: <http://capsi.com.au/core/CAPSICUM-tv#>
sarest: <http://www.knoesis.org/research/srl/standards/sa-rest/#>
di: <http://adage.unsw.edu.au/DigitalInteraction/#>
```

RDF[5], RDFS[6] and OWL[7] are the building blocks of ontologies, given in prefixes rdf, rdfs, and owl respectively. We reuse two ontologies from CAPSICUM framework related to business view (prefix: capsi-bv) and technical view (prefix: capsi-tv). Concepts from SA-REST (prefix: sarest) are used for service model definition and represented with prefix sarest. The prefix di represents concepts specific to the proposed Digital Interaction framework.

Information Model. The objective of the information models is facilitating organizations to represent their business objects. As defined by OMG's Business Object Management Special Interest Group, a business object is a representation of a thing active in the business domain, including at least its business name and definition, attributes, behavior, relationships, and constraints. It may contain resources, records, domain knowledge, people or product information related to an organization.

We extend capsi-bv ontology by defining di:Information as a subclass of capsi-bv:Concept. Any information concept related to an organization can be modelled as a subclass of capsi-bv:Concept and extended with related properties.

Service Model. Service is the main building block which links the user-defined interactions and information into actual execution. Our service model extends capsi-tv:Service in CAPSICUM technical layer to define di:Service. Components of the di:Service are defined using the SA-REST vocabulary [22] as shown in Fig. 4. For example di:Service has a parameter di:ServiceField of type sarest:Parameter and a method sarest:HTTPMethod. Other than the classes and properties defined in Fig. 4, di:Service consists of a set of attributes that define their access endpoints, versions etc. A service model has to be self-contained so we can create an executable workflow based on it.

---

[5] https://www.w3.org/RDF/.
[6] https://www.w3.org/TR/rdf-schema/.
[7] https://www.w3.org/OWL/.

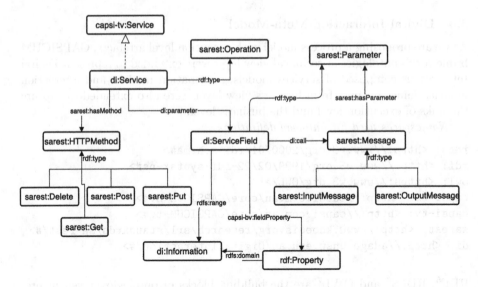

Fig. 4. Main components of the proposed service ontology

In Fig. 4 we also illustrate the relationship between di:ServiceField and di:Information model: A parameter to the service can be a di:Information or the parameter could be a property of di:Information.

We limit the scope of our prototype to REST-based services. But the core concepts of service ontology can be extended to cater different services required by an organization. The validity of this service model was tested by importing independent third-party service schemas and related information objects (e.g.- Xero APIs[8]) directly into this meta-model.

Interaction Model. An interaction is defined a mechanism in which inputs or outputs are exchanged between different entities. Some example interactions are messages or events passed within a computer system or human providing inputs through a user interface such as filling a form. Particularly human interactions are frequent and crucial to drive KIBPs. By modelling these an interaction, we make them flexible, malleable and interpretable.

The Interaction meta-model circled in Fig. 5 shows the di:Interaction concept as a subclass of capsi-bv:Interaction. Interaction is extended to three subclasses: form-based, message-based and event-based. Organizations can extend this further to incorporate other interaction types. Interactions contain di:InteractionField, which represents different components of the interaction. For example, in a form-based interaction di:InteractionField defines the various fields a user fills within the form. di:InteractionField is linked to information meta-model allowing to define the range of di:InteractionField as an information model or to map a property in the information model directly to di:InteractionField.

---

[8] https://github.com/XeroAPI/xero-schemas.

This way the semantics of the di:InteractionField such as its related domain, range, data type etc. are automatically accessible at execution.

Digital Interaction. The concept di:DigitalInteraction defined as a combination of Interaction and Service concepts, linked together via di:FlowLogic and di:ServiceInteraction-FieldMapping is shown in Fig. 5. The concept di:Service-InteractionFieldMapping is used to map inputs from interactions to the service parameters so that a service can be invoked automatically followed by interactions.

The concept di:FlowLogic defines the control flow between different components of the Digital Interaction. di:FlowLogic is authorized by a service or an interaction which initiates a flow. It contains a set of rules which evaluate a set of InteractionFields or ServiceFields and if they match expected values defined through the information model, respective service, interaction or Digital Interaction is triggered. For example, we can define a Boolean interaction field and create a di:FlowLogic to trigger two services depending on whether the value of interaction field is true or false.

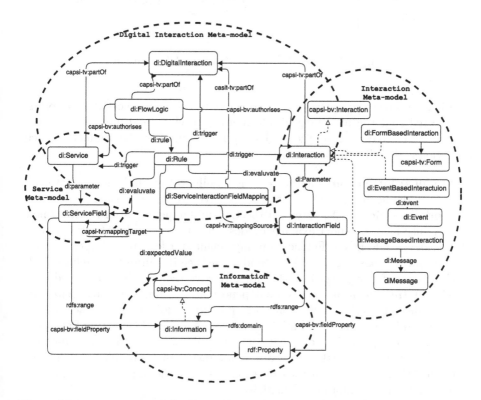

Fig. 5. Main components of the Digital Interaction meta-model with related Information, Service and Interaction model components

3.4   Tool Support

We extended the Capsifi Jalapeno platform and developed a prototype of the Digital Interaction Framework.

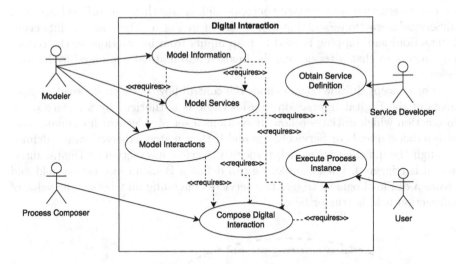

Fig. 6. Use case diagram for Jalapeno-DI extension

Figure 6 shows the use cases that are supported in Jalapeno-DI extension. It is expected that the modelling of information, services, and interactions takes place first before the composition of Digital Interactions can be conducted. Each operation is described below.

– **Model Information**: This use case is inbuilt to Capsifi Jalapeno platform. We can define any semantic concept, its attributes, and relations.
– **Model Services** - We extended the Capsifi Jalapeno platform with a new user interface to model existing or desired services, backed by the service ontology we designed. Further, we implemented a feature to import service models from existing OpenAPI standard service definitions, to reduce modelling effort for organizations that already have their services cataloged
– **Model Interactions** - Capsifi Jalapeno platform provides a user interface to model interactions and their corresponding fields. This interface has an advanced feature for Form-based interaction modelling by creating Pages and Forms by drag-and-drop different components such as text fields, drop-down, radio-buttons etc. Further, we can link interaction fields to information models via this interface, so at the execution level, the user inputs can be mapped automatically to information models.
– **Compose Digital Interaction** - Once the information, service and interaction models are created, we can use them to define Digital Interactions. We extended Capsifi Jalapeno platform's "Form-Flow" feature to

compose Digital Interactions. It provides a canvas to drag-and-drop predefined interactions and services and links them using di:FlowLogic and di:ServiceInteractionFieldMappings concepts.

- **Execute Process Instances** - Once a Digital Interaction is modelled, it can be exported in a machine-readable format and executed. Execution environment should support service invocation as well as inference of the semantic models.

- **Obtain Service Definitions** - Service developers can obtain and use service definitions, automatically exported as an OpenAPI standard documentation from service models. They act as requirement specifications for service developers, provided by modelers when a need for new service is identified.

4   Case Study

To demonstrate the capability of the proposed framework we modeled the example KIBP provided in Sect. 3.1 through Jalapeno-DI extension.

- **Model Information** We identified four high-level information concepts: Data Source, Dataset Format, Dataset and Prediction Model and their associated properties. Together they can capture domain knowledge and information sufficient to conduct an analysis.

- **Model Services** Our example leverages three services, modeled within Jalapeno-DI extension. They are 1. Import Dataset 2. Conduct Prediction 3. Export Result.

- **Model Interactions** We defined 5 interactions: Select data source, Specify dataset format, Import Dataset, Select Prediction Model, Conduct Prediction. Import Dataset and Conduct Prediction interactions provide parameters necessary for respective service executions, while other three aid in the decision making. All interactions are backed by information models to provide suggestions for decision making and to identify parameters user should provide.

- **Compose Digital Interaction** We model the Digital Interactions that starts with Select data source interaction, followed by Specify dataset format and Import Dataset. Import Dataset interaction triggers the Import Dataset service. Then Select Prediction Model interaction and Conduct Prediction service are linked respectively. Dataset returned from the Import Dataset service is mapped to Execute Model service. Export Results service is triggered immediately after the completion of the Execute Model service to generate a report for the user.
  Each link between two components of a DI is captured through di:FlowLogic. To link fields of Interactions with Services, di:ServiceInteraction-FieldMapping concept is used. For example, Data Source returned by Import Dataset service is mapped as the input for Conduct Prediction service.

Once this DI is designed, an execution engine is necessary to create graphical user interfaces from interactions and handle different service calls. Different users can use this DI to conduct individual prediction tasks. Detailed evaluation of the capabilities and limitations of the Digital Interactions framework can be found in our work published in Bandara et. al. [6].

5 Conclusion and Future Work

In the paper, we proposed a new ontology-based framework called Digital Interaction to support knowledge-intensive business processes management by providing agility and better domain knowledge representation.

By implementing Digital Interaction meta-model on top of CAPSICUM framework we enabled the linking of service concepts, interactions and Digital Interactions into the holistic enterprise architecture. We can define Digital Interaction as a part of a high-level business process or model how different organizational value streams and strategies are linked to these processes. It provides context and traceability for the services, information, and interactions we define. Hence we get one step closer to better alignment between business and IT architecture of the organization.

Marjanovic in her recent work [17] proposes a new theoretical model for ongoing improvements of KIBPs that support business intelligence and analysis. It composes of three phases: 1. Availability of latest technology infrastructure, 2. Tool support for individual decision makers to gain insights 3. Ability to share insights among decision makers across different instances of the same KIBP. From the experience we had in implementing the predictive analytic case study through Digital Interaction, we believe the proposed Digital Interaction framework can act as a stepping stone for realizing this theoretical model.

When considering phase 1, as the computations of DI are purely service based that are not coupled to particular technology or platform, enabling a rapid shift of technology infrastructure to reflect latest technologies available. To realize phase 2, semantic meta-model that contains organization information can be used to support and guide individual decision makers. As the semantic models are based on open world assumption, they can be frequently updated to reflect new information without changing other related artefacts.

To realize the phase three of Marjanovic's model we need to extend the information models to capture user insights, opinions and learn from previous Digital Interaction instances. Then a user can use that accumulated knowledge in future DI design and execution.

One limitation of our study is the restrictions imposed by extending the CAPSICUM framework. We lose certain level of flexibility, specially when designing flow logic, as we are building on top of CAPSICUM ontologies. It is a trade-off we made as we believe the value of Digital Interaction framework is enhanced by extending a framework that is already accepted and used by large scale organizations such as Australian Taxation Office and Australian Broadcasting Corporation.

Further, to harness the full potential of Digital Interactions we need a good execution platform that can access semantic models and drive different interactions dynamically.

The main challenge in adapting Digital Interactions framework for an organization is designing a good information model that reflect business objects. This model is unique to an organization and developing it from scratch can be challenging. Our framework is designed to link existing information models (e.g.- RDF Cube to model Dataset used in the case study) easily. Hence designing a repository of abstract information models and guidelines for specific KIBP domains such as data analytics, finance or marketing can lift the burden of information modelling and encourage many organizations to adapt Digital Interaction framework.

We consider this work as a foundation for a new approach to solve challenges related to KIBP management and execution. As future goals to achieve that objective, we propose to extend Digital Interaction to contain a knowledge layer that can enable knowledge workers to share their insights and experience, which can supports others in conducting similar KIBPs and decision making.

Acknowledgments. We are grateful to Capsifi, especially Dr. Terry Roach, for providing Capsifi Jalapeno platform and sponsoring the research which led to this paper.

References

1. Abelló, A., et al.: Using semantic web technologies for exploratory OLAP: a survey. IEEE Trans. Knowl. Data Eng. **27**(2), 571–588 (2015)
2. Baader, F.: The Description Logic Handbook: Theory, Implementation and Applications. Cambridge University Press, Cambridge (2003)
3. Baghdadi, Y.: Modelling business process with services: towards agile enterprises. Int. J. Bus. Inf. Syst. **15**(4), 410–433 (2014)
4. Bandara, M., Behnaz, A., Rabhi, F.A., Demirors, O.: From requirements to data analytics process: an ontology-based approach. In: Daniel, F., Sheng, Q.Z., Motahari, H. (eds.) BPM 2018. LNBIP, vol. 342, pp. 543–552. Springer, Cham (2019). https://doi.org/10.1007/978-3-030-11641-5_43
5. Bandara, M., Rabhi, F.A.: Semantic modeling for engineering data analytic solutions. Semant. Web J. (under review)
6. Bandara, M., Rabhi, F.A., Meymandpour, R.: Semantic model based approach for knowledge intensive processes. In: Stamelos, I., O'Connor, R.V., Rout, T., Dorling, A. (eds.) SPICE 2018. CCIS, vol. 918, pp. 215–229. Springer, Cham (2018). https://doi.org/10.1007/978-3-030-00623-5_15
7. Cauvet, C., Guzelian, G.: Business process modeling: a service-oriented approach. In: Hawaii International Conference on System Sciences, Proceedings of the 41st Annual, pp. 98–98. IEEE (2008)
8. Cohn, D., Hull, R.: Business artifacts: a data-centric approach to modeling business operations and processes. IEEE Data Eng. Bull. **32**(3), 3–9 (2009)
9. Coskuncay, A., Gurbuz, O., Demirors, O.: Transformation from business process models to process ontology: a case study. In: MCIS 2017 Proceedings, p. 40 (2017)

10. Coşkunçay, A., Gürbüz, Ö., Demirörs, O., Ekinci, E.E.: PROMPTUM toolset: tool support for integrated ontologies and process models. In: Dumas, M., Fantinato, M. (eds.) BPM 2016. LNBIP, vol. 281, pp. 93–105. Springer, Cham (2017). https://doi.org/10.1007/978-3-319-58457-7_7

11. Demirors, O., Celik, F.: Process modeling methodologies for improvement and automation. In: 2011 IEEE International Conference on Quaity and Reliability (ICQR), pp. 312–316. IEEE (2011)

12. Domingue, J., Roman, D., Stollberg, M.: Web service modeling ontology (WSMO)-an ontology for semantic web services (2005)

13. Filiz, C.Y., Demirors, O.: Utilizing process definitions for process automation: a comparative study. In: 2010 BPM and Workflow Handbook, Spotlight on Business Intelligence (2010)

14. Hepp, M., Roman, D.: An ontology framework for semantic business process management. In: Wirtschaftinformatik Proceedings, vol. 27 (2007)

15. Kumaran, S., Liu, R., Wu, F.Y.: On the duality of information-centric and activity-centric models of business processes. In: Bellahsène, Z., Léonard, M. (eds.) CAiSE 2008. LNCS, vol. 5074, pp. 32–47. Springer, Heidelberg (2008). https://doi.org/10.1007/978-3-540-69534-9_3

16. Le Clair, C., Moore, C.: Dynamic case management? An old idea catches new fire. Forrester Research (2009)

17. Marjanovic, O.: Improvement of knowledge-intensive business processes through analytics and knowledge sharing. In:International Conference on Information Systems, pp. 2820–2838 (2016)

18. Marrella, A., Mecella, M., Sardina, S.: Smartpm: an adaptive process management system through situation calculus, indigolog, and classical planning. In: KR (2014)

19. Rabhi, F., Bandara, M., Namvar, A., Demirors, O.: Big data analytics has little to do with analytics. In: Beheshti, A., Hashmi, M., Dong, H., Zhang, W.E. (eds.) ASSRI 2015/2017. LNBIP, vol. 234, pp. 3–17. Springer, Cham (2018). https://doi.org/10.1007/978-3-319-76587-7_1

20. Rao, L., Mansingh, G., Osei-Bryson, K.M.: Building ontology based knowledge maps to assist business process re-engineering. Decis. Support Syst. **52**(3), 577–589 (2012)

21. Roach, T.: CAPSICUM - a semantic framework for strategically aligned business architecture. Ph.D. thesis, University of New South Wales (2011)

22. Sheth, A.P., Gomadam, K., Lathem, J.: SA-REST: semantically interoperable and easier-to-use services and mashups. IEEE Internet Comput. **11**(6), 91–94 (2007)

23. Stein, S.: Modelling method extension for service-oriented business process management. Ph.D. thesis, Christian-Albrechts Universität Kiel (2009)

24. Weber, I., Hoffmann, J., Mendling, J., Nitzsche, J.: Towards a methodology for semantic business process modeling and configuration. In: Di Nitto, E., Ripeanu, M. (eds.) ICSOC 2007. LNCS, vol. 4907, pp. 176–187. Springer, Heidelberg (2009). https://doi.org/10.1007/978-3-540-93851-4_18

e-mentoring Activities in Online Programming Communities: An Empirical Study on Stack Overflow

Elham Kariri[✉] and Carlos Rodríguez[✉]

UNSW Sydney, Sydney, NSW 2052, Australia
{e.kariri,carlos.rodriguez}@unsw.edu.au

Abstract. Mentoring is widely acknowledged as an effective method for professional and academic development. The advances in the area of Information Technologies (IT) have positively impacted the mentoring process through a more technology-mediated form of mentoring known as e-mentoring or online mentoring. This form of mentoring has particularly had a great impact in improving learning opportunities in the context of online communities where mentors and mentees from around the world interact with each other in a mutually beneficial collaboration and learning experience. In this paper, we focus on online programming communities and we aim at identifying and understanding e-mentoring activities carried out in this context. We performed a qualitative study on a sample of 400 Q&A threads (i.e., questions and their corresponding answers) from Stack Overflow and identified a total of 31 different activities organized into 10 categories of activities. The results of our study provide insights into the e-mentoring activities performed in Stack Overflow, which can benefit both researchers and practitioners interested in understanding and improving e-mentoring in similar contexts.

Keywords: e-mentoring activities · Stack overflow Qualitative data analysis

1 Introduction

Mentoring has been applied as a personal empowerment as well as a developmental tool that addresses the main concerns of mentees through the provision of knowledge and advises that is critical in boosting competency and morale [3]. A key difference between e-mentoring and traditional mentoring is that they apply different approaches to the mentor-mentee relationships and interactions. For instance, in e-mentoring, mentors and mentees interact through online interaction platforms, unlike in traditional mentoring where mentors and mentees are usually located in one physical place [17]. Internet and computers, thus, play a major role in facilitating the online mentoring process.

The advancement in online programming communities has brought together a growing interest in leveraging such communities for mentoring purposes [11].

© Springer Nature Switzerland AG 2019
H.-P. Lam and S. Mistry (Eds.): ASSRI 2018, LNBIP 367, pp. 123–138, 2019.
https://doi.org/10.1007/978-3-030-32242-7_10

One example is Stack Overflow[1] (SO), where mentoring happens in the form of questions and answers (Q&A) [7,14]. Here, users (mentees) can ask questions about their programming concerns, while other expert users (mentors) provide the corresponding answers. Mentoring activities in this context include users sharing code examples, helping each other in code debugging, sharing best practices, among other activities. In order to effectively leverage on online programming communities like SO for the purpose of supporting e-mentoring, it is therefore of utmost importance to identify and understand such activities as well as to identify and categorize the profile of mentees and mentors involved.

Starting from the premise that Q&A is a form of mentoring in itself [7,14], in this paper, we aim to identify and understand e-mentoring activities happening in SO, as well as to characterize the skills of users that play the roles of mentors and mentees. To this end, we collected the top-voted 400 Q&A threads (i.e., questions and their corresponding answers) during the first quarter of 2018. We employed a qualitative research method based on content analysis described in [19]. The results of our analysis helped us identify a total of 31 different activities (e.g., *adding code examples*), which can be grouped into 10 different categories (e.g., *adding content for enriching answers*) according to the nature of the analyzed activity. The results of our study provide insights into the e-mentoring activities performed in this community, which can be leveraged by both researchers and practitioners interested in understanding and improving e-mentoring in similar contexts.

The rest of this paper is organized as follows. Section 2 presents related work. Section 3 describes the research methodology employed in this study. Next, Sect. 4 presents our findings. We elaborate on such findings in Sect. 5, where we also discuss identified opportunities (for both researchers and practitioners) and limitations of this study. We conclude this paper with Sect. 6 where we also discuss future work.

2   Related Work

Mentoring in online communities can be considered an example of peer-learning [23]. It is a form of knowledge and expertise acquisition where people help each other without necessarily having a formal relation, or received professional teacher training [23], and has been frequently observed in application software development [20].

From the *crowdsourcing* and *service science* perspective, researchers investigated the use of crowdsourcing for education [2,5], and education and learning as a service [1,4]. In the former, Anderson [2] explores crowdsourcing for higher education and proposes a design for distributed learning. Bradley et al. [5], instead, explore the use of both open data and crowdsourcing to create the Spectral Game, a game for molecules to interactive spectra matching. In the context of education as a service, Alabbadi [1] proposes education and learning as service where the use of cloud computing is proposed as a cost-effective alternative for

---

[1] https://stackoverflow.com.

sustainable education and learning initiatives. Similarly, Bora and Ahmed [4] propose the use of cloud computing for e-learning and discuss its benefits in terms of costs, software maintenance, security, among other dimensions.

In the domain of *online programming communities*, Feliciano et al. [10] examined the participation and experiences of students in GitHub[2] through a case study. The study found that GitHub can support students in their learning process through peer-reviews, comments and teaching resource suggestions. On a different front, Trainer et al. [24] explored the impact of social and technical dimensions of software on social ties and technical skills building in mentees. Among the main findings, the study reports that front-end, interdependent projects contribute to the development of technical skills and social ties, while back-end, modular projects contribute mainly to technical skills development.

Storey et al. [22] investigated social and communication channels and their role in shaping and challenging participation in software development. The study shows that, while communication channels do impact the participation culture in software development, not much is known as to how the participatory culture impacts the communication channels used by developers. The study also provides recommendations on how to choose the right communication tools, which considers, among other aspects, channel affordances, timing of tools and importance of learning how to use the selected channel.

In [26], Ye found peer support to be effective in the context of open source software communities through the means of Q&As via mailing lists. Ford et al. [11], instead, explored the deployment of just-in-time mentoring program on SO. In this study, novice participants of the community were redirected to an onsite Help-Room where experienced mentors helped them redraft their questions before submitting them to the Q&A forum. It was found that mentored questions have their score increased 50% on average when compared to non-mentored questions [11]. In a different study, Zagalsky et al. [27] explored R software community to understand how knowledge creation and curation takes place in SO and mailing lists. The study revealed that this is done in a participatory (i.e., through collaborations) and crowdsourced (i.e., working independently) form. The study also shows that there are a number of prolific contributors who were responsible for providing most of the answers.

Differently from the studies above, in this paper, we focus on identifying and understanding the activities carried out during e-mentoring interactions in an online programming community based on Q&As. To the best of our knowledge, this is the first study that explore and identify such activities in this context.

3   Research Methodology

This section describes the methodology used in conducting this study. In the following sections, we discuss the dataset used as well as the qualitative research method employed for the analysis.

---

[2] https://github.com.

3.1 Dataset

The dataset used in this study originated from SO. SO offers a Q&A platform that allows users to acquire and grow their programming knowledge and capabilities. The primary dataset was obtained from the threads originating from the questions asked and the corresponding answers provided by users of the platform. In addition, we also utilized the public profiles of users (in SO) to categorize the participants of such threads.

In order to select the Q&As to be included in our study, we collected the top-voted threads of Q&As from the full dataset of SO as of the first quarter of 2018. While this study is qualitative in nature, we used a minimum sample size given by $N = (384.16p)/(p + 383.16)$, where p is the total number of threads in SO (this formula takes into account a margin of error of 5% and confidence interval of 95%) [12]. With $p \approx 16,000,000$, the recommended minimum sample size is $N \approx 384$. We therefore collected a sample of size $N = 400$. For each top-voted question, we collected only the corresponding top-voted answer. This allows us to focus only on high-quality question-answer pairs.

3.2 Qualitative Data Analysis

We used content analysis techniques described in [19] to identify e-mentoring activities happening in Q&A threads of the selected sample. We focused on identifying the emergent themes (codes) referring to e-mentoring activities from the Q&As threads, which served as the basis for identifying the activity patterns and organizing them into categories. More specifically, in order to categorize an activity as an e-mentoring activity, we considered whether the interaction was performed in the context of an emerging understanding, knowledge application, generalization, testing of ideas or organization [6]. We identified initial activities (codes) that where further refined into categories of activities (see Fig. 1). Figure 2 outlines the steps for identifying e-mentoring activities and their corresponding categories. In order to categorize mentors and mentees, we analyzed the public profiles of the users that participated in the sampled threads. Here, we considered users asking questions as mentees, while users providing answers as mentors.

The coding and analysis was performed manually with the help of spreadsheets. The emerging categories for both activity identification and mentor-mentees categorization where reviewed and discussed in group meetings during various iterations to resolve any discrepancies in the meaning and interpretation of the identified categories.

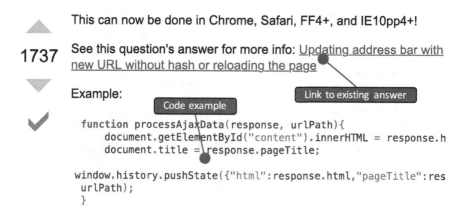

Fig. 1. Example of an answer posted on SO. Tags in red are examples of codes used during the analysis. The figure shows examples of activities such as providing a code example and adding a link to an existing answer. (Color figure online)

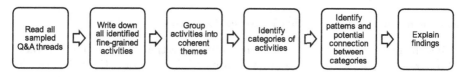

Fig. 2. Steps for the identification of e-mentoring activities and categories.

4   Findings

4.1   Mentors and Mentees in Stack Overflow

Figure 3 presents the background information of mentors and mentees that have been identified in the study. Among mentors, we identified that *moderator* represents the largest category (44%). *Full-stack developers* follow with a total of 32%. We noticed that *students* also play the role of mentors, although to a lesser extent (7%). Furthermore, only a handful of *educators/academic researchers* are involved as mentors. The analysis shows that this category represents only 1% of the total number of mentors in SO. Other categories of mentors include *database administrator* (5%), *mobile developer* (7%), *managing director* (1%), *system administrator* (1%), *c-suite executive (CEO, CTO, etc.)* (1%) and *other* (1%).

The largest category of mentees falls under *other* (50%). This category consists of users that left SO and the ones that did not provide any relevant information in their public profile that can help us with their categorization. *Beginner software developer* category is the second largest in number (31%). These two categories together make up the majority of the mentees found on this Q&A platform. Furthermore, *students* make up only 9% of all the mentees. It is also worth noting that even *experienced/senior developers* (3%) and *moderators* (2%)

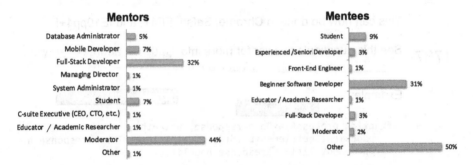

Fig. 3. Categorization of mentors and mentees in SO.

participate in the platform as mentees. Other categories of mentees include *front-end engineer* (1%), *educator/academic researcher* (1%) and *full-stack developer* (3%).

4.2 e-mentoring Activities in Stack Overflow

Using the methodology described in the previous section, we identified a total of 31 different activities from the 400 Q&A threads selected from SO. Such activities were organized into 10 categories as shown in Table 1. Below we discuss each of the categories and their corresponding activities.

Providing Critiques and Feedbacks. This category was found to have the highest number of observations, totalling to 490. 81% were made by users (both mentors and mentees) who wanted to vote on an answer, a question or a comment. This category of activities is particularly important in e-mentoring in that it provides an opportunity for mentors and mentees to analyze different answers and comments to their questions, and provide constructive criticism and structured feedbacks. According to study [8], such feedbacks are critical in SO because they enable the community to discuss issues in depth and therefore ensure that the best answers are found.

Motivating and Encouraging Good Community Practices. This category has the second highest number of observations (394). About 382 of them (97%) were made by users who wanted to provide compliments, offer thanks, opinions and encouraging comments. Motivating and encouraging users of online community to continue posting help enhance e-mentoring in that it promotes the interaction between mentors and mentees through continued communication [18]. For example, the mentor-mentee relationship may grow as a result of positive feedbacks and compliments. To a much lesser extent, 12 of them (3%) were made by users who wanted to put questions on hold in order to encourage improvements or edits on the answers given.

Table 1. Categories of e-mentoring activities in SO. The number shown in parenthesis for each activity is the number of threads on which the activity was performed. The last column reports on the number of observations of activities under each category. Notice that activities are non-exclusive, which means that a thread can fall into more than one type of activity. The number of observations for a category can be therefore higher than the total number of threads. For example, category *providing critiques and feedbacks* has 490 observations, which is computed as the sum of the observations for each activity under this category.

#	e-mentoring activities	Total number of observations
1	Providing critiques and feedbacks	490
	- Voting on a question, answer or comment (400)	
	- Marking a question, answer or comment as a favourite (77)	
	- Acknowledging/Citing useful answers for future readers (13)	
2	Motivating and encouraging good community practices	394
	- Providing a compliment (e.g., thanks) (382)	
	- Marking a question on hold to encourage editing (12)	
3	Adding content for enriching answers	368
	Adding:	
	- Code examples (280)	
	- Summaries (e.g., a brief before a long explanation) (14)	
	- Visual artifacts, such as bug/error image, data frame, state machine diagram, snapshot feature or expected output (24)	
	- Links to an existing answer (e.g., external application, project module, table, figure or graph) (41)	
	- External references (9)	
4	Improving quality of questions and answers	310
	- Editing a question or answer (e.g., to reword a sentence) (212)	
	- Correcting spelling, grammar error, code formatting (98)	
5	Helping in code debugging	210
	- Providing a correct code or solution (97)	
	- Suggesting a different method to correct a bug (96)	
	- Providing a possible solution for a bug (17)	
6	Explaining and clarifying answers	186
	- Clarifying a concept meaning (42)	
	- Providing an explanatory tutorial (95)	
	- Using a video/demo to explain an implementation (14)	
	- Providing code snippets with explanations (35)	
7	Sharing best development practices	179
	Sharing:	
	- Documentation guides about a platform (46)	
	- Developer blogs, articles, tutorials or projects (121)	
	- Links to academic publications such as e-book (2)	
	- Reference documentations (10)	
8	Managing posted information	177
	- Marking a question as duplicate (13)	
	- Closing a question (21)	
	- Creating a new tag or editing an existing one (143)	
9	Helping in organizing meetings and communications	112
	- Providing contact information (e.g., e-mail address) (2)	
	- Collaborating in discussions (107)	
	- Suggesting a new communication channel (e.g., chats) (3)	
10	Offering suggestions for improvement	55
	- Providing advice or tip (e.g., API versions) (14)	
	- Sharing other posted answers (41)	

Adding Content for Enriching Answers. One of the e-mentoring categories found is *adding content for enriching answers*. This category of e-mentoring activities had a total of 368 observations, making it the third largest category. It includes activities such as *adding code examples, summaries, visual artifacts* such as bug/error image, data frame, state machine diagram, snapshot feature or expected best run output, *adding a link to an existing solution* such as an external application, project module, table, figure or graph, as well as adding a list of *external references*. This category is an important one in that it allows the virtual interaction between mentors and mentees by providing an opportunity for peer mentors to add content and enrich answers which have already been provided by other mentors. Improving answers in this way can help, in turn, improve the quality of the knowledge acquired from the platform [3].

Improving the Quality of Questions and Answers. Another category of activities with a high number of observations is that of improving the quality of questions and answers. This category had a total of 310 observations, of which 68% were edited by either rewording it or improving the vocabulary used in the post. The rest of the observations (32%) targeted at correcting typos and code formatting. All these can be considered to be e-mentoring activities in that they are geared toward ensuring effective communication between mentors and mentees, thereby ensuring successful mentoring in the absence of face-to-face interaction [3].

Helping in Code Debugging. The results of our analysis shows, furthermore, that 210 observations are about *helping in code debugging*. This is a category of activities that involves identifying and understanding potential coding errors in programs and then providing a solution to fix them. The corresponding activities contribute to e-mentoring in SO in that they allow mentors to provide insights regarding how to debug and fix code errors, which is considered a key task in software development.

Explaining and Clarifying Answers. A total of 186 observations aimed at *explaining and clarifying answers*. Activities under this category help enhance the communication between mentors and mentees in SO. It can be viewed as a practice through which the answers of mentors to questions posted by mentees are further elaborated to favor clarity. For example, explaining and clarifying answers ensures that the essential meaning of the answers provided by the mentors is understood by the mentees (and the whole community), thereby mitigating the risks of potential misunderstandings.

Sharing Best Development Practices. This category has a total of 179 observations. Most of the observations within this category involves sharing a blog or article with best practices. Some of the activities under this category included providing guide documentation regarding a platform, link to academic publications (e.g., e-book) and reference documentations. These are considered e-mentoring activities in that they enable mentors to remotely provide useful learning materials to mentees. Sharing best practices within a domain is important in e-mentoring because it provides both mentors and mentees with an opportunity to learn from well-established practices and techniques in a particular domain.

Managing Posted Information. A total of 177 observations were found under this category. 80% of them involved creating a new tag for a question. The main activities under this category included marking questions that were found to be duplicate, closing questions that have already been answered, creating new tags for a question and editing an existing question. These activities help enhance the quality of e-mentoring in SO because it contributes to the curation of posts (and, therefore, knowledge) shared between mentors and mentees, as well as teach how to properly make contributions to the community. The latter is particularly important in SO, which rely on a code of conduct for participating in the community[3].

Helping in Organizing Meetings and Communications. Another important category of e-mentoring activities in SO consists in *helping in organizing meetings and communications*, which was observed 112 times. Activities under this category include collaborative discussion about positive experiences and opinions, alternative communication channels and sharing of contact information. All these activities contribute to e-mentoring in that they help establish proper and effective communication channels between mentors and mentees [6].

Offering Suggestions for Improvement. The activities under this category involve providing suggestions on how the answers and solutions provided by mentors to the questions from mentees could be further improved, e.g., through tips, advices and previously posted answers to similar questions. This is an essential category of activities for the enhancement of the effectiveness of e-mentoring because it helps in ensuring that the provided answers and solutions are as accurate as possible. Overall, 55 observations were made where *offering suggestions for improvement* was the main aim of the activities.

5   Discussion

To the best of our knowledge, this is the first study aims at identifying mentoring-related activities in SO as well as characterizing the profile of users that play the roles of mentors and mentees. In the following, we discuss and reflect upon the activities identified in the previous section, the opportunities for researchers and practitioners interested in these communities and platforms, and the limitations of this work.

---

[3] https://stackoverflow.com/conduct.

5.1   e-mentoring Activity Areas in Stack Overflow

The findings discussed in Sect. 4 allowed us to identify three key e-mentoring activity areas in SO, namely, *knowledge creation, knowledge curation*, and *mentor-mentee communication, organization* and *encouragement*. In the following, we discuss each of these areas along with the implications for e-mentoring.

Knowledge Creation. This area encompasses e-mentoring activities that are geared toward creating knowledge. While answering question is the main mechanism for creating knowledge in SO [27], other means also exist in the platform for complementing such knowledge creation instrument. One such alternative is *adding content for enriching answers*, which allows peer mentors to complement each others' contribution toward richer answers to mentees' questions. Artifacts used for enriching answers include code examples, external references (e.g., blogs) and visual artifacts such as diagrams and screenshots. Another form of knowledge creation includes *helping in code debugging*. This form of knowledge creation is not limited to just providing a solution for a code bug, but typically also involves detailed discussions on the underlying causes as well as key programming concepts related to a bug. Next, *sharing best development practices* can also be considered a mechanism for knowledge creation. This activity involves a range of artifacts including user and reference documentation, academic publications and tutorials that specifically target recommendations and best practices in the context of programming.

Table 2. Activities performed by mentors/mentees (represented as a table heatmap). The number in each cell reports the number of times a given mentor/mentee category performed the corresponding activity.

e-Mentoring activity areas in Stack Overflow / Categories of mentors and mentees		Knowledge creation			Knowledge curation					Mentor-mentee communication, organization & encouragement		# observations by categories of mentors and mentees	% participation by categories of mentors and mentees
	Categories of e-mentoring activities	Adding content for enriching answer	Helping in code debugging	Sharing best development practices	Providing critiques and feedbacks	Improving quality of questions and answers	Explaining and clarifying answers	Managing posted information	Offering suggestions for improvement	Motivating and encouraging good community practices	Helping in organizing meeting and communications		
Mentors	Database Administrator	1	7	25		10	19	6	1			69	5%
	Mobile Developer	28	6	2	5	18	8	6	14			87	7%
	Full-Stack Developer	221	69	43	2	28	42	7	13		2	427	32%
	Managing Director	5	1	5			1					12	1%
	System Administrator	1	5	3	1							10	1%
	Student	17	43	15			11	2	3			91	7%
	C-suite Executive	3			2	2		1	1			9	1%
	Educator or Academic Researcher	18										18	1%
	Moderator	71	79	86	4	125	50	85	11	12	52	575	44%
	Other				3	2		6	2			13	1%
Mentees	Student				44	19	22	4	5		7	101	9%
	Experienced/Senior Developer				19	2				5	8	34	3%
	Front-End Engineer				2		7					9	1%
	Full-Stack Developer					3		14		21		38	3%
	Beginner Software Developer				167	52	2	2	1	139		363	31%
	Educator or Academic Researcher				4					7		11	1%
	Moderator	3			8	3	9	4		1		28	2%
	Other				229	46	15	40	4	209	43	586	50%
# observations (by category of activity)		368	210	179	490	310	186	177	55	394	112	2481	

Knowledge creation in SO is mostly started by mentors (see Table 2). More specifically, it is widely performed by *moderators, full stack developers, students, mobile developers*, and *database administrators*. For example, we noticed that 60% of *adding content for enriching answers* activity is done by *full stack developers*, 19% by *moderators* and 21% by the remaining categories of mentors. In addition, we found that 38% of *helping in code debugging* activities is done by *moderators*, 33% by *full stack developers* and 21% by *student*. Moreover, sharing *best development practices* activities are done by 48% of *moderators*, 25% by *full stack developers* and 14% of the activities by *database administrators* from mentor categorization. Our analysis shows that the two most active categories of mentors in this area and across the three corresponding activity categories are therefore *full-stack developer* and *moderator*.

Knowledge Curation. The crowdsourcing, public nature of SO makes knowledge creation in this platform open to its community members. While such characteristic is typically seen as a key to leverage the power of the crowd [16], it comes with a number of challenges from a curation and quality control perspective [9]. We review next the activities that target knowledge curation of SO contributions made by the community.

One of the main activities for knowledge curation is *providing critiques and feedback*. It includes activities such as voting on questions, answers and comments, marking questions as favourite, and citing existing answers. Such feedback mechanisms help knowledge curation in the context of e-mentoring mainly in three ways. Firstly, it helps mentors and mentees assess the quality of their own posts (i.e., on their questions and answers). Secondly, it facilitates finding good questions and answers through the statistics associated to each post (e.g., number of votes and favourites). Thirdly, it allows for finding mentors (experts) in specific areas through SO's reputation system[4], which is based on the feedback mechanisms above.

Other activities in this area involve a more direct manipulation of the content of questions and answers for curation purposes. For example, the category *improving quality of questions and answer* involves activities such as question and answer editing (e.g., for understandability and technical correctness purposes) and spelling and grammar correction. These activities can be especially useful, e.g., for both mentees that are very new to a topic (e.g., for ensuring the use of the right terminology in posts) and non-native English speakers. Furthermore, *explaining and clarifying answers, managing posted information*, and *offering suggestions for improvements* are also categories that carry out knowledge curation activities. These categories involve a variety of curation activities including clarifying and explaining programming concepts (e.g., encapsulation in object-oriented programming), closing a question (e.g., out of scope question) and providing advice and tips (e.g., API versions).

While in the previous section we discussed that knowledge creation is mainly initiated by mentors, we can see that knowledge curation is carried out by both

---

[4] https://stackoverflow.com/help/whats-reputation.

mentors and mentees in a more evenly distributed manner as compared to knowledge creation (see Table 2). If we look at each activity category individually, we can notice that the category *providing critiques and feedbacks* is dominated by mentees, while the remaining categories is performed mainly by mentors. These results are in line with the observation that mentees in SO are actively involved in voting and favoriting questions and answers they find useful. The categories of *improving quality of questions and answers, explaining and clarifying answers, managing posted information* and *offering suggestions for improvement* typically require expertise and therefore are mainly performed by mentors.

The activities discussed in this section have tangible implications for the e-mentoring experience. For example, having a question edited for improving its understandability allows the original poster of the question to *learn by example* [13] on how to properly write questions both for a topic and within SO community. Similarly, questions marked as duplicate not only allows for discovering an already existing answer to the question but it is also an opportunity to remind mentees about the good practices for participating in the community (e.g., searching and researching before posting a question[5]). Finally, the gamification mechanisms put in place by SO offer gratification and acknowledgement for both mentors and mentees, which helps them keep engaged in the community [27].

Mentor-Mentee Communication, Organization and Encouragement. The third area emerged from e-mentoring activities in SO involves tasks that can be broadly classified as community management. It encompasses administrative, organizational and procedural aspects of online mentoring such as guiding discussions, participation encouragement, helping in finding consensus and promoting community best practices and policies. More specifically, the category *motivating and encouraging good community practices* involves activities such as the provision of compliments (e.g., thanks) and marking questions to encourage editing and improvement toward best practices. The implications of this category are two-fold. On the one hand, it serves as a incentive mechanism to promote participation of mentors and mentees through both extrinsic (e.g., increased reputation score in the platform) and intrinsic motivation (e.g., shared purpose) [9]. On the other hand, it helps encourage the improvement of quality of knowledge produced by the community through iterative enhancement [9] of both questions and answers.

From an organization and communication perspective, the category *helping in organizing meetings and communication* involves activities such as sharing contact information, collaboration in discussions and suggestions of alternative communication and collaboration channels. While these activities may not represent a direct form of mentor-mentee knowledge transfer, they do play an important role in the e-mentoring process. For example, in the context of social computing, study [25] discusses the interplay between SO and Github where, e.g., Github committers provide more answers and ask less questions, which

---

[5] https://stackoverflow.com/help/how-to-ask.

suggests a cross-fertilization between different platforms and channels that can contribute to expertise sharing in an e-mentoring context.

Mentor-mentee communication, organization and encouragement is widely performed by *beginner software developers*, *full stack developers*, and *others* in the mentee category (see Table 2). For example, we noticed that the majority of *motivating and encouraging good community practices* activities are done by *others* (53%) and *beginner software developers* (35%) in the mentee category. These results suggest that peer mentees tend to help each other in following good community practices. Under mentor category, the results shows that *moderator* is the most involved category in this area, mainly, in helping in organization and communication matters.

5.2   Opportunities for Researchers and Practitioners

Many opportunities are envisioned in the context of understanding and improving e-mentoring in online programming communities. On the research side, one potential direction that can emerge from our findings consists in further exploring how each of the identified activities contribute to e-mentoring in SO as well as in other similar online programming communities. For example, one interesting research question in this line is the understanding of how code examples benefit the e-mentoring process in these communities and whether the mechanisms currently in place are appropriate from an e-mentoring perspective. Given the typically short-lived interactions that happen between mentors and mentees in SO while performing these activities, it is also worth exploring the implications of such type of interactions and contrast them with traditional mentoring, which usually involves longer-lasting mentoring activities and mentor-mentee relationships. In addition, given that our findings on the characterization of mentors and mentees are based solely on information provided in public user profiles, more studies are needed (e.g., interviews) in order to better identify and characterize the actual profile of the users involved in e-mentoring activities.

Practitioners, on the other hand, can benefit from the reported findings by identifying opportunities for the development of new features for the platform to support common e-mentoring activities. For example, additional or improved features can be added to support widely performed activities such *improving the quality of questions and answers*, which can go beyond human-based curation and incorporate also automated techniques, e.g., based on NLP and AI [15, 21]. From the perspective of the category *adding content for enriching answers*, platforms such as SO could also rethink the way in which resources are managed within the platform. For instance, new features can be proposed that are able to categorize learning resources into bundles that target specific topics of interest for mentors and mentees participating in the community. Finally, more and better integration with development and collaboration tools (such as GitLab[6] and Slack[7]) can be added to the platform in order to provide an environment that

---

[6]   https://gitlab.com.
[7]   https://slack.com.

allows both mentors and mentees to seamlessly switch back and forth between the tools used during their e-mentoring activities.

5.3 Limitations of This Study

The study reported in this paper comes with its own limitations. Firstly, the dataset used in our analysis was limited to top-voted threads, and within each thread, to top-voted answers only. This decision, while helpful as a heuristic for choosing good questions and answers, brings together the risk of drawing conclusions that apply only to the dataset sampled for our study. Secondly, the characterization of mentors and mentees rely solely on the self-reported profile of the users participating in the selected threads. The implications of this is that our categorization may not capture the true profile of user, which may differ from the self-reported one for reasons such as lack of profile updates or simply because no profile information is provided by the user. Finally, this study is exploratory in nature and focuses on SO only. While this is a representative online programming community, the findings reported in this paper may not apply to other communities where e-mentoring may take place such as Github and Apache[8].

6   Conclusion and Future Work

This work explored e-mentoring activities in online programming communities through an empirical study on Stack Overflow's Q&As. The analysis of 400 threads of top-voted Q&As collected from this platform allowed us to identify a total of 31 different activities grouped into 10 categories, which create impact in three different areas, namely: knowledge creation, knowledge curation, and mentor-mentee communication, organization and encouragement. Our analysis found that, while *knowledge creation* activities are mainly performed by mentors, *knowledge curation* develops in a more participatory manner where both mentors and mentees jointly collaborate in curating knowledge in Q&As threads. Furthermore, *mentor-mentee communication, organization and encouragement* was found to be mostly initiated by peer mentees in an effort to encourage good community practices, organization and communication. We believe the results of this study will help in understanding better e-mentoring activities in this domain and motivate further research in this direction.

In future work, we plan to extend this research with further studies involving interviews with Stack Overflow's mentors and mentees with the aim of understanding the underlying motivations for participating in this form of e-mentoring, actual benefits of such participation, and opportunities for improving e-mentoring in online programming communities.

Acknowledgment. We would like to thank Prof. Boualem Benatallah, Dr. Ho-Pun Lam and reviewers for their valuable comments and feedbacks, which helped to improve this work.

---

[8] https://www.apache.org.

References

1. Alabbadi, M.M.: Cloud computing for education and learning: education and learning as a service (ELaaS). In: 2011 14th International Conference on Interactive Collaborative Learning, pp. 589–594. IEEE, Piestany (2011)
2. Anderson, M.: Crowdsourcing higher education: a design proposal for distributed learning. MERLOT J. Online Learn. Teach. **7**(4), 576–590 (2011)
3. Bierema, L.L., Merriam, S.B.: e-mentoring: using computer mediated communication to enhance the mentoring process. Innov. High. Educ. **26**(3), 211–227 (2002)
4. Bora, U.J., Ahmed, M.: E-learning using cloud computing. Int. J. Sci. Mod. Eng. **1**(2), 9–12 (2013)
5. Bradley, J.C., Lancashire, R.J., Lang, A.S., Williams, A.J.: The spectral game: leveraging open data and crowdsourcing for education. J. Cheminformatics **1**(1), 9 (2009)
6. Churchill, D., King, M., Webster, B., Fox, B.: Integrating learning design, interactivity, and technology. In: Carter, H., Gosper, M., Hedberg, J. (eds.) Proceedings of 30th ASCILITE-Australian Society for Computers in Learning in Tertiary Education Annual Conference, pp. 139–143. Macquarie University, Sydney (2016)
7. Cuban, L.J.: How Teachers Taught: Constancy and Change in American Classrooms, 1890–1990. Longman, Harlow (1984)
8. Dalip, D.H., Gonçalves, M.A., Cristo, M., Calado, P.: Exploiting user feedback to learn to rank answers in Q&A forums: a case study with stack overflow. In: Proceedings of the 36th International ACM SIGIR Conference on Research and Development in Information Retrieval, SIGIR 2013, pp. 543–552. ACM, Dublin (2013)
9. Daniel, F., Kucherbaev, P., Cappiello, C., Benatallah, B., Allahbakhsh, M.: Quality control in crowdsourcing: a survey of quality attributes, assessment techniques, and assurance actions. ACM Comput. Surv. **51**(1), 7:1–7:40 (2018)
10. Feliciano, J., Storey, M., Zagalsky, A.: Student experiences using github in software engineering courses: a case study. In: 2016 IEEE/ACM 38th International Conference on Software Engineering Companion (ICSE-C), pp. 422–431. IEEE, Austin (2016)
11. Ford, D., Lustig, K., Banks, J., Parnin, C.: "We don't do that here": how collaborative editing with mentors improves engagement in social Q&A communities. In: Proceedings of the 2018 CHI Conference on Human Factors in Computing Systems, CHI 2018, pp. 608:1–608:12. ACM, Montreal (2018)
12. Garcia, C., Jha, G., Verma, R.: The ultimate guide to effective data collection. https://europa.eu/capacity4dev/ict4dev/discussions/free-ebook-ultimate-guide-effective-data-collection
13. van Gog, T., Rummel, N.: Example-based learning: integrating cognitive and social-cognitive research perspectives. Educ. Psychol. Rev. **22**(2), 155–174 (2010)
14. Hargreaves, A., Fullan, M.: Mentoring in the new millennium. Theory Pract. **39**(1), 50–56 (2000)
15. Hirschberg, J., Manning, C.D.: Advances in natural language processing. Science **349**(6245), 261–266 (2015)
16. Howe, J.: The rise of crowdsourcing. Wired **14**(6), 1–4 (2006)
17. Packard, B.W.L.: Web-based mentoring: challenging traditional models to increase women's access. Mentor. Tutoring: Partn.Ship Learn. **11**(1), 53–65 (2003)
18. Ren, Y., Kraut, R.E., Resnick, P.: Encouraging commitment in online communities. In: Building Successful Online Communities: Evidence-Based Social Design, pp. 77–124. The MIT Press (2012)

19. Renner, M., Taylor-Powell, E.: Analyzing qualitative data. University of Wisconsin - Extension, Program Development and Evaluation (2003). https://learningstore. uwex.edu/assets/pdfs/g3658-12.pdf

20. Schilling, A., Laumer, S., Weitzel, T.: Train and retain: the impact of mentoring on the retention of FLOSS developers. In: Proceedings of the 50th Annual Conference on Computers and People Research, SIGMIS-CPR 2012, pp. 79–84. ACM, Milwaukee (2012)

21. Socher, R., Bengio, Y., Manning, C.D.: Deep learning for NLP (without magic). In: Strube, M. (ed.) Tutorial Abstracts of ACL 2012, ACL 2012, p. 5. Association for Computational Linguistics, Jeju Island, July 2012

22. Storey, M., Zagalsky, A., Filho, F.F., Singer, L., German, D.M.: How social and communication channels shape and challenge a participatory culture in software development. IEEE Trans. Softw. Eng. **43**(2), 185–204 (2017)

23. Topping, K.J.: Trends in peer learning. Educ. Psychol. **25**(6), 631–645 (2005)

24. Trainer, E.H., Kalyanasundaram, A., Herbsleb, J.D.: e-mentoring for software engineering: a socio-technical perspective. In: 2017 IEEE/ACM 39th International Conference on Software Engineering: Software Engineering Education and Training Track (ICSE-SEET), pp. 107–116. IEEE, Buenos Aires (2017)

25. Vasilescu, B., Filkov, V., Serebrenik, A.: StackOverflow and GitHub: associations between software development and crowdsourced knowledge. In: 2013 International Conference on Social Computing, pp. 188–195. IEEE, Alexandria (2013)

26. Ye, Y.: Peer to peer support for the reuse of open source software libraries. In: 2009 IEEE International Conference on Information Reuse Integration, pp. 284–289. IEEE, Las Vegas (2009)

27. Zagalsky, A., German, D.M., Storey, M.A., Teshima, C.G., Poo-Caamaño, G.: How the R community creates and curates knowledge: an extended study of stack overflow and mailing lists. Empir. Softw. Eng. **23**(2), 953–986 (2018)

iRecruit: Towards Automating the Recruitment Process

Usman Shahbaz[1], Amin Beheshti[1(✉)], Sadegh Nobari[2], Qiang Qu[3],
Hye-Young Paik[4], and Mehregan Mahdavi[1,5]

[1] Macquarie University, Sydney, Australia
usman.shahbaz@hdr.mq.edu.au, amin.beheshti@mq.edu.au
[2] Rakuten, Inc., Tokyo, Japan
s@sqnco.com
[3] Shenzhen Institutes of Advanced Technology, Chinese Academy of Sciences,
Shenzhen, China
qiang@siat.ac.cn
[4] University of New South Wales, Sydney, Australia
h.paik@cse.unsw.edu.au
[5] Asia Pacific International College (APIC), Sydney, Australia
mehregan.mahdavi@apicollege.edu.au

Abstract. Business world is getting increasingly dynamic. Information processing using knowledge-, service-, and cloud-based systems makes the use of complex, dynamic and often knowledge-intensive activities an inevitable task. Knowledge-intensive processes contain a set of coordinated tasks and activities, controlled by knowledge workers to achieve a business objective or goal. Recruitment process - i.e., the process of attracting, shortlisting, selecting and appointing suitable candidates for jobs within an organization - is an example of a knowledge-intensive process, where recruiters (i.e., knowledge workers who have the experience, understanding, information, and skills) control various tasks from advertising positions to analyzing the candidates' Curriculum Vitae. Attracting and recruiting right talent is a key differentiator in modern organizations. In this paper, we put the first step towards automating the recruitment process. We present a framework and algorithms (namely *iRecruit*) to: (i) imitate the knowledge of recruiters into the domain knowledge; and (ii) extract data and knowledge from business artifacts (e.g., candidates' CV and job advertisements) and link them to the facts in the domain Knowledge Base. We adopt a motivating scenario of recruitment challenges to find the right fit for Data Scientists role in an organization.

Keywords: Knowledge-intensive business processes
Data-driven business processes · Process data science
Process data analytics

1 Introduction

Business processes (BPs) - i.e., set of coordinated tasks and activities, carried out manually or automatically, to achieve a business objective or goal - are central

© Springer Nature Switzerland AG 2019
H.-P. Lam and S. Mistry (Eds.): ASSRI 2018, LNBIP 367, pp. 139–152, 2019.
https://doi.org/10.1007/978-3-030-32242-7_11

to the operation of enterprises [10,11]. Over the last decade, many BPs across and beyond the enterprise boundaries have been implemented. Recently, various technologies such as social media and Web 2.0 have made dynamic processes more prevalent. This enables the process workers in the front line to be more proactive and use their knowledge and best practices in the decision making process and to choose the best next steps. Such knowledge-intensive processes, controlled by knowledge workers who have the experience, understanding, information, and skills. In this context, a knowledge-intensive process defined as a set of coordinated tasks and activities, controlled by knowledge workers to achieve a business objective or goal. Recruitment process - i.e., the process of attracting, shortlisting, selecting and appointing suitable candidates for jobs within an organization - is an example of a knowledge-intensive process. Attracting and recruiting right talent is a key differentiator in modern organizations. Recruitment process involves many data-driven, collaborative and knowledge intensive steps to ensure the right fit for an organizational talent requirement.

One of the key challenges in the recruitment process, is the analysis of the resume and making inferences on different named entities and comparing these between candidates. Recruiters have limited time evaluating candidates pertinent to a role. To reduce this gap of making decisions based on limited information/data, we propose a novel approach where the relevant information about a candidate is presented in a contextual way and in a consistent manner irrespective of the way the resume is articulated or written. Our approach helps on the challenges in two ways. One that the information relevant to a candidate is extracted and presented as a summary view and secondly its complemented with linked entity domain knowledge. This will assist recruiters automatically extracting facts, information, and insights from the raw business artifacts, e.g., candidates' Curriculum Vitae (CV[1]) and job advertisements.

We adopt a typical scenario of recruitment challenges to find the right fit for the Data Scientist role. In our scenario we extract the information from resumes and link them to a domain Knowledge Base (KB[2]) to generate relevance and possible score to differentiate between candidates for the role. The unique contributions of this paper are:

- We put the first step towards automating the recruitment process and presents a framework (namely *iRecruit*) to imitate the knowledge of recruiters into a recruitment domain Knowledge Base (rKB), i.e., a knowledge base that consists of a set of concepts organized into the recruitment taxonomy (e.g., universities, organizations, jobs and best practices), instances for each concept and relationships among them.
- We present a set of domain specific algorithms to extract data and knowledge from business artifacts and link them to the facts in the domain knowledge.

---

[1] A Curriculum Vitae (CV) is a written overview of a person's experience and other qualifications for a job opportunity. It is akin to a résumé in North America.

[2] A Knowledge Base (KB) consists of a set of concepts organized into a taxonomy, instances for each concept and relationships among the concepts [6].

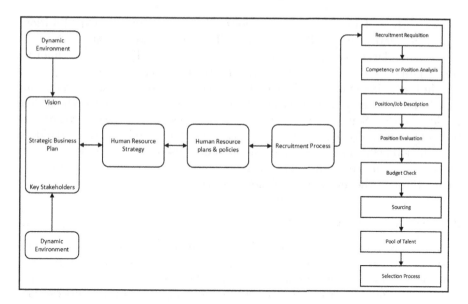

Fig. 1. Effective Recruitment and Selection Process [17]: an illustration on the HR processes in line with organization's strategic business plan.

The rest of the paper is organized as follows. In Sect. 2 we provide the background and related work. We present the framework for automating the recruitment process in Sect. 3. We discuss the implementation and the evaluation in Sect. 4 before concluding the paper in Sect. 5.

2   Background and Related Work

2.1   Recruitment Process

Competing for high-quality resource talent is becoming a prevalent issue for almost all the organizational leaders [24]. At the same time the recruitment process is a very expensive process for organizations. Recruiting for wrong fit can prove exceptionally costly not only due to monetary perspective but also it has serious consequences on employee morale and productivity [16,30]. For an effective recruitment plan, an organization needs to link its human resource strategy to its strategic business plan in conjunction with its vision and getting inputs from its key stakeholders [17]. Figure 1 illustrates the HR processes in line with organization's strategic business plan.

Screening right candidates is not only time consuming, but it is also resource intensive, since it demands knowledge intensity to make the correct selection decisions. Recruiters spend on average 6.25 s on a resume before they make Yes/No decision [1]. This is a very short time to make an informed decision on a candidate's profile with the relevant business skillset gap. Moreover, there are only six elements which are mostly looked at by the recruiters. These includes

Name, current Title/Company, previous Title/Company, previous Position's Start/End Dates, current Position's Start/End Dates and Education [1].

In particular, this may create a big challenge whether all the relevant information is properly structured in the resume for the recruiter to make the right decision in those six seconds. If the candidates have positioned their relevant information in different segments within the resume, chances are that the recruiters might miss this. Some of the recruitment techniques like the use of psychometric tests can potentially help organizations can fine tune matching right candidates with the job [23]. These techniques can used or abused by organizations in equal measure [21]; moreover these are costly and often overly used by untrained personnel through the availability of internet-based testing.

2.2   Data-Driven Processes

In our recent book [11], we provided a complete state-of-the-art in the area of business process management in general and process data analytics in particular. This book provides defrayals on: (i) technologies, applications and practices used to provide process analytics from querying to analyzing process data; (ii) a wide spectrum of business process paradigms that have been presented in the literature from structured to unstructured processes; (iii) the state-of-the-art technologies and the concepts, abstractions and methods in structured and unstructured BPM including activity-based, rule-based, artifact-based, and case-based processes; and (iv) the emerging trend in the business process management area such as: process spaces, big-data for processes, crowdsourcing, social BPM, and process management on the cloud.

2.3   Knowledge-Intensive Processes

Knowledge-intensive processes almost always involve the collection and presentation of a diverse set of artifacts and capturing the human activities around artifacts. This, emphasizes the artifact-centric nature of such processes. Many approaches [15,18,27,32] used business artifacts that combine data and process in a holistic manner and as the basic building block. Some of these works [18] used a variant of finite state machines to specify lifecycles. Some theoretical works [15] explored declarative approaches to specifying the artifact lifecycles following an event oriented style. Another line of work in this category, focused on querying artifact-centric processes [20].

Another related line of work is artifact-centric workflows [15] where the process model is defined in terms of the lifecycle of the documents. Some other works [26,29,31], focused on modeling and querying techniques for knowledge-intensive tasks. Some of existing approaches [26] for modeling ad-hoc processes focused on supporting ad-hoc workflows through user guidance. Some other approaches [29] focused on intelligent user assistance to guide end users during ad-hoc process execution by giving recommendations on possible next steps. Another line of work [9,22], considers entities (e.g., actors, activities and artifacts) as first class citizens and focuses on the evolution of business artifacts over time. Unlike these approaches, the iProcess framework [7], not only consider artifacts as first class citizens, but we take the information-items (e.g., named entities, keywords, etc.) extracted from the content of the artifacts into account.

2.4   Data Curation

In our previous work [5–7], we introduce the notion of *Knowledge Lake*, i.e. a contextualized Data Lake [4], as a centralized repository containing virtually inexhaustible amounts of both data and *contextualized data* that is readily made available anytime to anyone authorized to perform analytical activities. The term *Knowledge* here refers to a set of facts, information, and insights extracted from the raw social data using data curation techniques used to transfer an Information-Item into a Featurized-, Semantic- and Contextualized-Items [5]. The Knowledge Lake will provide the foundation for big data analytics by automatically curating the raw data in the Data Lake and to prepare them for deriving insights.

3   Towards Automating the Recruitment Process

The recruitment process as highlighted in Fig. 1 starts with the requisition step based on the organizational need for a specific skill against the strategic business plan and runs linear till the selection process. Talent pool that is established as an outcome of this process is generally compared relative to each other rather than the position description. Figure 2 illustrates an updated effective recruitment and selection process. There are generally two main contributing factors:

- One that it is time consuming and difficult to compare each of the candidates with the position description; and
- Secondly, since there is inherit requirement of building a rank order of candidates, so it sometimes takes precedence in developing the candidates ranking with respect to each other rather than relative to the position description.

We propose an analytical approach to this process to overcome the above two challenges. We propose that within the process there needs to be a feedback from the pool of talent stage to the position description where we can compare a candidates' resume as compared to the position description that has been established based on the organizational skills requirements. This helps us with the second challenge. This new process is shown in Fig. 3. For the first challenge we propose techniques within knowledge graphs, linking two graph nodes to automate the manual process of matching each of the candidates' resume to the position description and give a comparison score. We call this comparison score as 'Position Description Match Score'. Generating this score requires imitating the knowledge of recruiters and extracting data and knowledge from business artifacts.

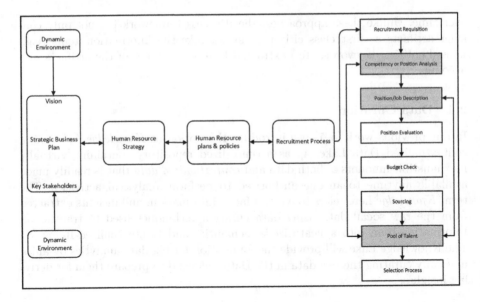

Fig. 2. Updated effective recruitment and selection process [17].

3.1 Imitating the Knowledge of Recruiters

We put the first step towards automating the recruitment process and presents a framework (namely *iRecruit*) to imitate the knowledge of recruiters into a recruitment domain Knowledge Base (rKB), i.e., a knowledge base that consists of a set of concepts organized into the recruitment taxonomy (e.g., universities, organizations, jobs and best practices), instances for each concept and relationships among them. We explain the techniques to construct the rKB domain knowledge. The rKB knowledge base includes the important entities such as organizations and their relevant information, universities and their profile including location and relevant information, countries and cities and relevant skills entities. To build this knowledge-base, we first identified the list of recruitment related categories and their related types/sub-types provided by recruitment guides[3]. Then we have focused on the recruitment for the computer science category and more specifically the data scientist role; and identified popular concepts and instances related to this category on the Web. For example, we have identified: concepts such as Programming Languages, Educations, Organizations and Technical Skills. Moreover, we have identified the best practices that recruiters follow and identified concepts such as Seniority Levels, Team Leadership, Statistical modeling (that data scientists are expert in), as well as reporting skills. Figure 3 shows a small snippet of the formulated rKB, which illustrates the above notions.

---

[3] https://builtvisible.com/recruitment-seo-guide/.

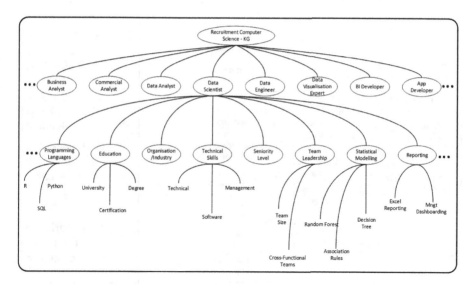

Fig. 3. A sample fragment of the rKB.

3.2   Extracting Data and Knowledge from Business Artifacts

We use our previous work [5,13,25] to extract data and knowledge from the business artifacts, including CVs in PDF, Candidates Website, and job advertisements. As a future work, we will use the proposed approach to construct a cognitive assistance to assist the recruiters in decision making and choose the best nest steps. It will also enable HR knowledge workers with the toolkit to extract knowledge from relevant talent documents and ask questions pertaining to individual's background industry knowledge and their academic relevance to the role. Figure 5 illustrates the features that our approach aims to extract from one side on the position description/business requirement and other side on the knowledgebase of the candidate's resume.

In our previous work [6], we have presented the notions of information-item (raw business artifact, e.g., a candidate CV), featurized-item (enabling automatic extraction of various features from Schema-based to Natural-Language-based and Metadata-based features), semantic-item (automatically enriched extracted features) and contextualized-item (automatically linking extracted data to the Domain Knowledge). Figure 4 illustrates how we generate featurized, semantic and contextualized items from raw business artifacts in the recruitment processes. Our approach is to extract features from the candidate resume from major sections such as career summary/ambition, Professional Experience, Education, Skills etc.

The features extracted from these resume sections can then be further grouped based on feature type such as Lexical/Natural Language based, Temporal, Geo etc. This enables us to enrich the extracted information from the

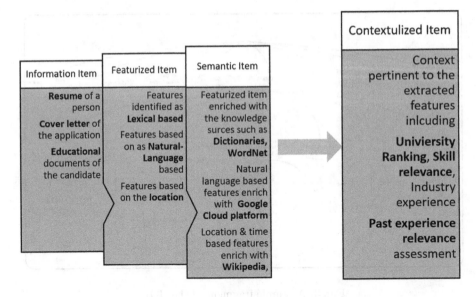

Fig. 4. Constructing a contextualized-item from a raw business process.

resume with external data sources (such as WikiData) and similar services such as, University Rankings[4,5], company reviews[6,7], educational certifications[8,9,10].

The set of features that are extracted from the resume sections include:

- Lexical-based features. This type is related to the vocabulary of a language such as topic, keyword, phrase, abbreviation, special characters, slangs, informal language.
- Natural-Language-based features. This category of features relates to entities that can be extracted by the analysis and synthesis of natural language (NL) and parts of speech, named entities like organisation type, industry vertical, job role, job tasks etc.
- Temporal-based features. This feature category is related to time space. Estimating total professional experience from the resume, number of years at a specific organisation, duration of the educational degree etc.
- Location-based features. This category is related to the mentions of locations in the resume of the candidate. (e.g., in Universities the text may contain 'Sydney'; a city in Australia, or worked at an organisation based in Melbourne, a city in Australia).

---

[4] https://www.timeshighereducation.com.
[5] https://www.topuniversities.com/qs-world-university-rankings.
[6] https://www.glassdoor.com.au/Reviews/index.htm.
[7] https://greatplacetowork.com.au/.
[8] https://www.acs.org.au.
[9] https://www.webopedia.com/quick_ref/computer-certifications.html.
[10] https://en.wikipedia.org/wiki/Academic/_certificate.

Next, we define a set of enrichment functions to enrich the extracted items. For instance, if education section contains BS Computer Science, the enrichment function 'Synonym' can be used to enrich this keyword with its synonyms such as Bachelor of Science from knowledge sources such as Wikidata. The result (e.g., set of synonyms) will be stored in the Enrichment Set. The proposed enrichment functions are built against the Lexical-based features, using knowledge sources such as WordNet[11] and dictionaries to enrich with their Synonyms, Stems, Hypernyms Hyponyms and more. Figure 6 illustrates the algorithm to Link entity nodes between candidate resume and position description.

We have provided curation services [13, 14] to automatically: (a) Extract features such as keyword, part-of-speech, and named entities such as Persons, Locations, Organizations, Companies, Products and more; (b) Enrich the extracted features by providing synonyms and stems leveraging lexical knowledge bases for the English language such as WordNet; (c) Link the extracted enriched features to external knowledge bases (such as Google Knowledge Graph[12] and Wikidata[13]) as well as the contextualized data islands; and (d) Annotate the items in a data island by information about the similarity among the extracted information items, classifying and categorizing items into various types, forms or any other distinct class. We model the contextualized data and knowledge as a graph [3, 19] of typed nodes (e.g. raw data and extracted features) and edges (relationships among items such as:

- $keyword \xrightarrow{(extractedFrom)} CV$,
- $keyword \xrightarrow{(similar\text{-}keywords)} keyword - set$,
- $Topic \xrightarrow{(extractedFrom)} CV$,
- $Topic \xrightarrow{(related\text{-}topics)} topic - set$,
- $University \xrightarrow{(extractedFrom)} CV$,
- $University \xrightarrow{(profile)} University - profilerank - per - subject$,
- $Company \xrightarrow{(extractedFrom)} CV$,
- $Company \xrightarrow{(profile)} ProductQuality, FinancialFactors, etc.$,
- $Organization \xrightarrow{(extractedFrom)} Job - Advertisement$,
- $Candidate \xrightarrow{(gradutaed\text{-}from)} University$,
- $Candidate \xrightarrow{(worked\text{-}in)} Company$, and
- $CV \xrightarrow{(relatedTo)} Job - Advertisement$.

To enable querying this large graph, we leverage our previous work [8], a SPARQL [12] query engine for analyzing large graphs, to organize the data and extracted-enriched-linked features. Technical details of these services and how we organize and query the data in the Knowledge Lake, can be found in [5][14].

---

[11] https://wordnet.princeton.edu/.

[12] https://developers.google.com/knowledge-graph/.

[13] https://www.wikidata.org/.

[14] https://github.com/unsw-cse-soc/CoreKG.

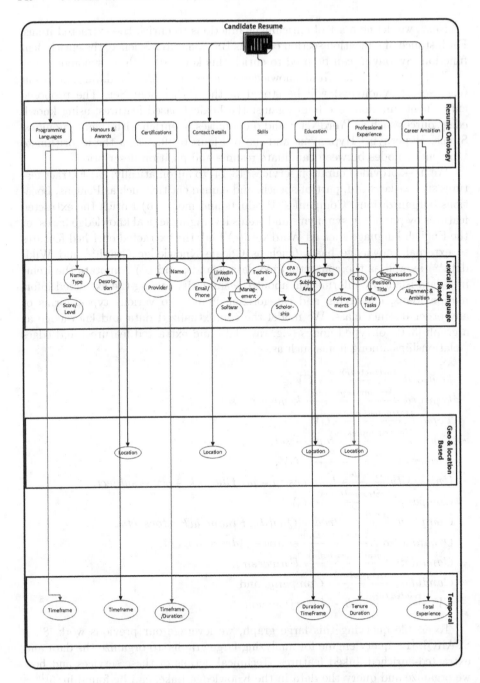

Fig. 5. Contextualizing the candidate resume (CV).

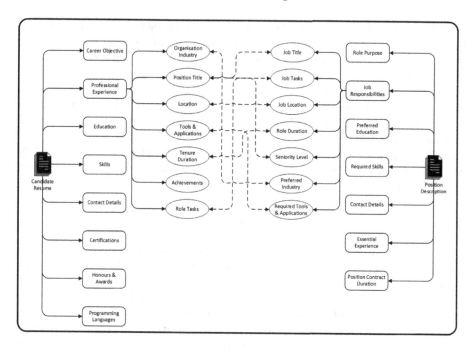

Fig. 6. Linking entity nodes between candidate resume and position description.

4   Evaluation and Experiments

We develop services to extract the raw data from business artifacts such as CVs, job advertisements, candidates profiles, Universities and Companies Job descriptions, and job search engine websites such as indeed.com and theladders.net. These services will persist the data in the knowledge lake [5]. To imitate the knowledge of recruiters and inspired by Google Knowledge Graph[15], we focused on constructing a recruitment domain Knowledge Base (rKB).

There are many systems that can be used at this level including our previous work (Curation APIs) [13], Google Cloud Platform (cloud.google.com/), and Microsoft Computer Vision API (azure.microsoft.com/) to extract information items from artifacts (such as CVs, personal home pages and company Websites).

We have identified many useful machine learning algorithms and wrapped them as services to enable us to summarize the constructed recruitment knowledge base [2,28]. Machine Learning (ML) combines techniques from statistics and artificial intelligence to create algorithms that can learn from empirical data and generalize to solve problems in various domains. One of the main challenges in Machine Learning is to enable users to subscribe and use ML application software in the cloud. This task is challenging as building ML services or AI-based application is different from building traditional SaaS services.

---

[15] https://developers.google.com/knowledge-graph/.

For example, for training models, each training problem is different and analysts need a toolbox to explore different algorithms and pick the best ones that apply to building a particular model. In this context, it is important to make these models available as a service so that others can easily replicate the training as well as the test environments. This will enable knowledge workers of all skill levels (e.g., an end-user with limited computer science background to data scientists) to access and reuse ML services in their processes. The evaluation of accuracy and performance of the Knowledge Lake and knowledge extraction services demonstrated in [5] and [13]. As future work, we will evaluate the usability of the approach regarding the intended application audience, i.e., the recruiters and expert users.

5 Conclusion and Future Work

Knowledge-intensive processes have flexible underlying process definition where the control flow between activities cannot be modeled in advance but simply occurs during run time [11]. Such processes, controlled by knowledge workers who have the experience, understanding, information, and skills. Recruitment process is an example of a knowledge-intensive process. Attracting and recruiting right talent is a key differentiator in modern organizations. Recruitment process involves many data-driven, collaborative and knowledge intensive steps to ensure a right fit for an organizational talent requirement. In such cases, the process execution path can change in a dynamic and ad-hoc manner due to changing business requirements, dynamic customer needs, and people's growing skills. In this paper, we put the first step towards automating the recruitment process. We presented a framework and algorithms to imitate the knowledge of recruiters into a domain knowledge base and extract data and knowledge from business artifacts (e.g., candidates' CV and job advertisements) and link them to the facts in the domain knowledge base. As a future work, we will use the proposed approach to construct a cognitive assistance to assist the recruiters in decision making and choose the best nest steps.

References

1. Ladders, inc.; job search engine. https://cdn.theladders.net/static/images/basicSite/pdfs/TheLadders-EyeTracking-StudyC2.pdf. Accessed 07 Nov 2018
2. Amouzgar, F., Beheshti, A., Ghodratnama, S., Benatallah, B., Yang, J., Sheng, Q.Z.: iSheets: a spreadsheet-based machine learning development platform for data-driven process analytics. In: Liu, X., et al. (eds.) ICSOC 2018. LNCS, vol. 11434, pp. 453–457. Springer, Cham (2019). https://doi.org/10.1007/978-3-030-17642-6_43
3. Batarfi, O., et al.: Large scale graph processing systems: survey and an experimental evaluation. Clust. Comput. 18(3), 1189–1213 (2015)
4. Beheshti, A., Benatallah, B., Nouri, R., Chhieng, V.M., Xiong, H., Zhao, X.: Coredb: a data lake service. In: Proceedings of the 2017 ACM on Conference on Information and Knowledge Management, CIKM 2017, Singapore, 06–10 November 2017, pp. 2451–2454 (2017)

5. Beheshti, A., Benatallah, B., Nouri, R., Tabebordbar, A.: Corekg: a knowledge lake service. PVLDB **11**(12), 1942–1945 (2018)
6. Beheshti, A., Benatallah, B., Tabebordbar, A., Motahari-Nezhad, H.R., Barukh, M.C., Nouri, R.: Datasynapse: a social data curation foundry. Distributed and Parallel Databases, August 2018. https://doi.org/10.1007/s10619-018-7245-1
7. Beheshti, A., et al.: iProcess: enabling IoT platforms in data-driven knowledge-intensive processes. In: Weske, M., Montali, M., Weber, I., vom Brocke, J. (eds.) BPM 2018. LNBIP, vol. 329, pp. 108–126. Springer, Cham (2018). https://doi.org/10.1007/978-3-319-98651-7_7
8. Beheshti, S., Benatallah, B., Motahari-Nezhad, H.R.: Galaxy: a platform for explorative analysis of open data sources. In: Proceedings of the 19th International Conference on Extending Database Technology, EDBT 2016, Bordeaux, France, 15–16 March 2016, Bordeaux, France, pp. 640–643 (2016)
9. Beheshti, S.-M.-R., Benatallah, B., Motahari-Nezhad, H.R.: Enabling the analysis of cross-cutting aspects in ad-hoc processes. In: Salinesi, C., Norrie, M.C., Pastor, Ó. (eds.) CAiSE 2013. LNCS, vol. 7908, pp. 51–67. Springer, Heidelberg (2013). https://doi.org/10.1007/978-3-642-38709-8_4
10. Beheshti, S.-M.-R., Benatallah, B., Motahari-Nezhad, H.R., Sakr, S.: A query language for analyzing business processes execution. In: Rinderle-Ma, S., Toumani, F., Wolf, K. (eds.) BPM 2011. LNCS, vol. 6896, pp. 281–297. Springer, Heidelberg (2011). https://doi.org/10.1007/978-3-642-23059-2_22
11. Beheshti, S., et al.: Process Analytics - Concepts and Techniques for Querying and Analyzing Process Data. Springer, Cham (2016). https://doi.org/10.1007/978-3-319-25037-3
12. Beheshti, S.M.R., Sakr, S., Benatallah, B., Motahari-Nezhad, H.R.: Extending SPARQL to support entity grouping and path queries. arXiv preprint arXiv:1211.5817 (2012)
13. Beheshti, S., Tabebordbar, A., Benatallah, B., Nouri, R.: On automating basic data curation tasks. In: Proceedings of the 26th International Conference on World Wide Web Companion, Perth, Australia, 3–7 April 2017, pp. 165–169 (2017)
14. Beheshti, S.M.R., Venugopal, S., Ryu, S.H., Benatallah, B., Wang, W.: Big data and cross-document coreference resolution: current state and future opportunities. arXiv preprint arXiv:1311.3987 (2013)
15. Bhattacharya, K., Gerede, C., Hull, R., Liu, R., Su, J.: Towards formal analysis of artifact-centric business process models. In: Alonso, G., Dadam, P., Rosemann, M. (eds.) BPM 2007. LNCS, vol. 4714, pp. 288–304. Springer, Heidelberg (2007). https://doi.org/10.1007/978-3-540-75183-0_21
16. Breaugh, J.A.: Employee recruitment: current knowledge and important areas for future research. Hum. Resour. Manag. Rev **18**(3), 103–118 (2008)
17. Compton, R.L.: Effective Recruitment and Selection Practices. CCH Australia Limited, Macquarie Park (2009)
18. Gerede, C.E., Su, J.: Specification and verification of artifact behaviors in business process models. In: Krämer, B.J., Lin, K.-J., Narasimhan, P. (eds.) ICSOC 2007. LNCS, vol. 4749, pp. 181–192. Springer, Heidelberg (2007). https://doi.org/10.1007/978-3-540-74974-5_15
19. Hammoud, M., Rabbou, D.A., Nouri, R., Beheshti, S., Sakr, S.: DREAM: distributed RDF engine with adaptive query planner and minimal communication. PVLDB **8**(6), 654–665 (2015)
20. Kuo, J.: A document-driven agent-based approach for business processes management. Inf. Softw. Technol. **46**(6), 373–382 (2004)

21. Kwiatkowski, R.: Trends in organisations and selection: an introduction. J. Manag. Psychol. **18**(5), 382–394 (2003)
22. Maamar, Z., Sakr, S., Barnawi, A., Beheshti, S.-M.-R.: A framework of enriching business processes life-cycle with tagging information. In: Sharaf, M.A., Cheema, M.A., Qi, J. (eds.) ADC 2015. LNCS, vol. 9093, pp. 309–313. Springer, Cham (2015). https://doi.org/10.1007/978-3-319-19548-3_25
23. Melamed, T., Jackson, D.: Psychometric instruments: potential benefits and practical use. Ind. Commer. Train. **27**(4), 11–16 (1995)
24. Ployhart, R.E.: Staffing in the 21st century: new challenges and strategic opportunities. J. Manag. **32**(6), 868–897 (2006)
25. Rastan, R., Paik, H.-Y., Shepherd, J., Ryu, S.H., Beheshti, A.: TEXUS: table extraction system for PDF documents. In: Wang, J., Cong, G., Chen, J., Qi, J. (eds.) ADC 2018. LNCS, vol. 10837, pp. 345–349. Springer, Cham (2018). https://doi.org/10.1007/978-3-319-92013-9_30
26. Reijers, H., Rigter, J., Aalst, W.: The case handling case. Int. J. Cooperative Inf. Syst. **12**(3), 365–391 (2003)
27. Salih, B.A., Wongthongtham, P., Beheshti, S., Zajabbari, B.: Towards a methodology for social business intelligence in the era of big social data incorporating trust and semantic analysis. In: Abawajy, J., Othman, M., Ghazali, R., Deris, M., Mahdin, H., Herawan, T. (eds.) DaEng-2015. LNCS, vol. 520, pp. 519–527. Springer, Singapore (2015). https://doi.org/10.1007/978-981-13-1799-6_54
28. Schiliro, F., et al.: iCOP: IoT-enabled policing processes. In: Liu, X., et al. (eds.) ICSOC 2018. LNCS, vol. 11434, pp. 447–452. Springer, Cham (2019). https://doi.org/10.1007/978-3-030-17642-6_42
29. Schonenberg, H., Weber, B., van Dongen, B., van der Aalst, W.: Supporting flexible processes through recommendations based on history. In: Dumas, M., Reichert, M., Shan, M.-C. (eds.) BPM 2008. LNCS, vol. 5240, pp. 51–66. Springer, Heidelberg (2008). https://doi.org/10.1007/978-3-540-85758-7_7
30. Shulman, B., Chiang, G.: When to use an executive search firm and how to get the most out of the relationship. Employ. Relat. Today **34**(1), 13–19 (2007)
31. Sun, Y.-J.J., Barukh, M.C., Benatallah, B., Beheshti, S.-M.-R.: Scalable SaaS-based process customization with *CaseWalls*. In: Barros, A., Grigori, D., Narendra, N.C., Dam, H.K. (eds.) ICSOC 2015. LNCS, vol. 9435, pp. 218–233. Springer, Heidelberg (2015). https://doi.org/10.1007/978-3-662-48616-0_14
32. Sun, Y., Su, J., Yang, J.: Universal artifacts: a new approach to business process management (BPM) systems. ACM Trans. Manag. Inf. Syst. **7**(1), 3:1–3:26 (2016)

Can Current Conceptions of Strategy Support the Formulation, Analysis and Execution of Service Strategies?

Hui-Ling Wang$^{(\boxtimes)}$

School of Management, Operations and Marketing, Faculty of Business,
University of Wollongong, Wollongong, NSW 2522, Australia
hwang@uow.edu.au

Abstract. A vast literature dating back many decades addresses the question of business strategies and their definition, formulation and execution. Relatively little has been done on the question of service strategies. Service strategies represent a sub-class of the general class of business strategies which require special attention for any organization engaged in the provision of services. This paper explores the extent to which current conceptions of strategy support the definition of service strategies.

Keywords: Strategy · Service strategy · Competitive advantage

1 Introduction

A significant amount of the research addresses the question of how can a firm perform better than its competitors. Porter [1] argues that competitive advantage is a key determinant of superior performance. Competitive advantage is obtained when a firm develops or obtains a set of attributes that allow it to outperform its competitors. Hence the sideline of competitive advantage perhaps is central to the discipline of strategic management [2–4].

Although there is a vast literature on strategic management, various conceptions of strategy, and strategic alignment, relatively little has been done on the question of service strategies. Service strategies represent a sub-class of the general class of business strategies which require special attention for any organization engaged in the provision of services. *More precisely, a service strategy is a high-level specification of the goals, plans and optimization objectives associated with the provision of either customer-facing services or internal business services.* **Example:** *Consider a hotel chain which might pursue a corporate strategy of being the preferred place to stay for elite business travelers. As a service strategy, the hotel chain might decide to offer a fully staffed front-desk at all hours of the day, to ensure a consistent high-quality check-in/checkout experience (in contrast to other hotel chains that provide lean staffing for the front desk during midnight hours).*

This paper makes inter-disciplinary contributions, bringing together the literature on strategic management and computing/information systems, in the following ways:

© Springer Nature Switzerland AG 2019
H.-P. Lam and S. Mistry (Eds.): ASSRI 2018, LNBIP 367, pp. 153–166, 2019.
https://doi.org/10.1007/978-3-030-32242-7_12

- It offers a novel framework for modelling service strategies.
- It offers a novel means of decomposing these strategies, specifically the optimization objective component of these strategies.
- It offers a first step towards the systematization of the strategy formulation problem, by focusing on strategic viability.

Sections 2, 3 and 4 review the relevant literature, setting the stage for the contributions listed above in the remainder of the paper.

2 Background

2.1 Strategic Management

Strategic management is concerned with resource allocation, strategic choice, organisational performance, and competitive advantage. Pearce and Robinson [5] define strategic management as *"the set of decisions and actions resulting in formulation and implementation of strategies designed to achieve the objectives of an organization."* Certo and Peter [6] define strategic management as *"a continuous, iterative process aimed at keeping an organization as a whole appropriately matched to its environment."* Ramos-Rodríguez and Ruíz-Navarro [7] identify economics, sociology and psychology as the roots of strategic management. Nag and colleagues [8] carry out a large-scale survey of strategic management scholars and offer the following definition of strategic management: *"The field of strategic management deals with (1) the major intended and emergent initiatives (2) taken by general managers on behalf of owners, (3) involving utilization of resources (4) to enhance the performance (5) of firms (6) in their external environments"* [8]. According to Furrer, Thomas and Goussevskaia [2], strategic management was initially a body of knowledge that would underpin practical advice to managers, but evolved into the endeavour to identify, from a positivist perspective, a theoretical framework with explanatory and predictive power.

2.2 Strategy

The prominent role of competitive advantage may stem from both the economic and military origins of the strategy literature [9]. According to Drucker [10] a strategy is a general view of what sort of *"business"* a company is or should be in. His contribution is significant because it reflects the fact that strategy ceased to be confined to the military environment. Subsequent researchers have viewed strategy as being part of business policy [11–13]. Later, Chandler [14] studies the relationship between the strategies (the way firms grew) and the structure (the pattern of organization devised) to manage such growth. Andrews [15] suggests that a firm need to address both the internal and external environment. His approach has become known as SWOT analysis (the acronym stands for strengths, weaknesses, opportunities and threats), that is managers should conduct an audit of the external environment to identify opportunities and threats, as well as conduct an audit of their internal environment to identify the strengths and weaknesses of the company. Driven in part by the seminal work of Ansoff [16] and Andrews [15], the discourse on strategy became increasingly popular.

Hofer and Schendel [17] define strategy via the correspondence between organizational purpose, resources, skills environment opportunities and risks. Glueck [18] emphasizes that all the major aspects of the enterprise need to be covered and joined in the plan and that all parts of the plan should be compatible with one another. Similarly, Bourgeois [19] defines strategy in terms of a firm's relationship with the environment to achieve its objectives. Thompson and Strickland [20] define strategy as the manner in which an organization accomplishes its objectives by deciding the means, assigning resources, and executing the plans thus obtained to produce results. Mintzberg [21] proposes a notion of five Ps. In this conception, a strategy can be a plan, a ploy, a pattern of behaviour, a position in respect customers or competitors, or the perspective of managers in a firm. According to Pearce and Robinson [5], the dimensions of strategy usually include: (1) requirement of top management decisions (2) allocation of large amounts of resources (3) the likelihood of long-term impact on the organization (4) a future orientation (5) multi-functional or multi-business consequences, and (6) consideration of factors external to the organization. Furrer and his colleges [2] sum up the popular of the two major streams of research- the first research stream seeking to understand how strategies are formulated and implemented and the second addressing the relationship between strategy and performance.

Chaffee [22] points out that "*virtually everyone writing on strategy agrees that no consensus on its definition exists*" (p. 89). This is an indication of the complexity of the strategy. Hambrick [23] suggests that this lack of consensus is due to the fact that strategy is multidimensional, situational and industry-specific. In summary, the notion of strategy is broad and admits a range of definitions

2.3   IT and Strategy

Many researchers have stressed the influence of Information and Communication Technology (ICT) and Electronic Commerce (EC) on organizational strategy and business processes [4, 24]). Scott Morton [24] emphasizes the importance of organizational transformation for the sustainability and survival of the enterprise. He has proposed five factors that influence an organization's strategic goals: strategy, structure, roles and skills, management processes and technology. A more recent study [25, 26] emphasizes technology-driven service strategy or service-oriented technology strategy. In this paper we use "*service strategy*" instead of these terms. Although strategy can be vary by industry [23], service strategy turns out to be an effective means of describing most service-oriented settings.

3   Service Strategy

Service strategies represent a sub-class of the general class of business strategies which require special attention for any organisation engaged in the provision of services. Demirkan and colleagues [25] suggest that service-orientation leverages technology in response to the increasing requirement for better business integration, flexibility, and agility. Hence service-oriented thinking is critical to creating new opportunities. The service-oriented thinking includes the allocation of resources, establishing practices and methods, sharing information, redeploying people, reconfiguring organization, storage data, transmission of data, as well as investing in technical solutions and technologies. Ultimately the goal is to effectively leverage technology and people to produce high business value [25].

Service strategy helps to design, formulate and implement technology management as well as identify organizational capabilities and strategic assets to provide value-added service. The value-added service strategy includes both internal and external stakeholders, as well as both internal and external business processes. Kaplan and Norton [27] believe that creating a value proposition is a part of business strategy. With internal stakeholders, such as employees, the internal value proposition delivery system are much simplifier than external value proposition delivery system. The three steps of deliver the internal value proposition are (1) choosing, (2) providing, and (3) communicating the value [28]. On the other hand, the problem with external stakeholders (for example, suppliers, customers or other stakeholders) can be more complicated. When a co-created value proposition involves a range of external providers, a meta-level management process of the entire extended enterprise needs to be carefully designed and implemented to enable the achievement of strategic and operational synergy [29].

4 The Hierarchical Level of Strategy

Organizations can develop strategies at a number of different levels. Hofer and Schendel [17] propose three hierarchical levels of strategy: corporate strategy at the highest level, followed by business strategy and functional strategy, in descending order. Each level of strategy is constrained by the one above it. In simple terms, corporate-level strategy helps decide what business sectors to compete in while business-level strategy helps decide how to compete within a particular business [22]. It has been argued that a distinct category of strategy, societal strategy, stands at a level higher than corporate-level strategy. Porter and Kramer [30] discuss the interdependence between corporations and society and observe that corporate decisions and activities sometimes have a direct and large impact on communities and society as a whole. Therefore, strategists and executives should take into account societal expectations and decisions, not only for the business itself, but also for the broader group of stakeholders that implicitly have a stake in the enterprise, extending to society in general [30]. Service strategy is emerging at multiple organizational levels in business [25]. In this paper, we describe the three conceptions of service strategy. Three are: (1) Strategy-driven service, in which service strategy acts as the corporate strategy. (2) Service design as strategy and (3) Service-driven strategies. A firm's service strategy should link well with its corporate strategy, functional strategy and societal strategy.

4.1 Service Strategy as Corporate Strategy

Andrews [15] defines corporate strategy as "*the pattern of decisions in a company that determines and reveals its objectives, purposes, or goals, produces the principal policies and plans for achieving those goals, and defines the range of business the company is to pursue, the kind of economic and human organization it is or intends to be, and the nature of the economic and non-economic contribution it intends to make to its shareholders, employees, customers, and communities.*" In other words, corporate-level strategy is formulated by the top management team to oversee the interests and operations of the organization as a whole.

When service strategy is the corporate strategy itself, service strategy defines the available resources and enables decisions on what services the firm can offer or which business segment to compete in. Service strategy is concerned with how a firm can create value across different business unit within a frim. Service strategy can sometimes focus on the overall scope and direction of the firm and make sure the various level of strategy are able to work together to achieve the goal with value-added outcome. Service strategy here requires the firm to invest and craft the business portfolio, and design the organization structure and system by using resources, human capital and relational capital available at its disposal.

4.2   Service Strategy as Business Strategy

Business-level strategy, sometimes also described as "*business unit strategy*" or "*line of business strategy*" [31, 32], deals with managing the interests and operations of a particular line of business [17]. Many corporations have to manage the complexity of a large number of highly heterogeneous lines of business; creating a range of strategic business units (SBUs) is one way to manage this complexity. The corporate-level strategy defines the available resources, a set of guidelines and objectives for the SBUs, based on which each SBU formulates its business-level strategies [32]. Business-level strategies are specific to particular industry settings [33]. Business-level strategies may be viewed as identifying ways in which a company would seek to attain competitive advantage through effective positioning [34], the five-forces model [34], generic strategies [35] and value chains [1].

When services strategy is part of firm's business strategy, service strategy is the means by which it sets out to achieve its objectives. Service strategy has become very important as it helps firms to decide how to add value to compete within a particular business. Huang and Rust [26] propose a technology-driven service strategy positioning map, and by using two key dimensions of service, (1) standardized vs. personalized and (2) transactional vs. relational and came up the four different types of service strategies, (1) McService Strategy (standardized/transactional), (2) Relational service strategy (standard/relational), (3) Customized transaction strategy (personalized/transactional), and (4) Adaptive Personalization strategy (personalized/relational).

4.3   Service Strategy as Functional Strategy

Functional-level strategy relates to a specific functionality within the enterprise. Examples of functional-level strategies include human resource management (HRM) strategy, operational strategy, technology strategy, pricing strategy, marketing strategy, technology strategy etc. A functional strategy defines the operational planning of functional procedures within an organization to support the business strategy [17].

Decisions involving functional-level strategy are often guided and constrained by strategic considerations accruing from strategies higher in the hierarchy (e.g., corporate-level or business-level strategies). The allocations of resources among different operations within the functional area are also constrained by business-level and corporate-level strategies. Functional-level strategies help determine the optimization of the functionalities as required to achieve business and corporate-level objectives [17].

When service strategy is part of firm's functional-level strategy, the service strategy becomes much simpler. For example, customer relationship management (CRM) technologies or business process management (BPM) are driven by functional-level strategy. These functionalities can in turn be aggregated to offer value-added services.

5   Service Modelling

Much of the discussion to follow is predicated on the underlying service modelling language. Most existing service modelling languages focus on modelling computational services, such as semantic web services. Eventually, we will focus on the Business Service Representation Language (BSRL) [36] which is the best option available with the representational richness to model both computational services, human-mediated business services and hybrids.

Most semantic web service modelling languages such as WSMO (http://www.wsmo.org/) and OWL-S (https://www.w3.org/Submission/OWL-S/) rely on the basic IOPE (Input-Output-Precondition-Effect) format.

A service model in BSRL consists of the following components:

- Service ID
- Preconditions
- Post-conditions
- Inputs
- Outputs
- Goals
- Assumptions
- QoS specifications, described as a set of <QoS-factor, range> pairs, where the range provides the upper and lower bounds of QoS factors with quantitative evaluations (note that upper and lower bounds might be equal), or is a qualitative value.
- Delivery schedule, specified as a set of <functionality, deadline> pairs.
- Payment schedule
- Penalties

6   Strategy Modelling

In this section, we will briefly review a strategy modelling scheme proposed in our earlier work [37]. A number of other strategy modelling schemes have been proposed, including the SERVALIGN framework [37] and BIM [38] but we will omit a detailed compare-and-contrast exercise here due to space constraints. We will then extend this modelling scheme to meet the unique needs of service strategy modelling. We will also offer an alternative taxonomy for service strategies.

The strategy modelling framework proposed in our earlier work [37] conceives of strategies being modelled in terms of the following four components:

1. *Strategic objectives*
2. *Strategic pre-requisites*
3. *Resource requirements*
4. *Strategic outcomes (there is also a slot for providing a detailed strategy description, but its contents do not actually play a role in characterizing a strategy).*

We note that there are interesting correspondences between our strategy modelling framework and the BSRL service modelling language. We note that strategic pre-requisites correspond to service preconditions in BSRL and strategic outcomes correspond to service post-conditions. In addition, strategic objectives are essentially key performance indicators (KPIs) to be optimized, and hence correspond to QoS specifications in BSRL.

There are also differences. Assumptions and goals, for instance, do not play a role in our strategy modelling framework (delivery and payment schedules, as well as penalties also do not figure, but, as noted earlier, we simplify matters by skipping these in the current discussion).

There are good reasons to include *assumptions* in a strategy modelling language. Assumptions are conditions whose truth is *assumed* during the execution of a strategy or a service. Assumptions are often confused with preconditions, but there are significant differences. Preconditions must be established as being true for a strategy or a service to be executed. Assumptions are conditions whose truth might never be truly known, but whose truth is assumed in the absence of evidence to the contrary. **Example:** *Most everyday contracts (insurance, rental contracts etc.) include a force majeure clause stating that the contract will be rendered null and void in the event of a natural disaster, an act of war or an act of terror.* These are not preconditions which would require that we establish at the start of the contract that such situations will not arise during the lifetime of the contract (clearly such things are impossible to predict). However, the clause stipulates that in the event that the assumptions turn out to be false during the lifetime of the contract (e.g., an act of war actually occurs), the contract ceases to be valid. Service strategies (and arguably all strategies, to varying degrees) are particularly reliant on assumptions. Service delivery is always a two-sided affair with both the service provider and the service consumer playing equally important roles. The online check-in service offered by an airline relies on the cooperation of the passenger checking in (provision of the correct information, willingness to print boarding passes etc.) for successful execution. A house painting service similarly relies on the assumption(s) that the home-owner will identify the walls to be painted, the colours to be used etc. and will deliver the contracted payment amount at the conclusion of the painting project. If the house painter has reason to believe, at any point during the execution of the project, that the home-owner might not pay (thus violating a crucial assumption), the house painter might be justified in aborting the project. Clearly, service strategies must explicitly articulate the assumptions that must be true for successful strategy execution. For example, the strategy of a business lender to offer near-instantaneous approval for small business loan applications lodged online is reliant on the assumption that the regulatory environment will continue to permit the online sharing of individual customer credit ratings by credit assessment agencies.

The role of goal specifications in service strategies is equally important. Our prior work on strategy modelling [37] makes provision for documenting the *outcomes* of a strategy, but does not distinguish between *desired outcomes* and *unintended (or collateral) outcomes*. For instance, the outcomes of engaging with an online air ticket purchase services include the fact that the client is in possession of a valid air ticket, but also the fact that the client bank balance is reduced (by the purchase price of the ticket). Being in possession of a valid ticket was a desired outcome, but being poorer by a certain amount was a necessary (but not necessarily desired) outcome. In strategy modelling, it useful, then, to distinguish between the desired outcomes (the *goals*) and the full set of outcomes of executing the strategy.

We have explored, thus far, two potential extensions to our strategy modelling framework that would be suitable for service strategy modelling: (1) goals and (2) assumptions. We will now take a necessary detour to present a novel taxonomy for service strategies, which will set the stage for a third extension to our strategy modelling framework to make it amenable to service strategy modelling.

A taxonomy of goals was proposed in [39] which provided for the following four types of goals:

1. **Achievement goals**: Here the intent is to make a condition true. Once it becomes true, the achievement does not specify what becomes of the condition thereafter (it might, for instance, become true for a transient instant, and then remain false).
2. **Maintenance goals**: Here the intent is to ensure that the truth of a condition is maintained (potentially in perpetuity).
3. **Avoidance goals**: These goals require us to avoid making certain conditions true.
4. **Optimization goals**: These require us to continually seek to maximize or minimize a function.

As elements of a service strategy, it would make sense to achieve, maintain or avoid certain conditions. It would also make sense to optimize certain objective functions (such as maximizing customer satisfaction). Thus, each of the categories of goals above could also be categories of strategies. However, these are firm-wide outcomes, i.e., they apply to the entire firm. None of these would be amenable to service-specific application, or be used to characterize how a specific class of services might be executed.

Service-specific strategies are in fact quite common. **Example:** *A firm might adopt a strategy of always allocating experienced service workers to calls or cases involving premium clients. This would not fit the definitions of either achievement, maintenance,* *avoidance or optimization strategies. Instead, these strategies are episodic, in that they apply to specific, potentially repeatable episodes.* This leads to the following extension to the taxonomy above:

5. **Episodic strategies:** Here the intent is to repeatedly make a condition true (or to optimize an objective function) every time a certain triggering condition becomes true.

Here, the episodes correspond to instances of service invocation. The conditions that are made true correspond to strategy-level, abstract descriptions of service post-conditions. The triggering conditions represent abstract descriptions of service triggers and preconditions.

Another component of the taxonomy that is particularly amenable to service strategies is cumulative strategies. **Example:** *A firm commits to ensuring that the average customer wait time (on the phone) at a customer contact centre never exceeds 3 min, or where a telecom provider commits to a call dropout rate of under 2%.*

6. **Cumulative strategies:** Here the intent is to articulate requirements that can only be verified by accumulating a measure over multiple episodes of service execution. Clearly cumulative strategies cannot be applied to individual episodes.

Armed with this taxonomy, we can now summarize our proposed service modelling language. The language includes our original proposal [37] augmented with assumption and goals. A further extension is that each component of this language can additionally be labelled using the elements of the taxonomy discussed above.

7   Strategy Decomposition and Monitoring Service Strategies

In the interests of brevity, we will briefly outline in this section how strategy decomposition underpins any approach to service strategy realization. We will also argue that strategy decomposition is key to service strategy monitoring. Service strategies (like all strategies) are expressed with an abstract vocabulary. Services are described using a far more fine-grained operational vocabulary. The key challenge in checking strategy realization is to be able to describe both strategies and services in the same vocabulary or ontology. One way to achieve this is to refine a strategy description to a level where it is articulated using the same vocabulary as services.

Dardenne et al. [39] have earlier defined a set of constraints on valid AND-decompositions of a goal into sub-goals. There are 3 constraints: (1) the set of sub-goals together with the parent goal must be logically consistent, (2) the conjunction of the sub-goals must logically entail the parent goal and (3) the set of sub-goals must be the smallest with respect to set inclusion that satisfies the first two constraints. We can use this formulation to decompose the truth-functional components of a service strategy – i.e., preconditions, outcomes, goals and assumptions.

The non-truth functional components, specifically the optimization objectives, present a harder challenge. Our approach here relies on using domain-specific libraries of objective decomposition patterns. Such a pattern might assert that $g(x)$ and $h(x)$ are sub-measures of measure $f(x)$. **Example:** *Let $f(x)$ measure customer satisfaction, while* *g(x) and h(x) measure the average phone wait time at the customer contact centre and the number of escalations respectively. Thus, minimizing f(x) requires us to minimize both g(x) and h(x). Let s be the parent strategy and s' and s" represent the refined strategies. Then, if s requires us to minimize f(x) and g(x) and h(x) are sub-measures as discussed above, then both s' and s" must have minimize g(x) and minimize h(x) as optimization objectives. This can be recursively applied at lower levels of refinement.*

8   The Formulation of Service Strategy

Ansoff [16] discusses two aspects of strategy: formulation and implementation. He argues that strategy and objectives together describe the concept of the firm's business. The interdependence of strategy, structure and the industry environment in which the organization competes would impacts the formulation of strategy [11, 14, 35]. In addition, strategy formulation involves complex social and political processes within an organization [40–42]. Pascale [43] argues that formulating a single strategy may sometimes prove to be inadequate, and that multiple strategies from multiple perspectives might be necessary. Mintzberg and Waters [44] argue that, in practice, strategies are rarely purely emergent or perfectly deliberate, but are typically somewhere in between those two extremes.

The formulation of service strategy can be either deliberate or emergent. The first service strategy formulation model as rational, structured, sequential and systematic. We will call it the structured model. The second service strategy formulation model is less formalized, unsystematic and unstructured. This type of formulation is also known as practice-based interpretations [45]. We will call it the emergent model.

Porter [35] suggests that strategy is deliberate. In fact, strategy formulation involves deliberation to obtain a plan of action that will develop a competitive advantage for the firm [14, 16, 34, 54]. However, Mintzberg [21] argues that strategies are not always the result of careful deliberation and planning but may emerge from what an organization does without any principled deliberation [21]. Mintzberg and Waters [44] introduce the distinction between deliberate and emergent strategy. Deliberate strategy, sometimes called planned, intended, espoused or prescriptive strategy, refers to the plans that managers develop; they can be regarded as statements of intent. On the other hand, emergent strategy is implicit in the actions that actually take place over a period of time. Although an emergent strategy has no specific objective, it might be as effective as a deliberate strategy [46]. The view that strategy is emergent is shared by contingency theorist [47, 48] who believe that organizations operate in a dynamic environment which may potentially make it impossible to lay out a strategy in advance [21]. Mintzberg [46] also notes that some successful companies do not start out with detailed strategic plans. Instead, they have an explicit goal of what the firm want to be in the future. In such firms, strategy emerges from the pattern of decisions they take in order to achieve their desired goals.

Whittington [9] identifies four generic approaches to strategy according to the intent of strategy and the process by which strategy is formed. Whittington [9] conceives of two kinds of objectives: the first category involves only profit-maximization objectives while second includes other objectives in addition to profit maximization.

The process of strategy formulation relies on Mintzberg and Waters [44] distinction between deliberate and emergent processes. The two categories coupled with the two dimensions leads to four-fold classification of perspectives on strategy - classical, evolutionary, processual and systemic [9].

While the literature on alternative conceptions of strategy is vast, very little has been done to address the problem of *strategy formulation*. Strategy formulation is a critical problem. Correctly or appropriately formulated strategies can lead to success and sustainability for the firm. Conversely, poorly formulated strategies can lead to the failure of the firm, or poor performance, even in settings where its resource base might otherwise be viewed as possessing all of the ingredients for success. It is important to ask the question: what is the genesis of a firm's strategies? Are there structured, principled processes that a firm might follow to arrive at the "right" set of *strategies for the firm?* At one level, strategies are the result of careful analysis, deliberation plus the "gut-feeling" of a firm's senior management. There is a vast space of possible answers to the question: where does the firm want to go? One might take Maslow's hierarchy of needs [49], re-interpret it for firms and use it as a scaffolding on which the firms strategies might be articulated. Ultimately, the reasoning involved and the data required are complex and highly domain-specific.

Our focus here is on a more manageable component of the strategy formulation problem – the problem of *strategic feasibility*. An important constraint on managerial thinking during strategy formulation is the feasibility of the strategies under consideration. Feasibility involves ensuring that the firm has the right resources, the right know-how, the right market conditions, the right regulatory environment and so on to achieve the strategies being formulated. For a successful airline, a strategy to become a leading maker of mobile phone handsets is probably not feasible (simply because of the time and effort required to acquire the internal resources/know-how for transitioning into an entirely new market and technology space). However, that same strategy might be feasible for a leading manufacturers of PCs, laptops and associated computer hardware (think of the history of Apple).

Establishing strategic feasibility is a complex problem in general. A complex set of resources, capabilities and know-how need to be considered. Very little work exists to provide guidance on how various combinations of these deliver on the diversity of strategic outcomes of interest. The problem is simpler in service-oriented settings which permit us to make the simplifying assumption that the complexity of firm resources, capabilities and know-how can be encapsulated in a carefully constructed service catalogue. Formally, the problem of determining the feasibility of a set of service strategies could be stated as follows:

Given:

1. *A service catalogue consisting of a set of service designs in an appropriate service description language.*
2. *A set of service strategies.*

Compute:

1. *A composition of some subset of the service catalogue that realizes all of the service strategies provided as input. This set of service strategies will be deemed to be feasible if such a composition exists.*

Note that this definition is deliberately general, and does not commit to the specifics of the service composition involved.

9 Conclusion

This paper represents the first steps towards a comprehensive framework for service strategies and strategic management. A number of open questions remain, such as strategy in supply chain collaboration [50], the use of constraint hierarchies to manage optimization objectives [51], the use of agent-based simulations of strategy models [52] and the use of belief change and belief merging operations in strategic re-alignment [53, 54].

References

1. Porter, M.E.: Competitive Advantage: Creating and Sustaining Superior Performance. Free Press, New York (1985)
2. Furrer, O., Thomas, H., Goussevskaia, A.: The structure and evolution of the strategic management field: a content analysis of 26 years of strategic management research. Int. J. Manag. Rev. 10(1), 1–23 (2008)
3. Hoskisson, R.E., Hitt, M.A., Wan, W.P., Yiu, D.: Theory and research in strategic management: swings of a pendulum. J. Manag. 25(3), 417–456 (1999)
4. Porter, M.E.: What is strategy? Harvard Bus. Rev. 74(6), 61–78 (1996)
5. Pearce, J.A., Robinson Jr., R.B.: Strategic Management: Strategy Formulation and Implementation, 3rd edn. Irwin, Homewood (1988)
6. Certo, S.C., Peter, J.P.: Strategic Management: A Focus on Process. McGraw-Hill, New York (1990)
7. Ramos-Rodríguez, A.-R., Ruíz-Navarro, J.: Changes in the intellectual structure of strategic management research: a bibliometric study of the Strategic Management Journal, 1980–2000. Strateg. Manag. J. 25(10), 981–1004 (2004)
8. Nag, R., Hambrick, D.C., Chen, M.-J.: What is strategic management, really? Inductive derivation of a consensus definition of the field. Strateg. Manag. J. 28(9), 935–955 (2007)
9. Whittington, R.: What is Strategy and Does It Matter?. Routledge, London (1993)
10. Drucker, P.: The Practice of Management. Harper and Row, New York (1954)
11. Bain, J.: Industrial Organization. Wiley, New York (1968)
12. Learned, E.P., Christensen, C., Andrews, K., Guth, W.: Business Policy: Text and Cases. Richard D. Irwin, Homewood (1965)
13. Thompson, A., Strickland, J.: Strategy and Policy: Concepts and Cases. Business Publications, Dallas (1981)
14. Chandler, A.: Strategy and Structure. MIT Press, Cambridge (1962)
15. Andrews, K.: The Concept of Corporate Strategy. Dow Jones-Irwin, Homewood (1971)

16. Ansoff, H.: Corporate Strategy: An Analytic Approach to Business Policy for Growth and Expansion. McGraw Hill, New York (1965)
17. Hofer, C., Schendel, D.: Strategy Formulation: Analytical Concepts. West Publishing Company, Eagan (1978)
18. Glueck, W.F.: Business Policy and Strategic Management, 3rd edn. McGraw-Hill, New York (1980)
19. Bourgeois, L.J.: Strategy and environment: a conceptual integration. Acad. Manag. Rev. **5**, 25–39 (1980)
20. Thompson, A., Strickland, J.: Strategy Formulation and Implementation. Business Publications, Dallas (1983)
21. Mintzberg, H.: Five P's for strategy. Calif. Manag. Rev. **30**(1), 11–24 (1987)
22. Chaffee, E.E.: Three models of strategy. Acad. Manag. Rev. **10**(1), 89–98 (1985)
23. Hambrick, D.C.: Some tests of the effectiveness and functional attributes of Miles and Snow's strategic types. Acad. Manag. J. **26**, 5–26 (1983)
24. Scott Morton, M.S.: The Corporation of the 1990s: Information Technology and Organizational Transformation. Oxford University Press, London (1991)
25. Demirkan, H., Kauffman, R., Vayghan, J., Fill, H.-G., Karagiannis, D., Maglio, P.: Service-oriented technology and management: perspectives on research and practice for the coming decade. Electron. Commer. Res. Appl. **7**, 356–376 (2008)
26. Huang, M.-H., Rust, R.T.: Technology-driven service strategy. J. Acad. Mark. Sci. **45**(6), 906–924 (2017)
27. Kaplan, R.S., Norton, D.P.: The strategy map: guide to aligning intangible assets. Strateg. Leadersh. **32**(5), 10–17 (2004)
28. Lanning, M., Michaels, E.: A business is a value delivery system. McKinsey Staff Paper, July, p. 41 (1988)
29. Skalen, P., Stefano, P., Cova, B.: Firm-brand community value co-creation as alignment of practices. Eur. J. Mark. **43**(3/4), 596–620 (2015)
30. Porter, M.E., Kramer, M.R.: Strategy and society: the link between competitive advantage and corporate social responsibility. Harvard Bus. Rev. **84**(12), 78–92 (2006)
31. Hannagan, T.: Management Concepts and Practices, 3rd edn. Prentice-Hall Inc., Harlow (2002)
32. Stoner, J., Freeman, E., Gilbreth, D.: Management, International edition. Prentice-Hall, Inc. (1995)
33. Hill, J.W., Jones, G.: Strategic Management Theory: An Integrated Approach, 3rd edn. Houghton-Mifflin, Boston (1995)
34. Porter, M.E.: How competitive forces shape strategy. Harvard Bus. Rev. **57**(2), 137–146 (1979)
35. Porter, M.E.: Competitive Strategy: Techniques for Analysing Industries and Competitors. Free Press, New York (1980)
36. Wang, H.L.: Dynamic re-alignment: understanding organizational response to changing business contexts using a conceptual framework for strategic alignment. In: The Proceedings of the 22nd Annual Conference of the Australian and New Zealand Academy of Management (ANZAM 2008), Auckland, New Zealand (2008)
37. Ghose, A.K., Lê, L.S., Hoesch-Klohe, K., Morrison, E.: The business service representation language: a preliminary report. In: Cezon, M., Wolfsthal, Y. (eds.) ServiceWave 2010. LNCS, vol. 6569, pp. 145–152. Springer, Heidelberg (2011). https://doi.org/10.1007/978-3-642-22760-8_16
38. Horkoff, J., et al.: Strategic business modeling: representation and reasoning. Softw. Syst. Model. **13**(3), 1015–1041 (2014)

39. Dardenne, A., van Lamsweerde, A., Fickas, S.: Goal-directed requirements acquisition. Sci. Comput. Program. **20**, 3–50 (1993)
40. Miles, R.E., Snow, C.C.: Causes of failure in network organizations. Calif. Manag. Rev. **34** (4), 53–61 (1992)
41. Pettigrew, A.M.: The Management of Strategic Change. Blackwell, Oxford (1988)
42. Hamel, G., Prahalad, C.: Strategic intent. Harvard Bus. Rev. **67**(3), 63–76 (1989)
43. Pascale, R.T.: Perspectives on strategy: the real story behind Honda's success. Calif. Manag. Rev. **26**(3), 47–72 (1984)
44. Mintzberg, H., Waters, J.A.: Of strategies, deliberate and emergent. Strateg. Manag. J. **6**(3), 257–272 (1985)
45. Fuglsang, L., Sørensen, F.: The balance between bricolage and innovation: management dilemmas in sustainable public innovation. Serv. Ind. J. **31**(4), 581–595 (2010)
46. Mintzberg, H.: Crafting strategy. Harvard Bus. Rev. **19**(2), 66–75 (1987)
47. Lawrence, P.R., Lorsch, J.W.: Differentiation and integration in complex organizations. Adm. Sci. Q. **12**(1), 1–47 (1967)
48. Donaldson, L.: The normal science of structural contingency theory. In: Clegg, S., Hardy, C., Nord, W. (eds.) Handbook of Organization Studies, pp. 57–76. Sage Publications, London (1996)
49. Maslow, A.H.: A theory of human motivation. Psychol. Rev. **50**(4), 370–396 (1943)
50. Sombattheera, C., Ghose, A., Hyland, P.: A framework to support coalition formation in supply chain collaboration. In: ICEB, pp. 1–6 (2004)
51. Guan, Y., Ghose, A.K., Lu, Z.: Using constraint hierarchies to support QoS-guided service composition. In: 2006 IEEE International Conference on Web Services (ICWS 2006), pp. 743–752 (2006)
52. Salim, F., Chang, C., Krishna, A., Ghose, A.K.: Towards executable specification: combining i* and AgentSpeak (L) (2005)
53. Ghose, A., Goebel, R.: Belief states as default theories: studies in non-prioritized belief change. In: European Conference on Artificial Intelligence, vol. 98, pp. 8–12 (1998)
54. Meyer, T., Ghose, A., Chopra, S.: Syntactic representations of semantic merging operations. In: PRICAI, vol. 2417, p. 620 (2002)

Innovation Track

A Statistical Approach to Explore the Effects of Business Model Change on Growth for the Airline Industry

Rajib Dutta[✉]

University of Wollongong, Wollongong, NSW 2522, Australia
rd754@uowmail.edu.au

Abstract. This article proposes an approach to answering questions on whether commonly observed changes made by the airline industry to their business model are effective for the growth of their business. We took a data driven evidence-based approach where we employed statistical models to test hypotheses articulated with an aim to answering the question how changes in business model influence the overall growth of the airline industry. Some of the models used in this data driven approach are time series models, especially, Autoregressive moving average of order (m, n) (ARMA (m, n)), vector autoregressive model of order p (VAR (p)) and generalized linear mixed models (GLMM).

Keywords: Service unbundling · Frequent flyer program · ARMA · VAR · GLMM

1 Introduction

This paper addresses a service innovation challenge/case study involving aspects of problems faced by the airline industry. These days introduction of low-cost airlines with extreme service unbundling is a common trend in the airline industry. This sometimes heavily influences the businesses of highly reputed full serviced airlines by eating up their existing price concerned customer base [1, 2]. In order to address this and sustain the competition, the full serviced airlines also make changes to their service model. Some of the recently seen changes by a few very successful and premium airlines are as follows [3].

1. Setting up regional airlines to serve many high-volume destinations.
2. Introducing low price full-serviced airlines with extreme service unbundling to retain existing price concerned customer base.
3. Providing limited access to the frequent flyer program to those customers who opted for any of the low-cost options with an aim to attract the premium customer base back to the full priced bundled services.

Making such major changes to the business model is only effective if this boosts the business in terms of overall growth, profitability and customer satisfaction. Therefore, it might be of great interest to the researchers to answer the question whether such

© Springer Nature Switzerland AG 2019
H.-P. Lam and S. Mistry (Eds.): ASSRI 2018, LNBIP 367, pp. 169–175, 2019.
https://doi.org/10.1007/978-3-030-32242-7_13

changes help the business to stand the competition by at least not incurring any plunge in the profitability and customer satisfaction. In this article we made an attempt to propose a statistical approach to address this question through testing of a set of hypotheses. To be specific, the first hypothesis addresses the business question "Is introducing a low cost career in a specific region reducing the growth in this region?". The second hypothesis answers the question "Does the low cost carrier adversely influence the business of full serviced airlines?" and final hypothesis addresses the question "Does the change in frequent flyer program also change existing customer's spending behaviors?".

2 Motivation and Related Work

A longitudinal study was carried out to assess the influence of service quality on profitability for airline industry in United States (US) [4] using data driven hypothesis testing approach. The four indices used to measure service quality in this study were ACSI (2016), AQR (2016), JD Power Airline Satisfaction Index and NSP (2016). They used return on investment (ROI) for measuring profitability. This study hypothesized about the effects of these four service quality indices on ROI over time and demonstrated a persistent positive association between service quality indices and ROI for US airline industry using data. Another empirical study was conducted to gauge how perceived service quality influences customer loyalty in terms of retention [5]. This also hypothesized about the effect of perceived serviced quality on customer loyalty and tested the same through building a scale to measure the perceived service quality and used the percentage of existing customer base retained during past one year as the measure of loyalty. It demonstrated that those airlines which have higher perceived service quality also have greater retention rate in general using statistical models on collected data. Similar other empirical studies [6, 7] also showed through hypothesis testing method that the importance of service quality for airline industry. Therefore, it is customary to assume that a significant change in an airline's business model may influence its service quality which may in turn affect profitability (measure of growth) and customer's spending behavior (measure of customer loyalty). Thus, the statistical methods applied in the proposed strategy in this study has been motivated by the earlier studies where similar or related problems had been addressed empirically through hypothesis testing by building appropriate statistical models.

3 Hypotheses

We assume that the business or specifically the airline in our case maintains all relevant business information related to profitability, customer's spending behavior and customer flying behavior. Specifically, the proposition is that the changes negatively influence the overall business growth of the airline in terms of earning profitability and maintaining customer satisfaction. It is now customary to estimate the magnitude of impact of each of these changes on the airline's business growth. Once we have these estimations it will be easy to identify the elements which most significantly impact the business and from there strategic decisions could be facilitated. We would address the following hypotheses to assess this proposition.

1. There is a significant drop in profitability coming from the geographic region where the regional airline had been introduced which persists over time after introduction of the regional airline (H_1) (analysis of structural break point in the profitability time series).
2. The profitability coming from full-priced airline and the profitability coming from low-price airline are cointegrated as well as negatively cross correlated; the nature of which persist over time (H_2).
3. The amount of spending by the existing customer base has dropped since the change in frequent flyer program has been introduced after adjusting for frequency of flying and distance travelled (H_3).

3.1   Intuition Behind the Hypotheses

H_1: The data on profitability for addressing this hypothesis need to be restricted to the geographic region where the regional airline was introduced. The data should span over a period in such a way that the point of introduction of the regional airline falls approximately in the middle so that there is enough number of observations for the time series exist before and after the time point when the regional airline was introduced. If there is a significant structural change in the time series close to the point of introduction of the regional airline which persists over time then it can be concluded that the introduction of the regional airline has an effect in this change assuming that the other market conditions remain adequately stable before and after this change was made.

H_2: In a similar way, if the market conditions do not change severely, we can study the cointegration between profits coming from low-price airline and full-priced airline to evaluate if one has the persistent influence on the other over time. Also, a cross correlation analysis between the two would indicate how one influences the other. If the profitability from low-price airline has a negative influence on the profitability from full-priced airline then it could be concluded that the introduction of low-price airline has a negative impact on the business.

H_3: Here, we assume that the amount of spending on air travel by a customer is a function of frequency of travel and distance travelled. Here, we will study the change in spending on air travel by the existing customers after adjusting for frequency of travel and distance travelled before and after the changes were made in frequent flyer program. If it turns out that there is a decline in amount spent on air travel after the changes were made in frequent flyer program then this is an indicative of customer behavior change triggered by the change in frequent flyer program.

4   Method

The nature of the hypotheses proposed here are temporal. Hence, the methods we will resort to are time series analysis and longitudinal analysis.

H_1: In order to test this hypothesis, we need to organize the data into two columns; one the equally spaced time indicator and the other corresponding profitability making it a time series on profitability. We will run a Sup test [8] for detecting the point of structural break along with its 95% confidence interval. Once the break point has been detected, the time series will be divided into two pieces; one from the beginning to the break point and the other from the break point to the end. Two separate ARMA (m, n) models [9] of appropriate order will then be estimated on these two time-series. The models would be of the following form.

$$y_t = \beta_0 + \sum_{j \in \{a:1 \le a \le m\}} \beta_j y_{t-j} + \sum_{j \in \{a:1 \le a \le n\}} \gamma_j \varepsilon_{t-j} + \epsilon_t$$

$$\text{Where} \in k_t \overset{iid}{\underset{\sim}{}} \mathcal{N}\left(0, \sigma_\varepsilon^2\right) \tag{1}$$

Here y_t is the profitability at time point t, ϵ_t is the residual at time t which is assumed to be a white noise process and β_j and γ_j are the coefficients (parameters) corresponding to the jth lag of y_t and ϵ_t respectively. The parameters of these two models will be tested for equality using Chow test [10]. If the parameters are found to be significantly different from each other then it can be concluded that the structural change in the profitability pattern over time has been persistent beyond the break point. If the time point of introduction of the regional airline falls within the 95% confidence interval of the break point, then it provides enough evidence to conclude that the change in profitability had resulted after the regional airline was introduced.

H_2: For this hypothesis, we will study two time series; first, the profit coming from full-priced airline and the second, profit coming from the low-price airline since the low-price airline was introduced. The two time series should have the same equally spaced time indicators. First, the cointegration between these two series will be evaluated. In order to do so we will first regress the series for profit coming from full-priced airline on the series for profit coming from low-price airline. The model would be of the following form.

$$y_t = \beta_0 + \beta_1 x_t + \epsilon_t \tag{2}$$

Where ϵ_t is non iid series with mean 0 and some covariance structure

Here, y_t is the profitability from full-priced airline while x_t is the profitability from low-price airline and ϵ_t is the residual at time point t. Then we will run an Augmented Dickey–Fuller (ADF) test [11] on ϵ_t series. If the residual series is found to be stationary by the ADF test, then it could be concluded that the two time-series are cointegrated. Next, we will build a vector autoregressive (VAR (m)) model of appropriate order 'm' depending on the nature of the data [12] of the following form.

$$y_t = \beta_{0y} + \sum_{j \in \{a:1 \le a \le m\}} \left(\beta_{jy} y_{t-j} + \gamma_{jy} x_{t-j}\right) + \epsilon_{y_t}$$

$$x_t = \beta_{0x} + \sum_{j \in \{a:1 \le a \le m\}} \left(\gamma_{jx} y_{t-j} + \beta_{jx} x_{t-j}\right) + \epsilon_{x_t}$$

$$\text{Where} \; \epsilon_{y_t} \overset{iid}{\underset{\sim}{}} \mathcal{N}\left(0, \sigma_{\varepsilon_y}^2\right) \text{and} \; \epsilon_{x_t} \overset{iid}{\underset{\sim}{}} \mathcal{N}\left(0, \sigma_{\varepsilon_x}^2\right) \tag{3}$$

If the cross-regression coefficients (γ's) of this model are significant then it can be concluded that the profit from low-price airline has a persistent impact on profit from full-priced airline.

H_3: We will be studying existing customer's spending behavior over time. This dataset should include an equally spaced time indicator, customer identifier, measurements on amount of spending for each customer at each time point, frequency of travel as well as distance travelled corresponding to each customer. For this we will estimate a linear mixed model [13] with spending amount as the response variable. We will use the time as the within customer predictor and frequency of travel as well as distance travelled as the between customer predictor variables. Also, we will include the higher order terms for time in order to capture any non-linear change in spending behavior over time. The model takes the following form.

$$y_{it} = \beta_{0i} + \sum_{k \in \{a:1 \leq a \leq m\}} \beta_{ki} t^k + \epsilon_{it}$$
$$\beta_{0i} = \gamma_{00} + \sum_{k \in \{a:1 \leq a \leq n\}} \gamma_{0k} x_k + \epsilon_{0i}$$
$$\beta_{pi} = \alpha_{p0} + \sum_{k \in \{a:1 \leq a \leq l\}} \alpha_{pk} x_k + \epsilon_{pi}$$

Where $p \in \{b : 1 \leq b \leq m\}$; $\epsilon_{0i} \overset{iid}{\sim} \mathcal{N}\left(0, \sigma_{\epsilon_0}^2\right)$, $\epsilon_{pi} \overset{iid}{\sim} \mathcal{N}\left(0, \sigma_{\epsilon_p}^2\right)$ and ϵ_{it} are non iid

with mean 0 and some covariance structure

(4)

Here, y represents the spending amount and x's represent the predictors; frequency of travel and distance travelled. As we only have two predictors in our case, then 'n' and 'l' can maximum go upto 2. This model will then be used to make estimation of the average spending amount at each time point after adjusting for frequency of travel and distance travelled. Once we obtain these estimations, we can detect any structural break point using the same method as in case of H_1. After we detect the break point, we will estimate two separate linear mixed models; one from the beginning until the break point and second from the break point to the end with the same form as depicted in Eq. 4. Finally, we will carry out the Chow test in order to find out if the parameters of these two models are significantly different. If it is found to be different and the time point when the change in frequent flyer program was made falls within the 95% confidence interval of the break point then we could conclude that the change in frequent flyer program has a persistent effect on the spending behavior of the customers.

5 Discussion and Future Direction

While this paper suggests a strategy on how to answer some of the business questions related to the challenges the airline industry commonly faces and identify the potential factors behind these challenges, it does not touch upon the questions on how to best design the optimum solutions in order to cater to some of the challenges as well as optimal long-term business strategies. For answering these questions, we need more granular analysis of customer's choice and preferences by conducting market research leading to development of best products and/or services. Preference aggregation techniques, such as those studied in the literature on belief merging [14, 15] can be of interest.

This paper proposes one of the potential strategies to making an educated judgment on how effective have the changes in the airline's business model been. Future studies need to make an attempt to demonstrate the appropriateness of this approach using a dataset from a real airline. Specifically, the data necessary to implement this strategy are the airline's profitability over time for the concerned geographic region as well as separately for full-serviced sector and low-priced sector of the airline. In addition, we also need data on spending behaviors, frequency of travel and distance travelled at individual customer level over time. Such information are very common to any airline business and are usually maintained on their customer relationship management (CRM) systems. Once the data have been collected, the statistical package 'R' can be adequately used for all analyses. First, the data need to be cleansed and then time series analyses and analyses using generalized linear mixed models need to be carried out using appropriate R packages such as 'forecast', 'robets', 'tseries', 'MTS' and 'glmm' to name a few. The results obtained from the analysis would then be used for making inferences in order to evaluate the proposed hypotheses. However, the biggest challenge could be getting access to the data. As the necessary data discussed here are core to any airline's business and very sensitive as well as confidential in nature, access to such data could be very restricted and not easily available. Hence, a suitable industry collaboration might be a prerequisite for getting access to the right data and hence evaluating the proposed hypotheses.

References

1. Pels, E.: Airline network competition: full-service airlines, low-cost airlines and long-haul markets. Econ. Low Cost Airlines Res. Transp. Econ. **24**(1), 68–74 (2008)
2. Alderighi, M., Cento, A., Nijkamp, P., Rietveld, P.: Competition in the European aviation market: the entry of low-cost airlines. J. Transp. Geogr. **24**, 223–233 (2012). Special Section on Theoretical Perspectives on Climate Change Mitigation in Transport
3. Graham, B., Vowles, T.M.: Carriers within carriers: a strategic response to low-cost airline competition. Transp. Rev. **26**(1), 105–126 (2006)
4. Nicole, K., Fernando, C.-P.: The quality effect on the profitability of US airline companies. Tourism Econ. **24**(3), 251–269 (2017)
5. Ostrowski, P.L., O'Brien, T.V., Gordon, G.L.: Service quality and customer loyalty in the commercial airline industry. J. Travel Res. **32**(2), 16–24 (2016)
6. Bawa, P.: Factors influencing the choice of domestic airlines in chandigarh-an empirical study. Asia Pac. Bus. Rev. **7**(2), 104–110 (2011)
7. Witt, C., Mühlemann, A.: Service quality in airlines. Tourism Econ. **1**(1), 33–49 (2016)
8. Andrews, D.W.K.: Tests for parameter instability and structural change with unknown change point: a corrigendum. Econometrica **71**(1), 395–397 (2003)
9. Brockwell, P.J., Davis, R.A.: Introduction to Time Series and Forecasting, 3rd edn. Springer, New York (1996). https://doi.org/10.1007/978-1-4757-2526-1

10. Gregory, C.C.: Tests of equality between sets of coefficients in two linear regressions. Econometrica **28**(3), 591–605 (1960)
11. Fuller, W.A.: Introduction to Statistical Time Series, 2nd edn. Wiley, New York (1996)
12. Dias, G.F., Kapetanios, G.: Estimation and forecasting in vector autoregressive moving average models for rich datasets. J. Econ. **202**(1), 75–91 (2018)
13. Zuur, A.F., Hilbe, J.M., Leno, E.N.: Beginner's Guide to GLM and GLMM with R: A Frequentist and Bayesian Perspective for Ecologists, 2nd edn. Highland Statistics Ltd, Newburgh (2013)
14. Meyer, T., Ghose, A., Chopra, S.: Syntactic representations of semantic merging operations. In: Ishizuka, M., Sattar, A. (eds.) PRICAI 2002. LNCS (LNAI), vol. 2417, p. 620. Springer, Heidelberg (2002). https://doi.org/10.1007/3-540-45683-X_88
15. Meyer, T., Ghose, A., Chopra, S.: Social choice, merging, and elections. In: Benferhat, S., Besnard, P. (eds.) ECSQARU 2001. LNCS (LNAI), vol. 2143, pp. 466–477. Springer, Heidelberg (2001). https://doi.org/10.1007/3-540-44652-4_41

Improving Airline Operations Efficiency via Flexible Business Process Management

Sumeet Kumar and Yingzhi Gou[✉]

Decision Systems Lab, School of Computing and Information Technology,
University of Wollongong, Wollongong, Australia
{sk521,yg452}@uowmail.edu.au

Abstract. This paper addresses the ASSRI-2018 Service Innovation Challenge case study relatine to inovation in the airline industry (available at: http://servicesciencesociety.org.au/downloads/ch.pdf). This paper offers a set of compelling examples motivating the need for on-the-fly generation of process instance variants. It then outlines a general approach that leverages some of our prior work on annotating process designs with expected post-conditions after every task [4] to position the variant generation problem as one of automated planning and intelligent search.

Keywords: Airline processes · Goals · Task post-conditions Process variants

1 Introduction

The operational processes of an airline are often complex, but the efficiency of these processes has an enormous impact on the cost structure of the airline. Many of the business processes used by an airline are amenable to flexible execution.

Consider the pre-flight departure process that starts with the boarding of passengers and the loading of luggage and culminates in the flight taking off. Many airlines tend to follow rigidly defined process models, which might require, for instance, that aircraft refuelling must occur after the loading of luggage. Indeed, between the three critical process steps of luggage loading, passenger boarding and aircraft refuelling, there are no critical constraints that would require any one of these to be necessarily sequenced before any of the others (although some might argue that it is marginally safer to not refuel the aircraft with passengers on-board). In snow-bound regions, aircraft also need to be de-iced by spraying certain chemicals on the control surfaces. The need to de-ice adds additional complexity to the problem. If de-icing is performed too early prior to take-off, the effect of the chemicals wears off and ice starts forming on the control surfaces again. Aircraft often get significantly delayed when a slight delay in boarding, luggage loading or de-icing leads to the aircraft missing out on

© Springer Nature Switzerland AG 2019
H.-P. Lam and S. Mistry (Eds.): ASSRI 2018, LNBIP 367, pp. 176–181, 2019.
https://doi.org/10.1007/978-3-030-32242-7_14

its take-off slot. This sometimes necessitates a second round of de-icing, slight delays in which might lead to the aircraft missing out on its second take-off slot and so on. In the meantime, having a fully loaded aircraft sitting on the tarmac for extended periods of time can lead to losses due to under-utilization of expensive capital equipment (an aircraft earns no revenue for the airline if it isn't flying) but also unnecessary fuel expense (a fully loaded aircraft needs to run its Auxillary Power Unit for keeping the lighting, air-conditioning and such going). We argue that the key to addressing this problem is flexible business process management, and in particular, the ability to dynamically re-sequence tasks at run-time. In the remainder of the paper, we shall show how an approach leveraging process designs annotated with task post-conditions, coupled with a novel notion of *process variant* enables us to achieve these ends.

2   Proposed Approach

We start by making the observation that the alternative sequences of tasks in the aircraft departure process example represent alternative *variants* of the original departure process. We then leverage the definition of a process variant in [11]. Specifically, that definition suggests that a process instance is a variant of another if both achieve the same goal, or goals that are OR-refined descendants/ancestors of each other. In making reference descendants and ancestors, we implicitly assume the existence of a background *goal model*. A goal model is typically a tree which describes how goals are decomposed into sub-goals and further into sub-subgoals and so on via AND-decomposition or OR-decomposition links. A goal model can be thought of as the representation of the know-how of an organization (in particular, AND-decompositions indicate that an organization has the capability of realizing the parent goals by achieving the decomposed subgoals).

We now need the capability to determine whether a given process instance achieves a given goal. Standard representations of process models (e.g., BPMN) and process instances involve sequences (or more complex coordination modes) of tasks. This alone provides insufficient information to evaluate goal realization. What we need, instead, is post-conditions associated with process tasks. The work of Santiputri et al. [14] shows how task post-conditions can be reliably mined from process logs and event logs. Hence acquiring these task post-conditions is a practical proposition. We also need to *accumulate* these post-conditions over task sequences to determine the final set of post-conditions that accrue at the end of the process. The ProcessSEER tool and framework by Hinge et al. [6] provides the machinery for achieving this, leveraging the idea of a *state update operator* which has its antecedents in the literature on reasoning about action.

Once we are able to compute the final set of post-conditions achieved via the execution of a process instance, the analysis of goal realization is a relatively straightforward proposition. All we need to do is determine if the goal of interest (stated formally) is logically entailed by the final set of post-conditions.

Equipped with the ability to *verify* that a given process instance is a variant of another, we now need the machinery to *generate* such variants. This machinery relies on some version of automated planning, as demonstrated in [4]. We shall summarize briefly below the notions of *semantically annotated process models*, *semantic execution trace*, *normative trace* and *semantic non-conformance*, drawing on definitions from [4]. These definitions leverage notions of expected or observed post-conditions. Belief change [3] or belief merging [9] operations can lead to a variety of novel conceptions of variant generation. QoS concerns can be brought to bear on the variant generation exercise in the spirit of [5]. Candidate variants can be integrated using techniques provides in [10].

We can now outline the flexible process execution machinery that we might want to use in our flight departure process example. We can conceive of the machinery continually searching through the space of possible process variants, seeking the optimal variant to deploy in the current setting.

Machinery such as this can play a significant role in making airline operational processes more efficient.

Definition 1 [4]. *A **semantically annotated process model** P is a process model in which each activity or event is associated with a set of effect scenarios. Each effect scenario es is a 4-tuple $\langle ID, S, Pre, Succ \rangle$, where S is a set of sentences in the background language, ID is a unique ID for each effect scenario, Pre is a set of IDs of effect scenarios that can be valid predecessors in P of the current effect scenario, while $Succ$ is a set of IDs of effect scenarios that can be valid successors in P of the current effect scenario.*

Definition 2 [4]. *A **semantic execution trace** of a process P is a sequence $\langle \tau_1, o_1, \tau_2, o_2, \ldots, \tau_m, o_m \rangle$ where each τ_i is either a task or an event, and each o_i is a set of sentences in the background language that we shall refer to as an observation that describes (possibly incompletely) the state of the process context after each task or event. We shall refer to the sequence $\langle \tau_1, \tau_2, \ldots, \tau_m \rangle$ as the identity of the execution trace.*

Definition 3 [4]. *A **normative trace** nt is a sequence $\langle \tau_1, es_1, \tau_2, \ldots es_{n-1}, \tau_n, es_n \rangle$, where*

- *$es_i \ldots, es_n$ are effect scenarios, and for each $es_i = \langle ID_i, S_i, Pre_i, Succ_i \rangle$, $i \in [2..n]$, it is always the case that $ID_{i-1} \in Pre_i$ and $ID_i \in Succ_{i-1}$;*
- *$es_n = \langle ID_n, S_n, Pre_n, \emptyset \rangle$ is the final effect scenario, normally associated with the end event of the process;*
- *$es_1 = \langle ID_1, S_1, \emptyset, Succ_1 \rangle$ is the initial effect scenario, normally associated with the start event of the process;*
- *Each of $\tau_1, \ldots, \tau_n$ is either an event or an activity in the process.*

We shall refer to the sequence $\langle \tau_1, \tau_2, \ldots, \tau_n \rangle$ as the identity of the trace nt.

Definition 4 [4]. *An execution trace $et = \langle \tau_1, o_1, \ldots, \tau_m, o_m \rangle$ is said to be **non-conformant** with respect to a semantically annotated process P if and only if any of the following hold: (1) There exists an o_i in et such that for all normative* *traces* $nt' = \langle \tau'_1, es_1, \ldots, \tau'_i, es_i, \ldots \rangle$ *for which the identity of* $\langle \tau_1, o_1, \ldots, \tau_i, o_i \rangle$ *is a prefix of its identity and* $o_j \models es_j$ *for each* $j = 1, \ldots, i - 1$, $o_i \not\models es_i$ *(we shall refer to this as* weak *semantic non-conformance). (2) If we replace non-entailment with inconsistency in condition (1) above, i.e.,* $o_i \cup es_i \models \bot$, *we obtain* strong *semantic non-conformance. In each case, we shall refer to* τ_i *as the* violation point *in the process.*

We can now outline the flexible process execution machinery that we might want to use in our flight departure process example. We can conceive of the machinery continually searching through the space of possible process variants, seeking the optimal variant to deploy in the current setting. Specifically, the search will be for variants that semantically conform (in the sense of the definition above) to a normative trace.

Machinery such as this can play a significant role in making airline operational processes more efficient.

In addition to the use of intelligent search and automated planning techniques (examples of which appear in [4], one can use simulation and executable specification environments such as those described in [13] to explore the space of possible variants.

3   Related Work

Cook et al. [1] offer a process validation framework, which involves comparing the event stream from the process model against the event stream from the log using string distance metrics. Rozinat and van der Aalst [12] developed the Conformance Checker as part of the ProM framework which, given a process design and a collection of its event log from execution, determines whether the process execution behavior reflects the designed behavior. Different from [12] and [1], our semantic conformance checking assumes that the instance of executed process is structurally correct. A number of proposals for goal-oriented process management exist [2,8]. Klein and Dellarocas [7] present a knowledge-based approach to exception detection and handling in work-flow systems. They define an exception as "any deviation from an 'ideal' collaborative process that uses the available resources to achieve the task requirements in an optimal way" [7]. In their exception management approach, the participant of an enacted process will be notified when there is an exception with the exception types and associated exception handler processes proposed by the work-flow designer, so that the participants are able to modify the instance of the process to resolve the exception and allow the process to continue. Our approach does not require that exceptions handlers be written for every possible exception.

4   Conclusion

As per the above-mentioned proposed approach, we can conclude that we are able to provide goal-oriented process variability approach using effect mining for the airline industry. This approach enables airline industry to study the depth and breadth of goal adherence and providing dynamic adaptation to the process execution on the fly.

References

1. Cook, J.E., Wolf, A.L.: Software process validation: quantitatively measuring the correspondence of a process to a model. ACM Trans. Softw. Eng. Methodol. **8**(2), 147–176 (1999). https://doi.org/10.1145/304399.304401
2. Ghose, A., Koliadis, G.: Actor eco-systems: from high-level agent models to executable processes via semantic annotations. In: Proceedings of the 31st Annual International Computer Software and Applications Conference, vol. 2, pp. 177–184. IEEE Computer Society, Washington, DC (2007). https://doi.org/10.1109/COMPSAC.2007.50
3. Ghose, A.K., Goebel, R.: Belief states as default theories: studies in non-prioritized belief change. In: Proceedings of 13th European Conference on Artificial Intelligence (ECAI 1998), Brighton, UK, pp. 8–12 (1998)
4. Gou, Y., Ghose, A., Chang, C.-F., Dam, H.K., Miller, A.: Semantic monitoring and compensation in socio-technical processes. In: Indulska, M., Purao, S. (eds.) ER 2014. LNCS, vol. 8823, pp. 117–126. Springer, Cham (2014). https://doi.org/10.1007/978-3-319-12256-4_12
5. Guan, Y., Ghose, A.K., Lu, Z.: Using constraint hierarchies to support QoS-guided service composition. In: Proceedings of 2006 IEEE International Conference on Web Services (ICWS 2006), pp. 743–752, September 2006. https://doi.org/10.1109/ICWS.2006.143
6. Hinge, K., Ghose, A., Koliadis, G.: Process seer: a tool for semantic effect annotation of business process models. In: IEEE International Enterprise Distributed Object Computing Conference, EDOC 2009, pp. 54–63. IEEE (2009)
7. Klein, M., Dellarocas, C.: A knowledge-based approach to handling exceptions in workflow systems. Comput. Support. Coop. Work **9**, 399–412 (2000)
8. Koliadis, G., Vranesevic, A., Bhuiyan, M., Krishna, A., Ghose, A.K.: A combined approach for supporting the business process model lifecycle. In: Proceedings of the 2006 Pacific Asia Conference on Information Systems, pp. 1305–1319 (2006)
9. Meyer, T., Ghose, A., Chopra, S.: Syntactic representations of semantic merging operations. In: Ishizuka, M., Sattar, A. (eds.) PRICAI 2002. LNCS (LNAI), vol. 2417, pp. 620–620. Springer, Heidelberg (2002). https://doi.org/10.1007/3-540-45683-X_88
10. Morrison, E.D., Menzies, A., Koliadis, G., Ghose, A.K.: Business process integration: method and analysis. In: Proceedings of the Sixth Asia-Pacific Conference on Conceptual Modeling, APCCM 2009, vol. 96, pp. 29–38. Australian Computer Society Inc, Darlinghurst (2009)
11. Ponnalagu, K., Ghose, A., Narendra, N.C., Dam, H.K.: Goal-aligned categorization of instance variants in knowledge-intensive processes. In: Motahari-Nezhad, H.R., Recker, J., Weidlich, M. (eds.) BPM 2015. LNCS, vol. 9253, pp. 350–364. Springer, Cham (2015). https://doi.org/10.1007/978-3-319-23063-4_24
12. Rozinat, A., van der Aalst, W.: Conformance checking of processes based on monitoring real behavior. Inf. Syst. **33**(1), 64–95 (2008). https://doi.org/10.1016/j.is.2007.07.001

13. Salim, F., Chang, C.F., Krishna, A., Ghose, A.K.: Towards executable specification: combining i* and AgentSpeak(L). In: Proceedings of the 17th International Conference on Software Engineering and Knowledge Engineering (SEKE 2005), pp. 739–742 (2005)
14. Santiputri, M., Ghose, A.K., Dam, H.K.: Mining task post-conditions: automating the acquisition of process semantics. Data Knowl. Eng. **109**, 112–125 (2017)

Author Index

Printed in the United States
By Bookmasters